School Pc

School Policy

Daniel L. Duke
University of Virginia

Robert Lynn Canady
University of Virginia

McGraw-Hill, Inc.
New York   St. Louis   San Francisco   Auckland   Bogotá
Caracas   Hamburg   Lisbon   London   Madrid   Mexico   Milan
Montreal   New Delhi   Paris   San Juan   São Paulo   Singapore
Sydney   Tokyo   Toronto

This book was developed by Lane Akers, Inc.

This book was set in Garamond by the College Composition Unit
in cooperation with Waldman Graphics, Inc.
The editors were Lane Akers and Tom Holton;
the production supervisor was Richard A. Ausburn.
The cover was designed by Carla Bauer.
R. R. Donnelley & Sons Company was printer and binder.

School Policy

1 2 3 4 5 6 7 8 9 0 DOC DOC 9 5 4 3 2 1 0

ISBN 0-07-018028-8

Library of Congress Cataloging-in-Publication Data

Duke, Daniel Linden.
    School policy / Daniel L. Duke, Robert Lynn Canady.
       p.   cm.
    Includes bibliographical references (p.) and index.
    ISBN 0-07-018028-8
    1. School management and organization—United States.
    2. Educational planning—United States.   3. Education and state—United States.
    I. Canady, Robert Lynn.   II. Title.
LB2805.D87   1991
371.2'00973—dc20   90-45186

About the Authors

Daniel L. Duke is Professor of Education at the University of Virginia. He received his B.A. from Yale University, where he was Scholar of the House and was elected to Phi Beta Kappa. After teaching high school social studies in Philadelphia, he attended the State University of New York at Albany, where he earned his Ed.D. in 1974. He served as a high school administrator for two years before joining the education faculty at Stanford University. During his fifteen years in higher education, he has been responsible for creating five new leadership preparation programs. Most recently he received a grant from the Danforth Foundation to create an innovative principal preparation program at the University of Virginia.

Professor Duke is the editor of the Series on Contemporary Educational Leadership of the State University of New York Press. He has authored twelve books and almost a hundred scholarly articles on topics ranging from school leadership and teacher evaluation to classroom management and alternative education. His most recent books include *School Leadership and Instructional Improvement* and *The Case for Commitment to Teacher Growth*. He currently is participating in a research project with colleagues in five other universities to determine strategies for helping improve the school experiences of at-risk youth.

Robert Lynn Canady is Associate Professor and Chair of the Department of Educational Leadership and Policy Studies at the University of Virginia. He received his Ed.D. degree from the University of Tennessee where he majored in Administration and Supervision with collateral studies in Educational Psychology and Industrial and Personnel Management. His major publications have been in the areas of grading practices, implementing programs for at-risk students, and restructuring schools through parallel block scheduling to increase teacher-directed instructional time and to reduce problems associated with "pullout programs."

Professor Canady has worked extensively with school districts not only in Virginia but also in twenty-four other states and for four summers with Dependent Schools in West Germany. He also serves as a Fellow in the National Center for Effective Schools Research and Development, University of Wisconsin. In addition to receiving the Phi Delta Kappa Distinguished Service Award and the Outstanding Professor Award in the School of Education, University of Virginia, he has received two universitywide awards for distinguished teaching and service.

Contents

11   *The Importance of School Policy*   *140*

Preface

School Policy resulted from our awareness that many of the policies that most directly affect students and teachers are the product of local initiative exercised by teachers, school administrators, central office personnel, superintendents, and boards of education. Put differently, Congress, the White House, state houses, state legislatures, and the courts are not the only sources of educational policy in the United States. In many ways, local school policies exert a much more immediate and consequential impact on students and teachers than do policies generated at higher levels. Perhaps our contention seems obvious. The fact remains, though, that this book is the first to deal with locally developed school policies in a comprehensive way. In addition, few graduate programs offer courses that focus on school policy, and programs that prepare teacher leaders and school administrators rarely stress these individuals' roles as local policymakers.

The policies on which we concentrate are ones that touch the lives of every student, parent, and teacher. They encompass such areas as curriculum, scheduling, grouping, programs for at-risk students, grading, homework, discipline, and personnel. What we conclude is that local policymakers confront a broad array of policy options. Furthermore, their choices of policies can greatly affect the educational experiences of students, particularly those considered to be at risk of failure and dropping out of school.

The recent publication of *Politics, Markets, and America's Schools* has helped to dramatize the negative consequences of over-centralization in education.[1] The authors provide evidence that increased student outcomes are associated with school-based policymaking and management. We wholeheartedly agree that the people best able to develop sensible educational policies are those closest to the classroom, not politicians, judges, and high-level bureaucrats. It should be the obligation of these individuals to oversee local policies and protect the public's interests, not to generate policies and suppress local initiative.

We intend this book primarily for persons currently involved in educational policymaking or preparing for leadership roles in schools and

[1]John E. Chubb and Terry M. Moe, *Politics, Markets, and America's Schools,* The Brookings Institution, Washington, D.C., 1990.

school systems. Researchers who study the impact of school policies also should find it of interest. To these individuals we offer a conception of "good policy" for schools—good school policy is policy that increases the likelihood that school goals will be achieved without adversely affecting any particular group of students.

Acknowledgments

Any project as ambitious as a book on school policy creates an enormous debt for its authors. We could not have undertaken the project without the blessing and support of our wives, Cheryl and Marjorie, and our children—Krista, Joshua, Jay, and Devan Duke and Carol, Donna, Robert, and Sarah Canady. In truth, it was our concern for the education of our own children that initially alerted us to the need for greater understanding of the impact of locally developed school policies. While family allowed us to commence the project, colleagues ensured that we completed it. We appreciate Suzan Cain and Mark Kindler's literature searches and the invaluable technical assistance of Joanne M. Reina, Michael D. Rettig, Rick Stiggins, Jeannette Pillsbury, and the editors. Sample policies were shared by Vicki Crews-Behr, Harriet H. Hopkins, and John J. English. Lane Akers offered much-needed encouragement and help in conceptualizing the book. Without his faith in our ideas, they would have remained just that—ideas. The act of fashioning scribbles into legible prose was performed most ably by Paula Price and Janet Webb.

McGraw-Hill and the authors would like to thank the following reviewers for their many helpful comments and suggestions: William Boyd, Pennsylvania State University; Sharon Conley, University of Arizona; Dick Elmore, Michigan State University; William Firestone, Rutgers University; Susan Fuhrman, Rutgers University; and Betty Merchant, University of Illinois.

We dedicate this book to all those individuals who recognize how policies can affect the lives of young people and who labor to ensure that the impact is as positive as possible. Policies must never mask the fact that we in education are dealing first with human beings, not regulations.

DANIEL L. DUKE

ROBERT LYNN CANADY

School Policy

1

The Emerging Field of Local School Policy

Anyone who has skipped or had to repeat a grade, been placed in or excluded from a special program, or been denied academic credit because of absences knows the importance of local school policies. While scholarly attention has tended to focus on federal and state education policy, those who attend and work in schools realize that their lives can be affected greatly by policy made at the school and district level. This book examines some of the territory of local school policy, particularly the policies affecting teaching and learning. These policies have the potential to affect the lives of students and teachers much more directly and immediately than do many state and federal policies. It is our belief that an understanding of local school policy, therefore, is essential for those concerned about increasing school effectiveness and student achievement, particularly for school administrators and board members.

The present chapter serves as an introduction to the emerging field of local school policy. The opening sections define and delimit the field and explain why the study of local school policy can be valuable. The next section provides an overview of the book and identifies the policy areas to be addressed in subsequent chapters. The chapter closes with an explanation of how local school policies will be discussed and analyzed.

WHAT IS SCHOOL POLICY?

To answer this question, it is first necessary to determine the meaning of *policy*. This is no simple task. Guba, for example, identifies eight quite distinct conceptions of policy.[1] They include the following:

1. Policy is an assertion of intents or goals.
2. Policy is the accumulated standing decisions of a governing body by which it regulates, controls, promotes, services, and otherwise influences matters within its sphere of authority.
3. Policy is a guide to discretionary action.
4. Policy is a strategy undertaken to solve or ameliorate a problem.

1

5. Policy is sanctioned behavior.
6. Policy is a norm of conduct characterized by consistency and regularity in some substantive action area.
7. Policy is the output of the policy-making system.
8. Policy is the effect of the policy-making and policy-implementing system as it is explained by the client.

Each of these conceptions has some value for the study of school districts and schools, but it is our judgment that the sixth conception of policy corresponds most closely to our understanding of local school policy. For present purposes, then, *school policy* refers to "any official action taken at the district or school level for the purpose of encouraging or requiring consistency and regularity." This definition implies intentionality on the part of those developing policy and thus encompasses Guba's first conception of policy as well.

We recognize that many local policy actions are subject to review and regulation by higher authorities, but the fact remains that considerable discretion for policy development rests with local schools and districts. This fact is due, in part, to what Berke and Kirst have referred to as the "religion of localism" in the United States.[2] It is useful to think of the study of school policy in terms of two key dimensions—discretion and constraint. The focus of this book will be upon (1) the amount of discretion available to school and district policymakers and (2) the range of options they have in matters related to teaching and learning. Where no realistic options exist, it is meaningless to speak of local discretion in policymaking.

School policy fits into what Pizzo refers to as an "ecology of public policies."[3] In other words, where the operation of public schools is concerned, a range of policy sources can be identified. Policies are derived from Congress, the Department of Education, the courts, state legislatures, intermediate agencies, school boards, and school-based personnel. To understand educational policy in the United States, it is necessary to understand each of these policymaking entities and the relationships among them. Up to now, most of the attention has been focused on policymaking at the federal and state levels; this book is intended to help correct the imbalance.

It is important to note the difference between *policy* and *practice*. As indicated earlier, *policy* refers to an official action for a specified purpose or purposes. School policies are deliberated and decided upon by individuals or groups vested with legitimate authority—school boards, superintendents, school administrators, standing or ad hoc committees, and those responsible for contract negotiations. Typically, these policies are written down and shared with those subject to and responsible for enforcing them.

Practices refer to the efforts to implement policies. As Lipsky noted in *Street-Level Bureaucrats,* it is not always easy to tell where policies end and practices begin.[4] Often, those responsible for implementation are permitted some degree of discretion. For example, a principal may establish a policy requiring all teachers to notify parents if their child is at risk of failing. The form that notification is to take may be left up to the faculty member. Some teachers may send home written forms, others may phone parents, and still others may arrange for conferences.

While we shall comment on practices from time to time, our primary concern in this book is on the policies themselves and the extent to which they constitute useful interventions for school improvement.

WHY STUDY LOCAL SCHOOL POLICY?

Why is the study of school policy of value to scholars and practitioners? We believe there are three reasons.

First, many of the education policies most likely to have a direct effect on the lives of students, parents, and teachers are local school policies. A state legislature may pass legislation concerning the allocation of resources for education, but the legislation does not become meaningful for clients, patrons, and employees until local policy decisions determine how the available resources will be utilized. In relatively few areas of school operations do federal and state mandates have a direct effect on school personnel or students. Typically, local policies must be developed to respond to the intent of the federal and state mandates. The fact that these local responses may vary considerably from district to district and school to school suggests a second reason for studying local school policy.

We have learned from research on school effectiveness that schools serving similar groups of students can differ greatly in areas such as student achievement, attendance, dropout rate, teacher morale, and school climate. Policies also vary across schools. It is reasonable to suspect that some relationship may exist between variations in school policies and variations in school outcomes. Support for this belief comes from studies by teams of California and British researchers who independently found that effective schools were characterized by certain types of locally developed policies.[5]

A third reason for studying school policies is the fact that the number of locally developed policies is likely to increase in the future. Interest in shared decision making, teacher empowerment, school-site management, and the restructuring of schools suggests that the locus of educational policymaking may be shifting. Studies of school improvement projects have consistently shown that teacher and parent involvement in planning and implementing change is a key determinant of success. A recent national study of principals' perceptions of the most important aspects of their jobs indicates that "policy development" is of above average importance in all schools except public elementary schools, where it is of average importance.[6] Recent Gallup polls of the public's attitudes toward the public schools have shown that a majority of the public favor a transfer of influence over educational decisions from the federal government to local school boards.[7] At the historic Education Summit in September 1989, President Bush endorsed this idea and called on bureaucrats at both the federal and state levels to reduce constraints on local education initiatives.

It thus appears as if ample justification exists for the systematic study of local school policy. Such study promises to shed light on school effectiveness, the process of school improvement, and the local control of education. In addition, as interest in at-risk students grows, questions need to be raised regarding the extent to which local school policies enhance or impede these youngsters' chances for success. Concern over the ability of schools to attract and retain talented teachers raises further questions about the possible relationship between working conditions for teachers and school policies. Some critics, in fact, suggest that the proliferation of federal and state education policies is to blame, in part, for contemporary teacher frustration and discontent.[8]

WHAT SCHOOL POLICIES SHOULD BE INVESTIGATED?

As the focus for educational improvement shifts to the local level, researchers have begun to identify key areas of school policy. In a study of superintendents' perceptions of control and coordination in twelve "effective" school districts in California, Peterson, Murphy, and Hallinger, for example, discovered a variety of policy targets.[9]

- Staff development
- School goals
- Teacher evaluation
- Supervision of instruction
- Use of particular instructional models
- Student assessment
- Teacher dismissal
- Curriculum content
- Time allocated to curriculum content
- Curriculum materials
- Principal evaluation

These researchers found that superintendents in each of the twelve "effective" districts reported that there were specific local mechanisms for controlling and coordinating many of these target areas. What the research did *not* show was (1) whether the specific mechanisms varied substantially from one "effective" district to another or (2) if they did, whether the less "effective" and the more "effective" districts were characterized by different mechanisms. In other words, it was unclear from this study whether the key to district effectiveness was the mere existence of policies covering certain aspects of the school's "technical core" (curriculum, instruction, and evaluation) or the special nature of the policies themselves. We must assume, however, that some policies are better than others.

In a provocative paper on the restructuring of American education, Cohen identifies a set of issues that need to be addressed at the school and district level if student achievement is to be raised.[10] These issues are

- Educational goals
- The way in which knowledge is organized into school curricula
- Instructional tasks and activities
- Instructional group size and composition
- Instructional time
- Personnel policies and practices

In an effort similar to Cohen's, the Resnicks isolated school variables that were (1) related to student achievement and (2) amenable to modification through local policymaking and practice.[11] Their list consisted of the following variables:

- Educational background of teachers
- Salary
- Instructional time
- Textbooks
- Class size
- Homogeneity/heterogeneity of classes
- Homework
- Tracking
- Course requirements

In the study of British schools cited above, a team of researchers identified "school organization and policies" as an important predictor of the success of nearly 2,000 students aged 7 to 11 in fifty randomly selected schools. Among the specific policies they reported to be influential were those concerning

- Staff involvement in decision making
- Curriculum
- Rewards and punishments
- Parental involvement
- Opportunities for students
- School climate

Rather than identifying types of school policies associated with desired student outcomes, Meyer, Scott, and Deal described the extent to which local policies were perceived to exist by (1) superintendents, (2) principals, and (3) teachers in thirty California districts.[12] Policy areas included the following:

- Type of curricular materials to be used
- Instructional methods or techniques teachers use
- Rules for student conduct on school grounds
- Written reports of student progress or grades
- Identifying students with learning disabilities
- Dealing with chronic student absence
- Ensuring that needy students have adequate food and clothing
- Criteria to be used in evaluating student learning
- Student conduct in classrooms

The study revealed that local policies or guidelines were perceived to exist by a majority of all three groups in every area except "instructional methods or techniques" and, in the case of superintendents, "student conduct in classrooms." As one might expect, perceptions varied somewhat across the three groups, with superintendents more likely to state that a "detailed explicit policy" existed in any given area. In general, teachers were the least likely to acknowledge the existence of formal policies.

The studies cited above permit us to isolate important areas of school policy upon which to focus our subsequent discussion and analysis. From the various lists, we have chosen eight policy domains. Each is related directly or indirectly to teaching and learning. Together they constitute a substantial portion of the agenda local policymakers must address if they hope to improve student achievement and enhance instruction.

The first policy domain, and the focus of Chapter 2, is curriculum. We contend that decisions regarding what students should learn are among the most important decisions made by local policymakers. Besides the content of courses, curriculum decisions include how content will be organized, the content choices available to students, and the extent to which content reflects local values. Once the curriculum has been determined, it is necessary to make decisions related to instruction. Of these, policies concerning the school schedule are crucial. It is our position that how time is allocated for instruction, or scheduling, is a key to understanding school effectiveness. Chapter 3 covers various aspects of scheduling, including optional formats, the handling of seat work, and programs that call for the removal of students from their regular classes for portions of the school day (pullout programs).

Chapter 4 builds on the previous chapter with an in-depth look at alternative policies for grouping students. Grouping encompasses strategies for combining students by ability, both within and across classes, and by educational interests. Programs designed to serve students with special needs are discussed in Chapter 5. Policy-related issues concerning these programs include eligibility, expectations, and resources. Programs range from alternative schools and dropout prevention centers to drug and alcohol treatment programs.

Recent years have witnessed a growing interest in accountability and assessment. Chapter 6 deals with the evaluation of student performance and related issues such as reporting student progress and grading. Homework serves as the focus for Chapter 7. Interest in homework policies has increased as educators have recognized the value of extending learning time and practice. Along with homework policies have come policies providing special assistance for students who have difficulty completing homework assignments.

Two areas where school policies have a long history are discipline and attendance. Most schools have some form of code of student conduct and guidelines governing absenteeism. Chapter 8 reviews the evolution of local discipline policies and a series of policy issues, including rules and consequences, disciplinary procedures, and comprehensive school discipline plans.

School policies can be no more effective than the personnel who help to develop and implement them. Chapter 9 looks at district policies related to teaching personnel. These include policies governing recruitment and selection, induction and assignment, supervision and evaluation, professional and staff development, teacher assistance and discipline, rewards and incentives, and teacher empowerment.

The concluding chapters do not deal with particular policy domains but, instead, focus on school policy in general. Chapter 10 discusses issues in the development and implementation of school policy. Matters such as who is and who should be involved in policymaking and why some policies are not implemented as originally intended are analyzed in order to provide a sense of the context in which local policies are created. Chapter 11 reviews the preceding chapters in order to assess the importance of school policy as a variable in school effectiveness and to determine the range of options available to local policymakers. The chapter closes with recommendations for further research in the area of school policy.

HOW WILL SCHOOL POLICIES BE ANALYZED?

While the eight chapters dealing with domains of school policies are, to some extent, distinct, we attempt to follow a general pattern in each. For example, each chapter opens with background information so that readers will have a sense of the historical development of each policy domain. Our primary task in these chapters is to identify the options, or the zone of discretion, available to local policymakers. Drawing on current research and professional judgment whenever possible, we try to point out the advantages and disadvantages of particular options. We are especially interested in policies that appear to benefit or harm particular groups of students.

Our analysis is guided by a conception of *good policy*. A *good school policy* is one that increases the likelihood that school goals will be achieved without adversely affecting any particular group of students. Policies may not always please or benefit everyone, but at the very least they should not harm certain groups of young people served by the schools.

Since school policies typically do not exist in a vacuum, we also attempt to look at the relationships among the various policies and the extent to which some complement or undermine others. The key to effective schools probably has less to do with the discovery of one best policy than with ensuring that all school policies are compatible, well-coordinated, and consistently followed.

A final word of caution: The study of local school policy, like policy studies in general, is an imperfect science at best. Since policymaking is often dictated by practical considerations, such as the availability of resources and the political need for compromise, policies may often appear limited or unimaginative to the casual observer. Scholars may be critical because they feel policymakers too frequently ignore research or respond too quickly to public pressure. We ask that readers try to view school policies in the light of the exigencies that prompted them in the first place. Doing so will help to foster greater understanding of the difficulties facing today's policymakers.

NOTES

1. Egon G. Guba, "The Effect of Definitions of *Policy* on the Nature and Outcomes of Policy Analysis," *Educational Leadership,* October 1984, pp. 63–70.
2. J. S. Berke and M. W. Kirst, "Intergovernmental Relations: Conclusions and Recommendations," in J. S. Berke and M. W. Kirst (eds.), *Federal Aid to Education: Who Benefits? Who Governs?* D. C. Heath, Lexington, Mass., 1972, p. 389.
3. Peggy Pizzo, "Slouching Toward Bethlehem: American Federal Policy Perspectives on Children and Their Families," in Edward F. Zigler, Sharon Lynn Kagan, and Edgar Klugman (eds.), *Children, Families, and Government,* Cambridge University Press, Cambridge, England, 1983, p. 12.
4. Michael Lipsky, *Street-Level Bureaucracy: Dilemmas of the Individual in Public Services,* Russell Sage Foundation, New York, 1980.
5. Joseph F. Murphy, Marsha Weil, Philip Hallinger, and Alexis Mitman, "Academic Press: Translating High Expectations into School Policies and Classroom Practices," *Educational Leadership,* December 1982, pp. 22–26; Peter Mortimore, Pamela Sammons, Louise Stoll, David Lewis, and Russell Ecob, *School Matters,* University of California Press, Berkeley, 1988, pp. 218–262.
6. Gary D. Gottfredson and Lois G. Hybl, "An Analytical Description of the School Principal's Job," Report No. 13, Center for Research on Elementary and Middle Schools, The Johns Hopkins University, Baltimore, 1987, p. 61.

7. Alec M. Gallup, "The 18th Annual Gallup Poll of the Public's Attitudes toward the Public Schools," *Phi Delta Kappan,* September 1986, pp. 44–50.
8. Arthur E. Wise, "Legislated Learning Revisited," *Phi Delta Kappan,* January 1988, pp. 328–333.
9. Kent D. Peterson, Joseph Murphy, and Philip Hallinger, "Superintendents' Perceptions of the Control and Coordination of the Technical Core in Effective School Districts," *Educational Administration Quarterly,* February 1987, pp. 79–95.
10. Michael Cohen, "Restructuring the Education System: Agenda for the 90's," unpublished paper, 1987.
11. Daniel P. Resnick and Lauren B. Resnick, "Understanding Achievement and Acting to Produce It: Some Recommendations for the NAEP," *Phi Delta Kappan,* April 1988, pp. 576–579.
12. John Meyer, W. Richard Scott, and Terrence Deal, "Research on School and District Organization," in J. Victor Baldridge and Terrence Deal (eds.), *The Dynamics of Organizational Change in Education,* McCutchan Publishing Corporation, Berkeley, Calif., 1983, pp. 409–425.

2

Curriculum

Schools exist, to a great extent, to impart knowledge and provide experiences deemed important for the perpetuation of society. Assessing the role that local policymakers—board members, school administrators, and selected teachers—play in determining the nature of this knowledge and these experiences is the purpose of the present chapter. *Curriculum* is an encompassing term referring to whatever it is that policymakers intend that young people will learn in school.

Glatthorn notes that curriculum, to be understood, must be subdivided into five distinct "types."[1] There is the "recommended curriculum," the opinions of scholars, professional groups, legislators, commissions, and the like about what should be taught. The "written curriculum" is the curriculum embodied in the approved state and district curriculum guides. The "supported curriculum" is the curriculum as reflected in and shaped by the resources allocated to deliver the curriculum. The "tested curriculum" includes the content for which students are held accountable on various tests. Last, the "learned curriculum" denotes all the changes in students' values, perceptions, and behavior that occur as a result of what they are taught in school.

Glatthorn's typology reveals the variety of individuals and groups that can influence curriculum decisions. A blue-ribbon commission may recommend that students learn Japanese, but the recommendation means little unless local school boards agree to allocate the funds needed to hire teachers of Japanese. A district curriculum guide may specify that all ninth graders learn the origins of the two-party system, but such learning is unlikely to occur if teachers fail to hold students accountable for it.

This chapter opens with an overview of the evolution of curriculum policymaking. The sections following deal with the major foci for local policymaking—school mission and curriculum goals, subject and course offerings, curriculum consistency, and curriculum responsiveness. These sections also include references to contemporary research on curriculum policymaking. The concluding section offers general guidance to those engaged in making curriculum decisions at the school and district level.

THE EVOLUTION OF CURRICULUM POLICYMAKING

In the early days of the republic, curriculum decisions were made on the local level. Educators believed that the curriculum had to be flexible if it was to meet the changing needs of various communities. The Tanners contend that the idea of a relatively fixed or permanent curriculum did not arise until the advent of state support for local schools.[2] As the role of the states grew, curriculum decisions became increasingly centralized. States began to develop lists of required learnings, prescribed courses, and graduate requirements.

The federal role in education remained relatively limited until midway through the twentieth century. At first, Washington's concerns focused primarily on protecting the right to a quality education for minority and disadvantaged students and promoting special programs. During the Reagan and Bush presidencies, though, the federal government began to take a greater interest in the overall quality of American education. Top-level efforts were aimed at increasing graduation requirements and making curriculum content more rigorous. The task of implementing this push for "educational excellence," however, was left to the states and local school systems.

The actual impact of the so-called excellence movement is debatable. When researchers studied the effectiveness of state-initiated reform legislation in seventeen California schools, they found that although the schools were able to return quickly and easily to more traditional academic courses, instructional methods and the contents of mathematics and science curricula failed to change in the manner hoped for by the reformers.[3] The study investigated the effects on at-risk students of these efforts to develop more rigorous curricula and concluded that the "push for excellence has not left at-risk students completely out in the cold, but the system's strategies for dealing with at-risk students need strengthening."[4]

A study of reform efforts during the eighties in Arizona, California, Florida, Georgia, Minnesota, and Pennsylvania noted that the most widely adopted changes were those aimed at raising student standards by increasing course requirements and expanding testing programs.[5] Raising student standards paved the way for greater centralization of curriculum and increased efforts to align curriculum, tests, texts, and teacher evaluation. The study's authors felt that parental pressure was compelling local school officials to make the curriculum more uniform across a school district.[6]

Teachers, too, have been affected by the reforms of the eighties. A Rand study of teachers' views of the effect of educational policies on their classroom practices found that many teachers were spending less time on subjects that were not covered on mandated standardized tests and resorting to lectures rather than discussions in order to cover more of the prescribed behavioral objectives.[7] The picture that emerges from this study is of steadily diminishing choices for teachers in the areas of curriculum and instruction. Almost half the teachers indicated that the single factor most likely to cause them to leave teaching was the "increased prescriptiveness of teaching content and methods."[8]

Despite the spread of state-initiated reforms and the frustrations of teachers faced with escalating responsibilities and shrinking autonomy, it would be wrong to conclude that local educators and board members no longer have a voice in determining what is taught. Several observers point out that the growth of state and federal policy need not result, automatically, in the loss of local control.[9] While the Rand study found a plethora of teacher concerns, other studies have suggested that many teachers still feel they are involved in making many curriculum decisions. John Goodlad found, for example, that teachers in the thirty-eight schools that were part of his "Study of Schooling" felt they exercised considerable influence over curriculum policies as well as policies related to instruction and student behavior.[10] When researchers investigated policies related to the mathematics curriculum in California—long regarded as a very "directive" state—they discovered considerable local latitude in determining what was taught.[11] A similar finding was reported in a more comprehensive study of policies in Bay Area school districts. Researchers here reported that a majority of the superintendents, principals, and teachers surveyed indicated that their district had locally developed policies or guidelines covering curriculum materials and the criteria to be used in evaluating student learning.[12] Administrators and teachers, however, varied somewhat in their judgments of the extent to which "detailed explicit policies" existed in these areas.

Boyd has attempted to account for the seemingly contradictory findings that local educators feel both in control and not in control of policy matters such as the school curriculum. His explanation reveals, on the one hand, episodic spurts of crisis-inspired policy initiatives at the state and federal levels and, on the other hand, cautious and continuous policy tinkering on the part of local educators and board members.[13] In other words, local policymakers periodically may feel that control of the curriculum has been grabbed from them by politicians faced with public pressure to alter what students are taught. When this pressure subsides, local policymakers resume considerable discretion over the curriculum.

Several observers of contemporary curriculum policymaking have attempted to identify the types of decisions over which local educators and board members are likely to exercise discretion. Kirst divides these decisions into ones dealing with (1) the nature and content of courses and (2) student access and course availability.[14] The first category covers issues such as the relationship between courses and subjects (*articulation*) and the assessment of curriculum adequacy. The second category includes graduation requirements, criteria governing admission to courses, and selection of courses for particular "tracks." Glatthorn focuses on issues of consistency.[15] His list of local curriculum concerns includes the extent to which individual schools within a district are able to modify district goals, reorganize fields of study, develop instructional objectives, select tests and instructional materials, and so on.

In order to take a closer look at the range of local policy options associated with the curriculum, we have drawn on both Kirst's and Glatthorn's lists and identified four general issues addressed by curriculum policy: (1) broad curriculum goals along with the stated mission of the school district, (2) course offerings and subject matter, (3) curriculum consistency, and (4) curriculum responsiveness.

CURRICULUM GOALS

Curriculum goals are defined by Glatthorn as the "general, long-term educational outcomes which the school system expects to achieve through its curriculum."[16] Goodlad groups these outcomes into four broad categories: academic, vocational, social/civic, and personal.[17] He surmises that it would not be unusual to find local policymakers specifying curriculum goals in all four categories. When students, teachers, and parents in his "Study of Schooling" were asked to indicate the relative importance of these outcomes, academic goals were chosen "most important" by all groups except high school students, who placed vocational goals first.[18] Personal goals were second in importance for all groups of teachers and parents.

Goodlad went on to create a "guiding framework for curriculum planning and teaching." This framework was based on the four broad categories of curriculum goals and included ten specific outcomes, each with various subcategories. The ten outcomes include the following:[19]

1. Mastery of basic skills and fundamental processes
2. Intellectual development
3. Career education—vocational education
4. Interpersonal understandings
5. Citizenship participation
6. Enculturation
7. Moral and ethical character
8. Emotional and physical well-being
9. Creativity and aesthetic expression
10. Self-realization

Goodlad's framework delineates the general boundaries within which most local choices of curriculum goals are made. If any controversy arises regarding the actual selection of goals, it is apt to concern either their prioritization or certain goals such as those dealing with values and psychological development. Some conservative special-interest groups, for example, oppose efforts by school systems to teach values or to address the emotional needs of students. The prioritization of curriculum goals typically does not become a matter of consequence until a school system is faced with declining resources. Kirst notes that during times of retrenchment, lists of goal priorities may be used as a basis for eliminating course offerings and teaching positions.[20]

When local policymakers consider curriculum goals, they often address the mission and philosophy of the school system as well. Mission statements and philosophies have attracted considerable attention in recent years as researchers have attempted to identify factors associated with effective organizations. Among the most frequently cited factors are clarity of organizational purpose and a sense of direction, attributes associated with mission statements and philosophies.

Examples of a mission statement and a philosophy for a large suburban school district appear below. These documents were drafted during a period of fiscal uncertainty, increasing pressure from conservative special-interest groups, and a turnover in board membership. The intention of the superintendent and the new board was to clarify their thinking about matters of educational significance and to send a signal to patrons and employees that district leaders possessed a vision of where the school system should be headed. They also hoped to provide a framework within which to make curriculum decisions necessitated by diminishing revenues and to specify how their district would continue to be distinctive.

Board of Directors' Philosophy

We believe that the children of our community are our most precious resource. It is the obligation of the School District to provide opportunities for each child—regardless of race, ethnic background, sex, or socioeconomic condition—to acquire the skills, knowledge, and attitudes that will allow him/her to become a contributing member of society.

We further recognize that schooling is more than preparation for the future. It is a substantial portion of every individual's life. We are obliged to make the school experience of each child as meaningful, safe, and secure as possible. We believe that academic growth is worth little if it comes at the expense of a child's self-esteem.

We believe that no single model of success should guide our efforts to educate the children of the School District. Our children should be exposed to various forms of excellence—in academics, the arts, athletics, business, industry, and family life. The strength of our community and our society depends on the cultivation of diverse gifts and talents in our children.

We believe that our school system should be sensitive to the needs, concerns, and aspirations of all segments of the community. We also believe that the welfare of the students of the School District must not be risked to serve the desires of any particular interest group.

School District Mission Statement (1987–1992)

The mission of this School District is to provide each student with opportunities to acquire the skills, knowledge, and attitudes necessary to become contributing members of society.

The special mission of the District for the period 1987–1992 is to develop and implement systems and procedures for preserving quality schooling during a period of fiscal uncertainty. These systems and procedures are designed to raise student achievement in selected areas, protect curriculum options for students, secure talented personnel, and provide constructive leadership at all levels of District operations.

During this five-year period, the School District also seeks to become a district of distinction in the area of vocational education, school-community relations, and the cultivation of student excellence.

An example of another type of mission statement comes from the Walla Walla (Washington) Public Schools. This statement was used as the basis for generating annual and ongoing district goals. Several of these goals related specifically to the curriculum.

Mission Statement

The mission of the Walla Walla Public Schools is to ensure each student the opportunity to develop knowledge, skills, and attitudes fundamental to effective citizenship and personal satisfaction. Our schools should provide each student with the basic skills essential to the lifelong learning process required to function in and contribute to society. Our schools should help students develop an acceptance and appreciation of themselves, others, and the essential interdependence between individuals, communities, and nations.

Ongoing Goals

In order to achieve the district's mission, Walla Walla Schools will

- maintain a balanced, challenging curriculum, with appropriate alternatives to match learning experiences with each student's ability, readiness, and style.
- attract and retain the best available staff and provide exemplary programs for their professional evaluation and development.

- continue to encourage, recognize, and reward excellence through goal setting and school improvement planning.
- provide educationally sound facilities for all students and programs.
- make maximum use of available resources through prudent programming and budgeting.
- maintain two-way communication with the community regarding educational needs, offerings, and responsibilities.

1985–1986 Goals

During the 1985–1986 school year, the Walla Walla School District shall

- evaluate the effects of developing middle schools on the educational program and faculty needs of the district.
- develop a maintenance program that will ensure the proper maintenance of existing facilities.
- resolve the facility needs at Green Park School.
- continue developing and planning a comprehensive thinking-skills program.
- evaluate the effectiveness of elementary school counseling programs and related alternatives.

As contemporary policymakers deliberate the proper mission of their school districts, they are forced to deal with several persistent curriculum issues. One concerns the desirability and feasibility of requiring all students to master a core of common learning. Is part of a school district's mission to ensure that all students are exposed to the same body of knowledge? How can this task be accomplished when, as Kirst has noted, there is considerable political and public pressure favoring curricular specialization and pluralism?[21] As schools are put under more and more pressure to develop special programs for at-risk students (see Chapter 5), it may become even harder to ensure that all students partake of common content.

Interest in a common curriculum has grown recently, despite the problems mentioned above. Much of the interest has been sparked by concern over declining student achievement and its impact on our nation's economic competitiveness. Another impetus has come from critics of contemporary efforts to help disadvantaged students. E. D. Hirsch, a representative of this group, argues that disadvantaged students are not being exposed in a systematic way to the key facts, idioms, and ideas that will permit them to function effectively in a modern western culture.[22] He urges policymakers to establish "cultural literacy" as a basic educational goal, and he provides a list of the specific information all students need to know in order to achieve the goal. Other advocates of a common curriculum prefer less specific examples of essential knowledge. Under the auspices of the Association for Supervision and Curriculum Development, a network of school systems committed to "general education" has been created.[23] While their lists of common curriculum themes and topics vary, each system is committed to providing every one of its high school students with a basic core of knowledge.

Related to the issue of a common curriculum is the viability of the comprehensive high school. In their efforts to accommodate an ever-expanding set of student interests and needs, many high schools have so diversified their curriculum that it is unlikely that their students are exposed to much of a common curriculum. Kirst questions whether the goal of providing programs to accommodate each student's special interests is affordable.[24] But if the goal of high schools is to become less "comprehensive," where should cuts in the curriculum be made? Those who advocate curtailing or eliminating vocational offerings are accused of being elitist. Supporters of diverse electives, on the other hand, are indicted for abandoning excellence. Local policymakers are left to determine the relative importance of curriculum depth, breadth, and quality.

COURSE OFFERINGS AND SUBJECT MATTER

Once decisions have been made concerning district mission and broad curriculum goals, it is possible to determine the courses and subject matter most likely to achieve this mission and accomplish these goals. Here, too, local educators and board members enjoy considerable discretion. As long as school districts meet basic state requirements, they are relatively free to decide their curriculum. Local policies may cover the specific subjects to be covered, the course offerings, subject-matter requirements for promotion or graduation, and curriculum organization.

Fairfax County (a large suburban district in northern Virginia), for example, adopted a policy specifying all the courses constituting a "standard" high school program.[25] The policy's stated intention is to ensure that "all schools offer a balanced curriculum," including "advanced courses for the gifted and talented, remedial and development programs for the academically unsuccessful, opportunities for fine and practical arts, and career exploration and preparation for all students." The policy goes on to state that the standard curriculum must meet the requirements established by the Virginia State Board of Education and the Southern Association of Colleges and Schools. Sets of approved course objectives are called for, along with the proviso that specific courses can be offered only if minimum enrollments are met.

Among the stated objectives of Fairfax's standard high school program are the following:

- Standardize course offerings so that a basic number of identified courses within each discipline will be offered in all high schools.
- Provide equal access for all students to a basic number of identified courses regardless of school size.
- Ensure a balanced curriculum so that students at various levels of achievement will be able to select appropriate courses to meet individual learning needs and satisfy all graduation requirements.
- Provide an appropriate sequence of study in curriculum areas.
- Ensure that all students meet minimum-competency requirements for high school graduation.
- Ensure implementation of basic skills programs in all schools to facilitate standardized and criterion-referenced test performance identified as acceptable by the Fairfax County School Board.

The Fairfax policy concludes with a comprehensive list of the general education and vocational education courses that constitute its standard program. The list is reproduced in its entirety to provide an example of the scope of offerings available in some school systems.

Course Listing for Fairfax County Public Schools

A . General Education Courses

Art

9120	Art 1
9130	Art 2
9140	Art 3
9145	Art 4

English

1130   English, Grade 9
1140   English, Grade 10
1150   English, Grade 11
1160   English, Grade 12
1196   Advanced Placement English
       (Literature and Composition *and/or* Language and
       Composition)
1200   Journalism 1
1300   Speech 1
1410   Theatre Arts 1
1420   Theatre Arts 2

Reading

1180   Developmental Reading*
1184   Reading (1)**

Foreign Language

5110   French 1
5120   French 2
5130   French 3
5105   Advanced Placement French Language
5106   Advanced Placement French Literature
5210   German 1
5220   German 2
5230   German 3
5205   Advanced Placement German Language
5310   Latin 1
5320   Latin 2
5510   Spanish 1
5520   Spanish 2

---

*Schools may meet reading needs on a broader basis by incorporating reading instruction into other subject areas. Alternatives to the course described above must provide a clearly defined plan for the organized teaching of reading skills. The principal must submit this plan to the area superintendent and the assistant superintendent for instructional services for approval.

**Schools may meet basic reading-skill needs through programs such as the Personalized Learning Program. Alternatives to the course described above must provide clearly defined reading elective options.

5530 Spanish 3
5505 Advanced Placement Spanish Language
5506 Advanced Placement Spanish Literature

Health and Physical Education
7005 Driver Education (in-car)
7015 Driver Education (in-classroom)
7300 Health and Physical Education, Grade 9
7410 Health and Physical Education, Grade 10
7510 Physical Education, Grade 11
7610 Physical Education, Grade 12
7700 Adaptive Physical Education

Mathematics
3121 General Mathematics
3130 Algebra 1
3131 Algebra I—Part I
3132 Algebra I—Part II
3143 Geometry
3135 Algebra 2
3137 Algebra 2—Trigonometry
3150 Trigonometry
3176 Analytic Geometry
3162 Mathematical Analysis
3163 Functions
3170 Calculus AB (advanced placement) *and/or*
3177 Calculus BC (advanced placement)
3184 Computer Science 1
3128 Consumer Mathematics
3180 Problem Solving and Programming

Music
9232 Beginning Band
9233 Intermediate Band
9234 Advanced Band
9239 Advanced Orchestra
9260 Treble Choir
9283 Concert Choir

Science
4210 Earth Science
4205 Earth and Space Science *or*
4305 LABS (Laboratory Approach to Biological Science)
4340 Advanced Placement Biology *and/or*
4440 Advanced Placement Chemistry
4310 Biology 1
4405 Consumer Chemistry
4410 Chemistry
4510 Physics 1 (PSSC)
45101 Physics 1 (Harvard project)

Social Studies***
    2210 World Geography****
    2340 World History****
    2360 Virginia and United States History
    2319 Advanced Placement American History
    2440 Virginia and United States Government
    2500 Sociology *or*
    2900 Psychology
    2451 Political Science

B Vocational Education Courses

Business Education
    6110 Introduction to Business
    6151 Typing 1
    6154 Typing 2
    6211 Shorthand 1
    6320 Accounting 1
    6612 Computerized Accounting/Accounting 2
    6440 Office Simulation
    6620 Office Technology 1
    6621 Office Technology 2
    6625 Word Processing
    6640 Business Data Processing 1
    6650 Business Data Processing 2
    6660 Information Processing
    6799 Cooperative Office Education

Health Occupations
    8331 Health Assistant 1
    8332 Health Assistant 2
    8357 Practical Nursing
    8331 Veterinary Aide

Home Economics
    8230 Contemporary Living 1
    8240 Contemporary Living 2
    8250 *Any two of the following semester courses:*
    8271 Single Living
    8272 Relationships
    8273 Gourmet Foods 1
    8274 Fashion Sewing 1
    8275 Restaurant Trades 1
    8276 Restaurant Trades 2

***Schools have the option to offer World Civilization (2375) and/or American Civilization (2315) in addition to the standard courses. By completing one of these courses, students meet the requirements for one credit in English and one credit in World History or in Virginia and United States History.
****Schools have the option to offer World Cultures (2351) in lieu of, or in addition to, World Geography and World History. By completing World Cultures, students meet the requirement for one credit in World History or World Geography.

8284 Child Development
8285 Child Care Occupations 1
8286 Child Care Occupations 2
8297 Housing and Interior Design

Industrial Arts
8433 Industrial Arts 1/Materials and Process Technology ·
8406 Industrial Arts 2
8416 Electricity, Electronics Technology
8412 Electronics
8435 Basic Technical Drawing
8436 Engineering Drawing
8437 Architectural Drawing

Marketing and Distributive Education
8120 Marketing 1
8130 Advanced Marketing
8140 Fashion Merchandising 1
8145 Fashion Merchandising 2
8160 Hotel and Motel Management

Trade and Industrial Education
8506 Basic Auto Mechanics
8590 General Maintenance Mechanics 1
8591 General Maintenance Mechanics 2
8901 Industrial Cooperative Training 1
8902 Industrial Cooperative Training 2

The following standard courses are offered to all students, but these courses may not be located in all schools:

8503 Air Conditioning and Refrigeration 1
8504 Air Conditioning and Refrigeration 2
8676 Auto Body 1
8677 Auto Body 2
8507 Auto Mechanics 1
8508 Auto Mechanics 2
8512 Bricklaying 1
8513 Bricklaying 2
8601 Carpentry 1
8602 Carpentry 2
8527 Cosmetology 1
8528 Cosmetology 2
8529 Cosmetology 3
8607 Commercial Photography 1
8608 Commercial Photography 2
8530 Drafting 1
8531 Drafting 2
8533 Electricity 1
8534 Electricity 2
8536 Electronics Technician 1

8034 Horticulture 1
8036 Horticulture 2
8356 Microcomputer/Photocopier Maintenance and Repair
8539 Machine Trades 1
8540 Machine Trades 2
8551 Plumbing 1
8552 Plumbing 2
8590 General Maintenance Mechanics 1
8591 General Maintenance Mechanics 2
8660 Printing 1
8661 Printing 2
8622 Television Communications 1
8623 Television Communications 2
8672 Welding 1
8673 Welding 2
8901 Industrial Cooperative Training 1
8902 Industrial Cooperative Training 2

Many districts do not mandate as extensive a program as does Fairfax County, but it is common to find local policies providing for advanced placement or honors courses, remedial courses, and electives. Local policymakers must also designate which courses do or do not lead to graduation credit or credit toward special diplomas. One of the most controversial areas of local curriculum policy concerns the issue of tracking. *Tracking* is the practice of clustering courses designed for students with common aspirations and abilities. Some districts specify that ability-based courses will be offered for required subjects such as English and mathematics. Evidence exists that tracking policies and practices vary across schools and districts.[26] The impact of tracking is discussed at greater length in Chapter 4.

Curriculum policies for elementary schools differ from those for secondary schools. In elementary schools, essential subjects and skill areas, rather than courses, are specified. The 1988–1989 elementary school curriculum guidelines for Prince George's County, Maryland, include detailed descriptions of curriculum units for each subject and grade. The following example pertains to social studies for fifth grade and fourth-and-fifth-grade combinations and includes essential learning outcomes and major curriculum topics:

Fifth-Grade and Fourth-and-Fifth-Grade Combinations: Social Studies

Unit I *ESTABLISHING AMERICA*

The unit focuses on the exploration of North America and English colonization. Essential learning outcomes for students are:

- Identify North American areas explored by England, France, and Spain.
- Give reasons for exploration and colonization.
- Tell when, where, and why Virginia, Pennsylvania, and Massachusetts were colonized.
- Compare and contrast the different ethnic makeups and lifestyles in these three colonies.

- Describe the economy of colonial America, what was consumed, and how it was produced.

Unit II *GOVERNING AMERICA*

This unit focuses on the origins and major characteristics of the Constitution. Essential learning outcomes for students are:

- Describe the significance of the American Revolution and the individual contributions of those who made it happen.
- Identify the characteristics and functions of the three branches of government.
- Describe the function of the Constitution and how the Constitution has been changed.
- Describe the American legislative process (how laws are made).
- Discuss the Civil War's significance for American government and the civil rights of Black Americans.

Unit III *EXPANDING AND CHANGING AMERICA*

This unit focuses on the movement of the American people westward and changes in the American people, as well as changes in America's economy. Essential learning outcomes are:

- Trace the westward movement of settlers, noting when and why they went.
- Identify major American inventors involved in movement and production.
- Identify ways factories (mass production) changed America (productivity, immigration, cities).

Besides outcomes and topics, Prince George's elementary curriculum guidelines specify "recommended minimum weekly instructional time allotments." Each student is expected to receive at least 650 minutes of reading and language arts instruction each week (1,800 total minutes of school). Thirty minutes of this time each day is to consist of direct instruction in reading for every student. The guidelines also call for daily mathematics instruction amounting to at least 225 minutes a week for primary and 250 minutes a week for intermediate students. Both groups are to receive 165 minutes a week of science, social studies, and health instruction and 45 minutes a week of art instruction. Music and physical education requirements vary according to the grade level and the week. The matter of how time is to be allocated is discussed in depth in the following chapter on scheduling.

Some curriculum policies deal with the relationship between courses and subject-matter areas—what we refer to as *curriculum organization.* Policies, for instance, may incorporate scope-and-sequence outlines covering the articulation of content across grade levels. Such policies often specify a hierarchy of objectives and prerequisites for upper-level courses. Besides the sequencing of content, policies guiding curriculum organization may indicate how particular content is to be incorporated into the curriculum. In recent years, educators have debated the merits of integrating curriculum mandates into existing courses as opposed to creating new courses. Among these mandates have been women's, black, global, and multicultural studies, computers, and thinking skills. Proponents of curriculum integration maintain that content dealing with matters such as multiculturalism and thinking skills is applicable to a variety of subject-matter areas and should not be treated as a separate course. Advocates of separation counter that existing courses are already overcrowded, and integration can result in a lack of sufficient attention to key subjects.

An issue related to curriculum integration is the issue of the interdisciplinary nature of knowledge. A case can be made that discipline-based courses lead students to view content as fragmented and disconnected. As a result, they may fail to appreciate how knowledge from various disciplines can be applied in the process of solving complex problems. Local policymakers seem most willing to endorse interdisciplinary content for elementary and middle school programs. High schools, though, have resisted interdisciplinary curriculum proposals, in part because of the autonomy of their academic departments.

CURRICULUM CONSISTENCY

Once policymakers have determined the purposes and general components of the curriculum, they often consider issues related to curriculum implementation. Chief among these issues is curriculum consistency. To what extent should teachers within a school or across different schools in a district be expected to cover the same content? In what ways can such expectations be enforced without diminishing the teacher's status as a professional? Questions like these arise because opportunities for students to learn are linked directly to the subject matter to which they are exposed.

Research on curriculum implementation suggests that teachers vary greatly in the amount of time they devote to particular subjects. In one study at the elementary level, the average daily minutes spent on five subjects by six teachers were compared.[27] The time allocated for reading ranged from 26.5 to 95.5 minutes, for mathematics from 29.1 to 49.9 minutes, for language arts from 25.3 to 72.0 minutes, for science from 2.0 to 43.2 minutes, and for social studies from 2.4 to 43.2 minutes.

One reason for such variance may involve teachers' judgments of what their students are capable of learning. Many teachers who work with the disadvantaged have low expectations for their students and therefore expose them to relatively more of the least challenging content.[28] This practice has been criticized for its tendency to foster self-fulfilling prophecies.

Researchers at Michigan State spent years studying how teachers influenced the curriculum. They concluded that individual teachers ultimately may decide what topics will be taught, to whom they will be taught, when and how long each topic will be taught, and how well topics will be learned, but district policies still play a role in shaping the curriculum.[29] In analyzing data on the fourth-grade mathematics curriculum collected from district curriculum directors in five states, for example, the researchers found that the vast majority of districts in four out of the five states had local testing policies and district curriculum objectives. In all five states, at least 70 percent of the students were in districts that mandated textbooks. About half the districts had guidelines governing how much time should be spent on fourth-grade mathematics.[30]

The mere existence of policies, of course, does not guarantee curriculum consistency. Besides the obvious discretion teachers exercise once the classroom door is closed, there is the problem of policy disjointedness. Districts rarely develop policies in a comprehensive way. Instead, policies are added as needed, often in response to transient external pressures. As a result, policies in a domain such as curriculum are not always compatible. One area in which districts have begun to address this problem is in the relationship between curriculum objectives, textbook content, and the items on tests used to assess student achievement. Efforts to ensure compatibility across these three areas often are referred to as *curriculum alignment*. Some districts now have policies that mandate curriculum alignment.

Komoski reported on a curriculum-alignment study in Flint, Michigan.[31] Researchers compared district mathematics objectives with the material covered in district mathematics textbooks at the second-, fourth-, sixth-, and eighth-grade levels. While 95 percent of the district's mathematics goals were covered in the second-grade texts, the figure fell to 69 percent by the eighth grade. In some cases, over half the lessons in a textbook had nothing to do with the district's curriculum objectives. If Flint's teachers stick to textbook content while district tests of mathematics achievement are geared to district objectives, it is easy to understand why test results in Flint may be lower than necessary.

One way to reduce the likelihood of a poorly aligned curriculum is to exercise care in selecting texts. Many districts require that all teachers use the same or comparable texts. These texts typically are selected by textbook adoption committees made up of teachers and curriculum specialists. In twenty-two states, selections must be made from lists of texts approved at the state level.[32] There is some reason to believe, though, that policies governing local textbook adoptions do not always function as well as they should. For example, in one study of the criteria used by seventy committees, Farr and Tulley found that textbook review forms averaged seventy-three criteria and that all criteria were weighted equally![33]

An example of a district policy governing textbook adoption comes from Mesa Unified School District in Arizona. The policy, adopted in 1986, begins as follows:

> *Selection of Textbooks.* The Governing Board shall adopt textbooks and other supplementary books for the schools as recommended by the Superintendent.
>
> Consistent with Board policy, and within any applicable state law and State Board of Education rules, the involvement of parents, teachers, directors, and principals shall be encouraged in textbook selection.

The policy goes on to specify a process for selecting elementary textbooks.

> *Elementary Textbook Adoption Process (K–8).* A textbook adoption procedure for Grades K–8 shall be conducted in each subject area corresponding to the recommendations by the Arizona Department of Education, unless otherwise directed by the Superintendent.
>
> The adoption procedures shall be conducted under the supervision of the Assistant Superintendent for Curriculum and Instruction and the District director or consultant for the subject in question. Principals and teachers shall be involved in making the study and recommendations. Parents or guardians shall also be involved at some point in the study.
>
> The criteria for study, selection, and recommendations shall include
>
> • Assurance that the District goals and objectives can be realized.
> • Provision for evaluating the following, whenever applicable:

1. Philosophy
2. Format
3. Readability
4. Skill, scope, and sequence
5. Interest
6. Manuals
7. Supplementary materials
8. Legal concerns
9. Objectionable content
10. Research
11. Cost

- An evaluation format.

Specific criteria shall be developed under the leadership of the director and submitted to teachers and principals for modification before the actual survey of material is made.

The recommended adoption procedures, and a timetable of events, shall be submitted to the Superintendent for approval before December 1 of each year. The recommended materials must be placed on exhibit for the public for sixty (60) days and then receive official Governing Board approval.

Once the need for a new textbook is determined, it is the function of the director concerned to notify the department chairperson and teacher(s) of the course regarding the need for evaluating textbooks. A minimum of three (3) books should be analyzed and a textbook selected for each course.

Upon completion of the study, a copy of the evaluation shall be approved by the department head, the principal, and the District consultant or director and submitted to the Assistant Superintendent for Curriculum Instruction.

The Assistant Superintendent has the responsibility for making all books considered for adoption available to the Board and the community for a period of at least sixty (60) days. The Assistant Superintendent shall inform the Board of the books being considered and the location where the materials shall be displayed and available for examination. It is also the responsibility of the Assistant Superintendent to submit the request to the Superintendent and the Board. A summary of the evaluations, together with department comments, shall be made available upon request.

It is a requirement that the same text be used throughout the District for the course offering.

Textbook adoption policies such as Mesa's are an important step toward greater curriculum consistency. Consistency can also be a concern in areas of the curriculum other than textbook selection. Consistent treatment of sensitive topics, such as minority contributions to western culture, theories of creation, and the etiology of AIDS, has become particularly important in light of the increased activity of special-interest groups in education. Schools that cannot ensure that controversial topics will be handled in a balanced and unbiased way may find their authority to cover the content challenged. Other challenges may result from inconsistencies in student assignments and expectations across similar courses. As noted earlier, a key to educational equity is seeing that all students are held accountable for basic academic content. The extent to which local school policies are useful in promoting such curriculum consistency remains to be determined, however.

CURRICULUM RESPONSIVENESS

A district's curriculum is a curious amalgam of the old and the new. On the one hand, the curriculum attempts to preserve that which is deemed valuable in traditional culture. On the other hand, it attempts to respond to new developments and to prepare students for the future. Local policymakers may be criticized for their slowness in changing the curriculum or for changing it so much that cultural continuity is lost. In light of such pressures, it is prudent for school systems to develop policies governing the approval of new courses and the changing of curriculum content.

Appendix A is an example of a course-approval policy from Fairfax County, Virginia. The policy specifies four sets of procedures: (1) procedures for requesting approval to add to the school's offerings a course previously approved by the State Department of Education and included on the district's current list of approved courses, (2) procedures for requesting approval of a new course not on the district list of approved courses and for which no additional funding or staffing is required, (3) procedures for requesting approval of a new course for which additional funding or staffing is required, and (4) procedures for approval of a new course proposed by the central administration. Provision is made to pilot new courses and evaluate them prior to final approval. While policies such as Fairfax's may seem cumbersome, they increase the likelihood that adequate review and reflection will precede the addition of any new curriculum offering. Such steps are essential when resources are limited and curriculum demands are great.

During the last decade, school districts have been pressured into offering more drug and alcohol education, more multicultural and global studies, more thinking skills, more foreign languages, and more AIDS awareness instruction. Blue-ribbon commissions have also called for upgrading mathematics, science, and vocational education. As a result, complaints are being voiced that policymakers are too quick to increase teachers' curriculum responsibilities. Content is being added to the curriculum without eliminating outdated or less crucial material. Eventually, such practices lead to a bloated curriculum where *no* content receives sufficient emphasis. In their efforts to respond to changing curriculum needs, local policymakers need to consider ways to winnow current content as they accommodate new material.

Local policymakers can be *too* responsive to pressures for curriculum change. One of the most notable examples of questionable responsiveness involves the censorship of curriculum materials.[34] On the one hand, local policymakers must be careful not to treat the demands of certain special-interest groups as if they necessarily represented the will of the community. On the other hand, the welfare of students and the principles of free speech and academic freedom may be at odds with the desires of a large segment of local citizens. In the latter case, local policymakers may be faced with making unpopular decisions in order to protect students' access to a wide range of ideas and perspectives. It is therefore essential for school systems to have a policy ensuring the orderly review of challenges to curriculum materials.

DETERMINING CURRICULUM POLICIES

Having looked at various dimensions of curriculum policymaking, we now review the major themes that emerge from our analysis.

The first theme—one to be found in subsequent chapters as well—is choice.

Despite increased media attention to the centralization of curriculum decisions, it appears that local policymakers still have a variety of substantive curriculum choices to make. These choices range from mission statements and general curriculum goals to course approval and textbook selection. It would be a mistake, therefore, to regard curriculum policymaking as a process totally dominated by state and federal officials.

A second theme involves control. To what extent should local policymakers attempt to control what is taught? The salience of this question has increased in recent years as concerns have mounted over educational equity. Evidence indicating inequities in exposure to content for different groups of students has compelled policymakers to consider how to ensure that all students have access to a rigorous and comparable academic program. Since curriculum control by policymakers presents a potential challenge to the autonomy and professional judgment of teachers, it is vital that teachers play a role in setting any policies designed to minimize inequities in curriculum coverage. There is little value in standardizing the curriculum if, in so doing, we alienate teachers and reduce the attractiveness of careers in teaching.

Achieving the right balance between control and flexibility is no easy task. Assuming that it is desirable for local policymakers to establish *some* parameters governing content, the question becomes, What are the most effective and least demeaning mechanisms for ensuring curriculum consistency? Mission statements and broad curriculum goals are helpful to a point, but they lack the capacity to ensure compliance. Our distinction between primary and supporting policies becomes important at this point. In order to achieve a district's curriculum mission, it may be necessary to create supporting policies linking curriculum coverage to the evaluation of students, teachers, and programs. Such policies are designed to promote district curriculum goals through the control of outputs. Other supporting policies may focus on controlling inputs. Examples of the latter include policies for hiring teachers with certain subject-matter expertise and acquiring textbooks aligned to district curriculum goals.

As we cover other domains of local policy, it should become increasingly apparent that determining policies related to student learning and the quality of instruction must not be regarded as a series of discrete decisions. The preceding paragraph suggests that many of the policies required to support the implementation of primary policies derive from other domains—such as the evaluation of student performance and personnel. It is of little value for local policymakers to consider curriculum policies without simultaneously reviewing a variety of associated policies. In our judgment, the seven policy domains addressed in the following chapters all relate, in key ways, to the implementation of district curriculum policies and the realization of a district's mission.

NOTES

1. Allan A. Glatthorn, *Curriculum Leadership,* Scott, Foresman and Company, Glenview, Ill., 1987, pp. 4–15.
2. Daniel Tanner and Laurel Tanner, *Curriculum Development,* Macmillan, New York, 1975, p. 189.
3. Allan Odden and David Marsh, "How Comprehensive Reform Legislation Can Improve Secondary Schools," *Phi Delta Kappan,* April 1988, p. 597.
4. Ibid., p. 598.

5. William A. Firestone, Susan H. Fuhrman, and Michael W. Kirst, "The Progress of Reform," Center for Policy Research in Education, New Brunswick, N.J., 1989, p. 22.

6. Ibid.

7. Linda Darling-Hammond, "Valuing Teachers: The Making of a Profession," *Teachers College Record* 87, no. 2 (1985): 209.

8. Ibid.

9. Robert E. Floden, Andrew C. Porter, Linda E. Alford, Donald J. Freeman, Susan Irwin, William H. Schmidt, and John R. Schwille, "Instructional Leadership at the District Level: A Closer Look at Autonomy and Control," *Educational Administration Quarterly,* May 1988, p. 97.

10. John I. Goodlad, *A Place Called School,* McGraw-Hill, New York, 1984, p. 190.

11. John Schwille, Andrew Porter, Linda Alford, Robert Floden, Donald Freeman, Susan Irwin, and William Schmidt, "State Policy and the Control of Curriculum Decisions," *Educational Policy,* March 1988, p. 37.

12. John Meyer, W. Richard Scott, and Terrence Deal, "Research on School and District Organization," in J. Victor Baldridge and Terrence Deal (eds.), *The Dynamics of Organizational Change in Education,* McCutchan, Berkeley, Calif., 1983, pp. 418–419.

13. William Lowe Boyd, "The Politics of Curriculum Change and Stability," in Baldridge and Deal, pp. 243–244.

14. Michael W. Kirst, "Policy Implications of Individual Differences and the Common Curriculum," in Gary D. Fenstermacher and John I. Goodlad (eds.), *Individual Differences and the Common Curriculum,* NSSE Yearbook, pt. 1, 1983, pp. 293–295.

15. Glatthorn, op. cit., p. 146.

16. Ibid., p. 15.

17. Goodlad, op. cit., p. 37.

18. Ibid., p. 38.

19. Ibid., pp. 51–56.

20. Kirst, op. cit., pp. 296–297.

21. Ibid., p. 297.

22. E. D. Hirsch, Jr., *Cultural Literacy,* Houghton Mifflin, Boston, 1987.

23. Arthur D. Roberts and Gordon Camelti, *Redefining General Education in the American High School,* Association for Supervision and Curriculum Development, Alexandria, Va., 1984.

24. Kirst, op. cit., p. 298.

25. Our appreciation to Harriet Hopkins for sharing Fairfax County Regulation 3201 with us.

26. Michael S. Garet and Brian DeLany, "Students, Courses, and Stratification," *Sociology of Education,* April 1988, pp. 61–77.

27. Thomas L. Good and Jere E. Brophy, *Looking in Classrooms,* 4th ed., Harper & Row, New York, 1987, p. 36.

28. Jeannie Oakes, "Keeping Track, Part I: The Policy and Practice of Curriculum Inequality," *Phi Delta Kappan,* September 1986, pp. 15–16; Stewart C. Purkey and Robert A. Rutter, "High School Teaching: Teacher Practices and Beliefs in Urban and Suburban Public Schools," *Educational Policy* 1, no. 3 (1987): 387.

29. Floden et al., op. cit., p. 101.

30. Ibid., p. 107.

31. P. Kenneth Komoski, "Needed: A Whole-Curriculum Approach," *Educational Leadership,* February 1990, p. 78.

32. Roger Farr and Michael A. Tulley, "Do Adoption Committees Perpetuate Mediocre Textbooks?" *Phi Delta Kappan,* March 1985, pp. 467–471.

33. Ibid., p. 470.

34. Perry A. Zirkel and Ivan B. Gluckman, "The Constitution and the Curriculum," *Principal,* September 1988, p. 60.

3

Scheduling

Scheduling has become a critical variable in ensuring curriculum coverage and organizing schools for instruction, in part because of the proliferation of supplementary programs and special personnel. During the past twenty-five years, school staffs and program offerings have been expanded. Expansion has meant greater complexity concerning the allocation of time for instruction.

Determining how students and teachers should be scheduled has traditionally been a primary responsibility for local policymakers. Among the factors they must weigh are (1) the shape and size of the school building, (2) the type of schedule to which the community is accustomed, (3) the needs and desires of teacher-specialists, (4) teacher strengths and weaknesses, and (5) funding.

In this chapter, policy issues concerning scheduling for instructional purposes will be examined. Scheduling will not be treated as the mere assignment of staff members, students, activities, and space; instead, it will be viewed as a mechanism for dealing with a variety of issues of teaching and learning. After establishing the importance of scheduling to the delivery of quality instruction, four specific issues will be treated.

Some researchers have reported that many elementary school students, particularly low-achieving students, spend up to 70 percent of their school day "waiting."[1] This "waiting time," sometimes disguised as *seatwork,* is often meaningless[2] and costly.[3] Seatwork and its implications for scheduling is the first issue treated.

Not only are teachers being told to reduce unproductive class time, but they are also being asked to work with students of all abilities in the same class and to increase individual student success rates. The second issue treated, therefore, is the relationship between ability-grouping practices, scheduling policies, and student outcomes.

Teachers, parents, and school administrators routinely suggest that if classes were smaller, achievement would rise. This hypothesis has yet to be conclusively proven, however. The third issue treated is the relationship between school scheduling policy, class size, and student achievement.

"Pullout programs" continue to grow, and, although some of these programs have merit, they can result in a reduction in the role of classroom teachers in making decisions about students. Such programs also can fragment the school day for both students and teachers and often stigmatize students who participate in them. The fourth issue treated, therefore, is how to design schedules to minimize the negative by-products of "pullout programs."

Various scheduling models for elementary, middle, and secondary schools are also discussed in this chapter to illustrate some of the options available to school leaders concerned with the four issues presented. The chapter closes with several recommendations for educators charged with the task of developing and assessing local policies related to scheduling and the allocation of instructional time.

THE EVOLUTION OF SCHEDULING

The school schedule is the vehicle for allocating time, space, staff, and resources for the delivery of instruction. The schedule symbolizes what educators believe to be important in a school; in essence, the schedule reveals the school's priorities. *School scheduling,* the allocation of instructional time, is the primary expression of the school's academic focus.

Much of the recent interest in the study of time and learning may be traced to the conceptual framework provided by Carroll. The major idea supporting this model is that in a curriculum time should be a variable unit while achievement levels should be constant. Believing that time-allocation decisions are related to student achievement, Carroll incorporated time utilization into his "Model of School Learning" (MSL).[4] Carroll theorized that the following five factors were related to the time needed to learn a given subject:

1. *Aptitude,* defined as "the amount of time an individual needs to learn a given task under optimal conditions"
2. Ability to understand instruction
3. Quality of instruction
4. *Perseverance,* or "the amount of time an individual is willing to devote to active learning"
5. *Opportunity,* or "the amount of time allowed for learning"

According to Carroll, aptitude, ability, and perseverance reside within the individual. Opportunity to learn and quality of instruction are conditions external to the individual and, consequently, hold the most promise for manipulation by school policymakers. Acknowledging the complexity and elusiveness of quality of instruction, Carroll determined that opportunity for learning was the more clear-cut and easily understood variable for manipulation.[5] Policymakers are key persons in determining opportunities for students to learn, and the school schedule is the primary vehicle for providing those opportunities.

Although relatively few systematic studies of scheduling exist, the importance of scheduling to teaching effectiveness has been recognized by several researchers. In their identification of effective schools in Michigan, Brookover and others indicate that scheduling was an important factor in achieving a school climate conducive to student learning.[6] Levine and Stark studied the implementation of the Chicago Mastery Learning Reading Program in one Chicago and three New York elementary schools. One factor they found to be related to student achievement was a principal who was able to schedule in such a way that teachers and students were aware of academic expectations.[7] In a study designed to determine the organizational factors that contribute to student achievement in reading and mathematics for poor and black elementary school students, Sizemore found that scheduling was of crucial importance.[8]

Traditionally, scheduling for instruction has been largely the concern of secondary school principals. In recent years, however, elementary programs have increased in complexity. With the advent of mainstreaming, compensatory education, and special programs, elementary school scheduling has grown beyond the simple establishment of opening, closing, and recess times; class periods; lunchtimes; and teacher assignments. English captures the feelings of many elementary school principals in the following quotation:

> "The grammar school is dead; it doesn't exist anymore," groaned one seasoned elementary principal after trying to schedule for pull-outs. "It's been replaced with a highly complex, difficult-to-manage organization that's as complicated as anything at the secondary level."[9]

Many contemporary books written for principals refer to the importance of scheduling. For example, Hencley, McCleary, and McGrath believe that organizing for instruction, or *scheduling,* is the most important function of the elementary school principal because student achievement outcomes may be dependent on the way in which time is allocated for instruction. In their words:

> Although sound organization does not in itself guarantee effective programs, it is an essential element in maximizing effectiveness; and worthwhile programs can be seriously affected, even destroyed, by poor organization.[10]

Neale, Bailey, and Ross suggest that school faculties charged with increasing school effectiveness begin by considering the manner in which their schools are organized for instruction.[11] Faber and Shearron conclude that the organizational plan selected for an elementary school has a direct effect upon student outcomes in terms of achievement, morale, and self-esteem. In their view, scheduling reveals more about educators' attitudes toward teaching children than philosophical statements.[12] Saville also points out that "effective organization of the teaching-learning process in the elementary school is very necessary and requires careful planning."[13] Hughes and Ubben draw the following conclusions:

> The school schedule is considered by many to be the command performance of the principal. It is here that the ability to conceptualize, to organize, and to carry out detailed planning is most visible. If well done, the schedule will strongly support the instructional and curricular program of the school. On the other hand, if poorly designed, the schedule will be a road-block to a balanced curriculum and instructional flexibility.[14]

SEATWORK AND SCHEDULING

One area where the impact of scheduling on instruction can be detected is seatwork, or the independent work assigned to students while the teacher is engaged in other activities. Particularly at the elementary level, the time available for seatwork is a function, in part, of the overall school schedule. Because students' independent work can constitute a large percentage of instructional time in many schools, it is vitally important that this time be well spent. There is little evidence to indicate that such is the case.[15]

Rupley and Blair, summarizing the suggestions of several researchers, made the following recommendations for the organization and implementation of effective reading seatwork activities:

1. The needs of the students should determine the use of the activities.
2. Students should be given relevant purposes and directions for learning.
3. Students should be provided with practice examples to assure they understand the task and how to respond.
4. Teachers should have established procedures for assisting students who experience difficulty with the assignment.
5. Teachers need to monitor students' seatwork and give feedback as needed.
6. Students should complete activities in various types of groups (individual, partner, small-group, and cooperative).
7. Seatwork tasks should reinforce reading skills that have been previously taught.[16]

In studying primary teachers' seatwork assignment and supervision practices, Rupley and Blair found that (1) approximately 50 percent of the teachers assigned the seatwork before assigning the reading lesson to the whole class; (2) few teachers used written directions, and no teachers used an assignment sheet; (3) 50 percent of the teachers gave the purposes for the assignment, but only 10 percent gave practice examples; (4) all of the teachers required students to complete their seatwork by themselves; and (5) one-third of them provided some assistance during seatwork time.[17]

Seatwork is not only difficult to assign and monitor in an educationally effective way, but it can also have deleterious effects upon low achievers. Anderson and other researchers at Michigan State's Institute for Research on Teaching suggest that the basic skills of reading and math are easily acquired when practice meets with a high level of success and the material is introduced gradually, in small increments. Failure results when low-achieving students are assigned seatwork that is too difficult for them. These students then focus on completing their tasks as quickly as possible and looking busy. They found that students in lower reading groups respond poorly to seatwork activities in general. Those who need the most practice and reinforcement thus get the least out of the activity.[18]

David Berliner sums up the problem with seatwork as follows:

> What are students doing when they do seatwork? It appears some are not doing much at all. What others do is done without much thought. And most are doing their seatwork to finish it as quickly as possible.[19]

Classroom research suggests that the assignment and monitoring of seatwork by teachers in elementary school is not effectively managed. There is some indication that seatwork practices may have disproportionally negative effects upon low achievers. An elementary school scheduling system that dramatically decreases the need for seatwork activities is presented later in this chapter to illustrate the relationship between the allocation of instructional time by teachers and school scheduling policy.

ABILITY GROUPING AND SCHEDULING

The effect of grouping on student achievement and student self-esteem has been a controversial topic in education for many years. Recent studies in this area suggest that the positive academic-achievement effects of homogeneous grouping are limited to very specific cases. Other evidence indicates that children put in low-ability groups suffer a loss of self-esteem and may, in fact, receive less instructional attention from the teacher.[20] It is our contention that scheduling policies, especially at the elementary level, play a role in decisions regarding grouping. This point becomes clearer in a later section when we discuss alternative schedules.

While grouping is discussed in greater detail in Chapter 4, it is useful to review some of the findings of research on the subject.

Noland and Taylor conclude from their metaanalysis of fifty studies reported between 1967 and 1983 that "ability grouping does not improve overall student achievement and does damage overall student self-concept."[21] They discovered that though students of both high and low academic ability benefited slightly from instruction in homogeneous groups, students of average ability suffered.[22] Their analysis by school subject revealed that

> For both cognitive and affective measures, when the subject was reading, ability grouping had positive effects. . . . for all other subjects which were investigated, the affective scores of the students who were ability grouped for instruction were lower.[23]

They also found that students relegated to the lower groups suffered the greatest damage to their self-concepts.[24]

Wilkinson's review of the grouping literature led her to conclude the following:

> Homogeneous grouping is detrimental to learning of students assigned to low groups, a consequence of the prevalent pullout practice in the way Title I has been implemented in the classroom.[25]

Winn and Wilson add to the mounting criticism of ability grouping for instruction.

> Research does not support the popular practice of ability grouping. Students are placed in groups through diverse and questionable means. Usually they do not escape the group unless it is to be assigned to a lower ability group. Teachers generally teach students in lower groups at a lower cognitive level and expect less from them because of their group placement. This often leads to a self-fulfilling prediction that attitudes will be poor and performance less than predicted.[26]

After examining the extensive data provided by John Goodlad's "Study of Schooling," Jeanne Oakes concluded "The curricular and instructional inequalities that accompany tracking may actually foster mediocre classroom experiences for most students and erect special barriers to the educational success of poor, black, and Hispanic students."[27]

After examination of more than 100 studies, Slavin and other researchers at the Center for Research on Elementary and Middle Schools at Johns Hopkins University tentatively advanced the following elements of effective ability-grouping plans:

1. Students should remain in heterogeneous classes at most times and be regrouped by ability only in subjects such as reading and mathematics where reducing heterogeneity is particularly important. Students' primary identification should be with a heterogeneous class.
2. Grouping plans should be based upon students' skill in the specific subject, not on overall IQ or achievement.
3. Grouping plans should include frequent reassessment of student placements and should be flexible enough to allow for easy reassignment after an initial placement.
4. Teachers should actually vary their level and pace of instruction to correspond to students' levels of readiness and learning rates in regrouped classes.
5. In within-class groupings, numbers of groups should be kept small to allow for adequate direct instruction from the teacher for the group.[28]

While research on the effects of ability grouping has not yet come up with any conclusive answers, decisions at the school level still must be made regarding how to group students. Local policymakers cannot ignore the fact that the "most consistent finding in the ability group research over the past 50 years is that parents and teachers believe that ability grouping works and that it is good for children."[29] School scheduling policy can facilitate or inhibit efforts to group students by ability on a selective basis. Scheduling options, in turn, may be a function of class size.

CLASS SIZE AND ACHIEVEMENT IN SCHEDULING

The effect of class size on student achievement has been the subject of much controversy and examination. The first known investigation of the subject was published in 1893. By 1954, Blake found that there had been a total of 267 studies on class size.[30] A review of 85 of them revealed that 35 found small class size related positively to student achievement and 18 found large class size related positively to achievement. The remaining studies were inconclusive.[31]

Narrowing the field down to 22 scientifically acceptable studies, Blake found that small class size and student achievement related positively in 72 percent of these studies; large class size and achievement were related positively in 3 of the 22; and no significant differences were reported in another 3. Design flaws, however, were found in many of these studies.[32] Less conclusive findings were reported by Educational Research Service:

> Research findings on class size to this point document repeatedly that the relationship between pupil achievement and class size is highly complex.
> There is general consensus that the research findings on the effects of class size on pupil achievement across all grade levels are contradictory and inconclusive.
> Research to date provides no support for the concept of an "optimum" class size in isolation of other factors.
> Existing research findings do not support the contention that smaller classes will of themselves result in greater academic achievement gains for pupils.
> There is research evidence that small classes are important to increased achievement in reading and mathematics in the early primary grades.

Few if any pupil benefits can be expected from reducing class size if teachers continue to use the same instructional methods and procedures in the small classes that they used in the larger classes.[33]

Questioning the above findings, Glass and others undertook another review of class-size literature, using metaanalysis to compare students' achievement in classes of two different sizes.[34] Glass picked seventy-seven studies for metaanalysis. The focus for his study was a comparison of achievement in large and small classes; for example, the reading achievement of students taught in classes of fifteen pupils was compared with the achievement of pupils in classes of thirty. This analysis revealed that student achievement increased as class size decreased, with the most dramatic increase occurring among the students who were taught in groups of fifteen or fewer students.[35]

Although teachers may have applauded the Glass findings, some researchers were less than enthusiastic. Researchers at Educational Research Service (ERS), for example, were commissioned to respond to the work and found the following five weaknesses:

1. The use of metaanalysis resulted in an oversimplification of results.
2. Too few studies were used, and conclusions were overgeneralized.
3. The interpretations of the findings were sometimes contradictory.
4. The conclusion confused the class-size issue.
5. Bold generalizations served to negate the need for further research.[36]

Shapson and others investigated the effect of class size on the achievement of sixty-two groups of fourth- and fifth-grade Toronto students in reading, mathematics, art, and composition.[37] Their most important finding, according to Shapson, was in the area of teacher morale and attitudes. Teacher morale was significantly higher in the smaller classes, and the authors suggested that "in the future," emphasis could be placed on providing teachers with training in specific instructional strategies most appropriate for different class sizes.[38] In essence, Shapson agrees with the findings of the ERS group but believes that teachers must learn special teaching methods for small-group instruction if achievement gains are to result from smaller class sizes.

Cahen, Filby, McCutcheon, and Kyle also explored the question of how class size influenced teaching and learning.[39] In their studies, class size was reduced by one-third in selected classes at midterm. Research methods included "naturalistic observations, field notes, and interviews as well as systematic behavioral observation and some achievement test data."[40] They reported that, in general, small class size was related to increased student achievement. Students in smaller classes received more individual attention from the teacher, had a higher time-on-task rate, and experienced fewer discipline problems.[41] Like Shapson, however, Cahen and colleagues found little change in the way in which classes were conducted and recommended in-service training in techniques found effective in small-group instruction.

In a 1986 update of the earlier ERS review, Robinson and Wittebols drew the following conclusions relative to the relationship between class size and student achievement:

1. Research to date provides no support for the concept of "optimum" class size in isolation from other factors.
2. There is evidence that small classes increase pupil achievement in reading and mathematics in the early primary grades.
3. There is some evidence that pupils of lesser ability tend to achieve more in smaller classes. The evidence is mixed for students of average or higher academic abilities.
4. Research indicates that smaller classes can have a positive effect on the academic achievement of economically disadvantaged and ethnic minority students.
5. Research indicates that few if any pupil benefits can be expected from reducing class size if teachers continue to use the same instructional methods and procedures in smaller classes that they use in larger classes.[42]

Limited support for the thesis that small class size and student achievement are related exists in the research literature just reviewed. Some researchers report a positive relationship between large class size and achievement; others find no significant differences relative to class size. In the most extensive study, the aforementioned metaanalysis of class-size research, Glass and his colleagues conclude that student achievement increases as class size decreases. Significant increases in achievement were found when classes consisted of fewer than twenty students, with the greatest advantage occurring when class size was limited to fifteen or fewer students.

Scheduling relates to class size in several ways. At the elementary level, scheduling policies that facilitate the use of specialty teachers can help reduce class size at certain times during the day. At the secondary level, schedules divide the school day into periods. Schedules that include a greater number of periods increase the possibility of smaller classes. Policymakers should be aware, however, that tradeoffs may have to be made to reduce class size in these cases. For example, students may experience more interruptions and teachers may be compelled to increase their number of "preparations."

THE ISSUE OF "PULLOUT PROGRAMS"

Increased levels of federal and state involvement in public education have prompted educators to focus on supplementary programs as a means of improving education. One significant intervention resulted when schools were enlisted in the "war on poverty" under the Johnson administration. To provide equal educational opportunities for poor children, Congress enacted the Elementary and Secondary Education Act (ESEA), which provided for compensatory education programs. These programs were aimed at overcoming the negative environmental factors thought to be associated with the lack of academic motivation and lower achievement among children from poor families. Remedial and special programs for enhancing the "cognitive, social and emotional development"[43] of low-income and low-achieving students were introduced into elementary school programs. According to the guidelines of Title I of ESEA, these compensatory programs were to be in addition to, rather than in place of, existing instructional programs.[44]

Another piece of legislation that had great impact on the policymakers responsible for scheduling was the Education of All Handicapped Law of 1975 (P.L. 94-142), commonly referred to as the "mainstreaming law." Enacted primarily in response to lobbying efforts on behalf of the 4 million handicapped children whose parents felt they were not receiving the educational services they needed,[45] the law charged public schools with responsibility for providing these children with special services such as speech therapy, physical therapy, and occupational therapy in the "least restrictive environment."[46] As provisions of this law have been implemented, special-education students (including the health-impaired, the hearing-impaired, the visually impaired, the learning-disabled, the mentally retarded, and the emotionally disturbed) have spent more and more time in regular classrooms. Special services have been provided in resource classes for only a part of the school day.

The growth in state and federal mandates has resulted in a large increase in the use of support personnel in schools. Students receiving a special service are typically "pulled out" of mainstream instructional activities and taught individually or in small groups by the appropriate specialist. Scheduling for instruction around the various "pullout programs" has become a complex undertaking for the regular classroom teacher. Regular classroom or base teachers, already juggling twenty-five or more students, must now accommodate various support personnel and their "pullout programs." Movement in and out of classrooms has increased. Teachers, especially at the elementary level, have expressed frustration at being "traffic directors."[47] The following comment is apt to be heard in elementary school lounges throughout the country: "I don't have an hour a day when I have all my students in my classroom together. Two or three are always assigned to some program—Chapter 1, talented and gifted, speech therapy, reading resource, or what have you."

Moreover, remedial programs that require students to miss instruction by the base teacher have produced only limited gains in terms of student outcomes. Too often, these programs are poorly integrated with regular classroom activities. There is growing evidence that remedial programs that are personal, highly specific, and focused on keeping the student in a regular group and competitive with the group produce the best results in terms of long-term student growth.[48]

The intent of compensatory and special-education programs was to increase educational opportunities for disadvantaged and handicapped students. Regardless of one's belief about the success of such efforts, one effect is certain: Their implementation has resulted in fragmentation of the school day. Pullout programs, therefore, have become a concern of local policymakers who determine how instructional time should be allocated.

SCHOOL SCHEDULING OPTIONS

The preceding sections identified several issues that must be considered by local policymakers as they determine how instructional time should be allocated. Seatwork, ability grouping, class size, and pullout programs are matters that affect, and are affected by, the school schedule. A schedule that places elementary students with the same teacher all day does little to facilitate between-class grouping and increases the likelihood that seatwork might be overassigned. Secondary school schedules that are divided into larger numbers of discrete "periods" enable teachers to offer a greater array of small specialty courses. Certain schedules can accommodate pullout programs more easily than others.

This section reviews some of the scheduling options available at the elementary, middle, and high school levels.

Descriptions of School Schedules

ELEMENTARY AND MIDDLE SCHOOL SCHEDULING OPTIONS

Many more options exist for the organization of time in elementary and middle schools than many observers have realized. After describing some of these options, a form of scheduling that ameliorates many of the problems associated with the issues of seatwork, grouping, class size, and "pullout programs" will be presented.

In the traditional *self-contained classroom* a given number of students is assigned to a teacher for the entire day. The classroom teacher is responsible for instruction in nearly all subject areas. Children receiving special services are "pulled out" from the classroom for that instruction. The class may also receive supplementary instruction in physical education, art, music, and other specialties from resource staff, if such staff members are available. Schedules for resource teachers may be created by the principal, but these schedules are often negotiated by the teachers themselves. Proponents of this form of scheduling cite its flexibility and the close relationship it fosters between teacher and pupil as its major strengths.

Several scheduling plans have attempted to lessen academic diversity by grouping students by ability. A variation of the self-contained classroom, the *nongraded classroom* permits students to be grouped by skill level rather than chronological age. The age span within an individual classroom varies with the particular plan. Children move up from one level to the next after they have met predetermined exit criteria. The *Joplin Plan* creates a nongraded instructional organization for part of the school day. Students are regrouped by ability for language arts and reading instruction regardless of their chronological age. The majority of their day, however, is still spent in self-contained rooms. Many schools assign students to heterogeneous homerooms within a grade level and then schedule students by ability for parts of the day. This typically occurs for an extended period for both language arts and mathematics. For example, in a grade level with three teachers, children might be divided into three language arts or reading groups, "high," "middle," and "low," with each group instructed by one of the three teachers. Later in the day, students would be regrouped by ability in mathematics. Instruction in heterogeneous groups is given only in the basic skills.

Efforts have been made to ameliorate the problems associated with "pullout programs." In the *closed time option,* part of the school day is protected from "pullouts." Typically, reading and/or mathematics time blocks are freed from interruptions. In a *rotational schedule for "pullouts,"* children who participate in such programs are scheduled on a rotating basis so as not to miss the same subject each day. Some schools have attempted to solve this problem by putting all children participating in "pullout programs" into one classroom. The pullout, or resource, teacher then comes into the classroom to provide *in-class services* to these children while the regular classroom teacher is working on the same subject.[49]

Practitioners also offer suggestions for reorganizing schedules in efforts to reduce class size. Hawkinson reports that small-group instruction was facilitated in the Hatch School in Oak Park, Illinois, by reassigning teaching personnel.[50] In the Hatch School, all certified reading teachers, including specialists and resource teachers, were assigned to teach fifteen or fewer students during a 3-hour time block each morning. Large-group instruction occurred during the afternoon session, when specialists and resource teachers returned to their special assignments during the afternoon sessions. Pamela Noli, principal of Howard Elementary School in Madera, California, scheduled "a one-hour math tutoring program after the regular school day . . . to provide individualized help to students."[51]

Parallel block scheduling is a relatively new option that can resolve many of the issues associated with scheduling in elementary and middle schools. Canady and others suggest that parallel block scheduling provides opportunities for small-group instruction while minimizing the disruptions associated with "pullout programs."[52] Canady and Hotchkiss state that organization is critical to a successful school operation, and effective organization is achieved primarily through the scheduling process.[53] According to Canady, equal time allocations for all students, small class size, academic focus, direct instruction in reading and mathematics, and uninterrupted time for instruction are among the benefits accruing to students in schools using parallel block scheduling.

In a parallel block schedule, blocks of time are allotted for essential and/or desired small instructional groups parallel to, or concurrent with, blocks of time when other instructional activities and support services are scheduled. In elementary and middle schools, the reduced instructional groups usually are in the areas of reading/language arts and mathematics. These groups of fourteen or fewer students average approximately one-half of the typical classroom number. Students are scheduled to attend various "pullout" programs during the block of time that coincides with the time allocated for the direct instruction of reduced groups in reading and mathematics.

Parallel block scheduling is characterized by the following elements:

1. Schedules for instruction in reading, mathematics, special programs, and support services are coordinated by an administrator or designee (either an individual or a committee).
2. Large blocks of uninterrupted time are allocated for reading and mathematics; and time periods, subjects, and instructional groups are consistent from day to day.
3. Large-group instruction is provided, usually in extension centers, so that base teachers may work with reduced groups during reading and mathematics.
4. Support services are scheduled during times other than the times allocated for direct instruction; "pullout" services are scheduled out of extension activities.
5. Instruction in reading and mathematics is provided in reduced groups. Ideally,

base teachers work with one group while all other students attend extension-center instruction and/or support services.

6. The instructional programs of extension-center teachers, support personnel, and base teachers are coordinated.
7. The instructional program of the base teacher takes precedence over other scheduling considerations.

While several of the characteristics listed above also may be characteristic of a traditionally scheduled school, all must be present for the efficient and effective operation of a parallel block schedule.

Parallel block scheduling addresses the issues of seatwork, ability grouping, class size, and pullout programs. Its primary objectives include the following:

1. To provide an academic focus by building the schedule around specific instructional programs
2. To give base teachers decision-making authority and responsibility regarding their students' placement and grouping requirements
3. To coordinate the programs of base and support teachers
4. To prevent fragmentation of the instructional program for regular and special students
5. To strengthen the instructional program of the base teacher
6. To provide instruction in reading and mathematics in reduced groups
7. To reduce the stigma associated with selected "pullout programs"
8. To increase the amount of time-on-task for students
9. To reduce the need for unsupervised seatwork activities
10. To reduce discipline problems associated with independent seatwork groups
11. To provide, with the extension center, something special for the "average" child
12. To assure equality of teacher instructional time for each instructional group

HIGH SCHOOL SCHEDULING OPTIONS

Various scheduling plans have been employed in secondary schools over the past few decades. In many of the plans, attempts were made to increase flexibility of time and class size and to accommodate student and teacher needs. The more complex scheduling models initially received enthusiastic receptions, but typically gave way to the traditional six- or seven-period schedule. Today there is a renewed interest in reforming high school scheduling because of increased graduation requirements, expanded curricula, and concern over declining student achievement. Among the models being discussed in the contemporary literature are (1) *intensive scheduling*,[54] which involves scheduling students into one class at a time, usually for 3 or 4 hours each day, for approximately 4 or 5 weeks; (2) a rotating extra-period day;[55] (3) a slide concurrent schedule; (4) a flexible modular schedule;[56] (5) a trimester scheduling plan;[57] and (6) a block plan.[58] Brief descriptions of each of these plans are offered below:

According to Anderson, most secondary schools today use concurrent scheduling. The term *concurrent scheduling* refers to the fact that the daily schedule for each student consists of several classes, each meeting for approximately 50 minutes. This means that each class accounts for approximately 250 minutes a week. The courses continue for 18 or 36 weeks. *Intensive scheduling,* by contrast, involves scheduling students into one class at a time, usually for 3 or 4 hours each day, for approximately 4 or 5 weeks. The student in the intensively scheduled school is exposed to a subject for approximately the same amount of time as the student under the concurrent method; however, the exposure is compressed into fewer weeks. Not every subject, of course, may necessitate intensive scheduling. Subjects such as band, vocal music, foreign languages, and physical education may continue to be scheduled concurrently in a rotating period of time, possibly when selected groups of teachers involved in the intensively scheduled classes are released for planning.[59]

Because of a recent increase in the number of traditional academic courses required for graduation in many districts, classes in the arts and vocational areas are being "pushed out" of the curriculum for many students. In a traditional six-period day, there simply is insufficient time for such areas of study, particularly for the college-bound student. Here is where a rotating extra-period schedule can help. This scheduling option is organized around the traditional six-period day except that each of the periods is longer—perhaps 55 to 60 minutes instead of 45 to 50 minutes. Each of these six periods is replaced on a rotating basis once every 7 days by an additional course. For example: on Day 1, a student attends Periods 1, 2, 3, 4, 5, and 6; on Day 2, the student attends Periods 1, 2, 3, 4, 5, 7; on Day 3, the student attends Periods 1, 2, 3, 4, 6, 7, and so on. The rotating seven-period schedule for Winfield (Kan.) High School, for example, (1) requires that a student skip a class once every 7 days; (2) provides each student with an opportunity to earn twenty-eight units (over a 4-year period); and (3) ensures each student an opportunity to take as many as 9.5 credits of electives.[60]

A *slide concurrent schedule* represents a variation of the rotating extra-day schedule. Each period slides to a different time in the day on a rotating basis. For example, if the school has a seven-period day, on Day 1, classes meet in the following pattern: Periods 1, 2, 3, 4, 5, 6, and 7. On Day 2, the classes meet in the following pattern: Periods 7, 1, 2, 3, 4, 5, and 6. On Day 3, the pattern is Period 6, 7, 1, 2, 3, 4, and 5, and so on until the cycle is complete. Several variations of the slide concurrent schedule have been tried. Some schools may slide only every other day. Day 1 would consist of Periods 1, 2, 3, 4, 5, 6, and 7. Day 2 would consist of Periods 7, 6, 5, 4, 3, 2, and 1. In this alternative, Period 4 remains the same each day, a provision that is useful in designing lunch schedules, accommodating certain programs such as band (which may require students from various grade levels to meet at a common period), and helping schools using itinerant teachers.

Major arguments for the various slide schedules are that students scheduled for certain problematic periods, such as the first and last periods of the day, are not penalized as they are with fixed schedules. Also, planning periods for teachers are rotated so that no group of teachers monopolizes preferred periods.

A complex format, flexible modular scheduling is characterized by classes of varying lengths. Flexible modular scheduling may range from a simple alteration of period length and subject order to a complex system in which new schedules are generated daily and picked up by students each morning.[61] Three types of grouping, with different goals and instructional methods, typically are encompassed in flexible-modular-schedule models. Most models call for (1) *large-group instruction* (LGI), designed primarily to motivate students to investigate the particular content; (2) *small-group discussion* (SGD), designed primarily to encourage open inquiry, clarification, and debate around the issues and ideas of the content; and (3) *independent study* (IS), conducted by individual students or a small group of students with the teacher acting as a guide or adviser. Some schools today also use cooperative-learning strategies in addition to, or in some instances in lieu of, the SGD and IS modes.

Another scheduling option is the trimester plan, which requires the 180-day school year to be divided into three 60-day trimesters. Usually, each day contains four class periods, and each trimester-long course earns students one-half credit. In the Warren County, North Carolina, High School plan, all students and teachers are rescheduled at the beginning of each trimester. The plan's advantages include (1) decreased demands on resources, (2) greater flexibility in scheduling and making changes, (3) reduction in the number of students who must repeat a failed course for an entire year, and (4) greater efficiency in the use of time. The disadvantages include (1) class periods that may be overlong for some subjects, (2) a breakup of courses traditionally seen as whole units, (3) a decrease in the number of days available for teachers and students to work together to build relationships, (4) difficulties presented for transfer students, and (5) the necessity of building three different schedules during the school year.[62]

Used most often in junior high and middle schools, the block plan is similar to the back-to-back scheduled periods implemented during the 1960s in selected secondary schools in the United States. The plan also has some of the features of the parallel block scheduling option described earlier; however, secondary block plans usually do not include reduced instructional groups as part of the model. The *secondary block plan* typically includes a pair of teachers assigned to two classes for the homeroom period plus four academic core courses, such as language arts/social studies and mathematics/science. The plan's advantages include (1) flexibility in the allocation of time for instruction, (2) joint planning by teachers, (3) special attention to the teacher's role in counseling students, and (4) increased possibilities for integrating subject matter.[63] The plan, however, cannot easily accommodate itinerant teachers, and it often requires teachers with dual certification. A further disadvantage is that it is sometimes difficult to schedule single-period classes around the core blocks of time.

The newest recommendation for high school scheduling is the so-called Copernican Plan, offered by its author as a mechanism for restructuring American secondary education.[64] Similar to parallel block scheduling, the Copernican Plan is based on large blocks of time (greater than a typical "period") and some degree of concentration on one subject at a time. The plan is offered as a means for avoiding the kind of juggling of multiple courses that distresses many students and results in fragmentation of the curriculum. It is too early to know how the Copernican Plan will function on a regular basis.

DETERMINING SCHEDULING POLICIES

The school schedule can express the philosophy, goals, priorities, and prejudices of a school. Local policymakers, including principals, should not regard the choice of a schedule as a routine chore to be foisted off on the assistant principal or guidance counselor. Although these individuals certainly should be involved in the scheduling process, local educational leaders should consider the adoption of a schedule as an important policy decision.

As has been shown, a variety of scheduling options exists. Our review of the research and analysis of the key issues related to scheduling lead to the following considerations for those involved in determining school schedules:

- Of the several factors associated with learning—aptitude, ability, quality of instruction, opportunity to learn, and perseverance—*opportunity to learn,* or the amount of time allowed for learning, holds the most promise for control by policymakers. The design of the school schedule is critical in determining opportunities for learning. In most schools, there is time within the school day that could be used more productively; therefore, a schedule should enhance the productive use of time by teachers and students.
- Research suggests that regrouping into ability groups for specific classes such as reading or mathematics may be effective in raising student achievement without negatively impacting self-esteem *if* students spend most of their school day in a heterogeneous group. Research does *not* support extensive ability grouping for long periods of the school day. Schedules should reflect these findings.
- Many teachers believe they can be more effective with a smaller group of students than with a larger group; a schedule should therefore be sufficiently flexible to allow teaching-group sizes to be reduced during selected periods of the day. Factors which should be considered in deciding appropriate teacher-student ratios are (1) the particular talents of the teacher, (2) the teaching style of the teacher, (3) the objectives of the lesson, (4) the content to be taught, (5) the age and characteristics of the students, and (6) the learning characteristics and needs of the students.
- School schedules can be constructed in such a way as to assist teachers in using teaching time more productively, but the schedule cannot guarantee that teachers will demonstrate productive teaching functions. Evidence in the literature suggests that many teachers need assistance in using teaching time and small groups.
- Base teachers should be responsible and accountable for the academic progress of the students assigned to their classes; therefore, base teachers should play a major role in the decision-making process regarding the scheduling and coordination of various "pullout" support services.
- "Pullout" services should focus on keeping students in regular educational programs and should be scheduled with the realization that direct instruction by the classroom teacher is of primary importance. The stigma associated with participation in various "pullout programs" can be diminished by reducing the visibility of such groupings. (For example, in parallel block scheduling, where half the children leave the room at the same time for a variety of services, there is less attention drawn to those attending remedial programs.)
- Students learn more in teacher-directed instruction than they do in independent, unsupervised activities; therefore, a schedule should support increased time for teacher-directed interaction and instruction.
- There is some research suggesting that at-risk students in middle, junior, and senior high schools may profit from spending large blocks of time during the

day with one teacher. For these students, it may be more important that they experience a sense of belonging to "a group" and be "known" by a single teacher than to be mixed and moved about in six or more classes during a school day. Again, persons responsible for designing schedules for middle, junior, and senior high schools may want to consider how scheduling can facilitate the needs of at-risk students.

- Many high schools today have increased the number of credits required for graduation and, with this increase, subjects such as art, vocal music, band, speech, debate, and some vocational subjects have been adversely affected because students cannot schedule them during the school day. Persons responsible for high school schedules are urged to consider several of the models suggested in this chapter, which give both teachers and students flexibility in designing individual student programs. Two schedule designs which can increase the number of periods for course offerings are the rotating extra-period day schedule and the flexible modular schedule.

The importance of the school schedule in communicating the academic focus of a school cannot be overstated. The problems in education today are complicated, and research into the nature of these problems does not suggest simple answers. Designing school schedules that promote sound educational practices is a challenge that has received too little attention in the past. The school schedule has great untapped potential for assisting policymakers in improving learning opportunities for all students.

NOTES

1. *Becoming a Nation of Readers,* U.S. Department of Education: The National Academy of Education, the National Institute of Education, the Center for the Study of Reading, 1985, p. 74.
2. Ibid.; for additional information on questionable use of instructional time, see: John L. Goodlad, *A Place Called School,* McGraw-Hill, New York, 1984, pp. 319–331; and David C. Berliner, "The Half-Full Glass: A Review of Research on Teaching," in *Using What We Know About Teaching,* Philip Hosford (ed.), Association for Supervision and Curriculum Development, Alexandria, Va., 1984, p. 54.
3. Nora K. Jachym, Richard L. Allington, and Kathleen A. Broikon, "Estimating the Cost of Seatwork," *The Reading Teacher,* October 1989, pp. 30–35.
4. John B. Carroll, "A Model of School Learning," *Teacher's College Record* 64 (1963): 723–733.
5. Ibid.
6. Wilber Brookover et al, *School Social Systems and Student Achievement,* Praeger, New York, 1979, p. 148.
7. Daniel U. Levine and Joyce Stark, *Instructional and Organizational Arrangements for Improving Achievement at Inner City Schools,* ERIC Document Reproduction Service, Chicago and New York, ED 221 636, (1981): 12.
8. Barbara A. Sizemore, *An Abashing Anomaly: The High Achieving Predominantly Black Elementary School. Executive Summary,* ERIC Document Reproduction Service, Pittsburgh, ED 236 275 (1983): 16–20.
9. Fenwick English, "Pull-Outs: How Much Do They Erode Whole-Class Teaching?" *Principal,* May 1984, pp. 32–36.
10. Stephen P. Hencley, Lloyd E. McCleary, and J. H. McGrath, *The Elementary School Principalship,* Dodd, Mead and Company, New York, 1970, p. 203.
11. Daniel C. Neale, William J. Bailey, and Billy E. Ross, *Strategies for School Improvement,* Allyn and Bacon, Boston, 1981, 23–25.
12. Charles F. Faber and Gilbert F. Shearron, *Elementary School Administration,* Holt, Rinehart and Winston, New York, 1970, pp. 138–142.

13. Anthony Saville, *Instructional Programming,* Merrill, Columbus, Ohio, 1973, p. 61.
14. Larry W. Hughes and Gerald W. Ubben, *The Elementary Principal's Handbook,* Allyn and Bacon, Boston, 1984, p. 203.
15. *Becoming a Nation of Readers.*
16. William H. Rupley and Timothy R. Blair, "Primary Teachers' Assignment and Supervision of Students' Reading Seatwork," *Reading Psychology* 7, no. 4 (1986): 285.
17. Ibid.: 286–287.
18. Linda M. Anderson et al., "A Qualitative Study of Seatwork in First Grade Classrooms," *Elementary School Journal,* November 1985, p. 133.
19. David Berliner, "When Kids Do Seatwork, What Do They Do?" *Instructor,* November/December, 1986, p. 15.
20. Robert E. Slavin, "Ability Grouping and Student Achievement: A Best-Evidence Synthesis," *Review of Educational Research* 57, no. 3 (1987): 328.
21. Theresa Koontz Noland and Bob L. Taylor, "The Effects of Ability Grouping: A Meta-Analysis of Research Findings," paper presented at the annual meeting of the American Educational Research Association, San Francisco, April 16–20, 1986. Reproduction supplied by ERIC ED 269 451, p. 33.
22. Ibid., p. 27.
23. Ibid., p. 27.
24. Ibid., p. 16.
25. Louise Cherry Wilkinson, "Grouping Low-Achieving Students for Instruction," in *Designs for Compensatory Education: Conference Proceedings and Papers,* Washington, June 17–18, 1986, Reproduction supplied by ERIC ED 293 295.
26. Wynona Winn and Alfred P. Wilson, "The Affect and Effect of Ability Grouping," *Contemporary Education* 54, no. 2 (1983): 123.
27. Jeanne Oakes, "Keeping Track, Part 2: Curriculum Inequality and School Reform," *Phi Delta Kappan,* October 1986, p. 148.
28. Slavin, op. cit.
29. Noland et al., op. cit., p. 31.
30. *Class Size, Research Summary 1951–68* National Education Association, Research Division, Washington, 1968, p. 3 (ERIC Document Reproduction Service, ED 032 614, 1968).
31. Howard V. Blake, "Class Size: A Summary of Selected Studies in Elementary and Secondary Schools," Ed.D. dissertation, Teachers College, Columbia University, New York, 1954. As quoted in *Class Size: A Summary of Research,* Educational Research Service, Washington, 1978, p. 9.
32. Ibid., p. 9.
33. Ibid., pp. 68–69.
34. Gene V. Glass, Leonard S. Cahen, Mary Lee Smith, and Nikola N. Filby, *School Class Size,* Sage Publications, Beverly Hills, 1982, p. 41.
35. Ibid.
36. Leonard S. Cahen et al., *Class Size Research: A Critique of Recent Meta-Analyses,* Educational Research Service, Arlington, Va., 1980, p. 17.
37. Stan M. Shapson et al., "An Experimental Study of the Effects of Class Size," *American Educational Research Journal* 17 (1980): 141–151.
38. Ibid., p. 151.
39. Leonard S. Cahen, Nikola Filby, Gail McCutcheon, and Diane W. Kyle, *Class Size and Instruction,* Longman, New York, 1983, p. 3.
40. Ibid., p. 4.
41. Ibid., pp. 201–206.
42. Glen Robinson and James H. Wittebols, *Class Size Research: A Related Cluster Analysis for Decision-making,* Educational Research Service, Arlington, Va., 1986, pp. 203–204.
43. Erwin V. Johanningmeier, *Americans and Their Schools,* Rand McNally, Chicago, 1980, p. 295.
44. Ibid.
45. Ibid., p. 299
46. Cecil D. Mercer, *Children and Adolescents with Learning Disabilities,* Charles E. Merrill, Columbus, Ohio, 1979, p. 320.
47. Barbara Taylor, "Let's Pull Out of the Pullout Programs," *Principal* 61 (1985): 52.
48. Robert E. Slavin, "Making Chapter I Make a Difference," *Phi Delta Kappan,* October 1987, pp. 110–119.

49. Thanks to Joan Daly-Lewis, former principal of Miller Avenue Elementary School, Shoreham, N.Y., for her summary of the above scheduling options.

50. Howard Hawkinson, "Hatch School—Not at Risk," *Phi Delta Kappan* 65 (1984): 181–182.

51. Karen Klein, "The Research on Class Size," *Phi Delta Kappan* 66 (1985): 578–579.

52. Robert Lynn Canady, "A Cure for Fragmented Schedules in Elementary Schools," *Educational Leadership,* October 1988, pp. 65–67; Robert Lynn Canady and Phyllis R. Hotchkiss, "School Improvement Without Additional Cost," *Phi Delta Kappan,* November 1984, pp. 183–184; Robert Lynn Canady and Jane R. McCullen, "Programming for Flexibility: Attack the Class Size Issue and Fragmented School Programs with These Scheduling Ideas," *AIGE Forum,* Spring 1981, pp. 1–7; Anne P. Sweet and Robert Lynn Canady, "Scheduling for a Differentiated Reading Program," *Reading Horizons,* Fall 1979, pp. 36–41; Robert Lynn Canady, "Grouping and Time Management Strategies Designed to Improve Reading Instruction," in *Essays: Management Strategies for Improving Reading Instruction,* McGraw-Hill, Monterey, Calif., 1980, n.p.; Robert Lynn Canady and Alfred R. Butler IV, "Designing a Middle School Schedule," *American Middle School Education,* Fall 1981, pp. 29–35; Robert Lynn Canady and Jane R. McCullen, "Elementary Scheduling Practices Designed to Support Programs for Gifted Students," *Roeper Review: A Journal on Gifted Education,* February 1985, pp. 142–145; Robert Lynn Canady and Elaine Fogliani, "Cut Class Size in Half Without Hiring More Teachers," *The Executive Educator,* August 1989, and Robert Lynn Canady, "Parallel Block Scheduling: A Better Way to Organize a School," *Principal,* January 1990.

53. Robert L. Canady and Phyllis R. Hotchkiss, "Scheduling Practices and Policies Associated with Increased Achievement for Low-Achieving Students," *The Journal of Negro Education* 54 (1985): 344.

54. John K. Anderson, "Intensive Scheduling; An Interesting Possibility," *The Clearing House,* September 1982, pp. 26–28.

55. Dan R. Flummerfelt, "Getting the Best of Both Worlds," *NASSP Bulletin,* December 1986, pp. 118–119.

56. Jeri J. Goldman, "Flexible Modular Scheduling: Results of Evaluations in Its Second Decade," *Urban Education,* July 1983, pp. 191–209.

57. Michael F. Williams, "The Trimester Scheduling Plan: Flexibility in the High School Curriculum," paper presented at the annual meeting of the American Association of School Administrators, Atlanta, Ga., February 22–25, 1985. Reproduction supplied by ERIC ED 266 553, EA 018 250.

58. Sol E. Sigurdson, "Two Years on the Block Plan: Meeting the Needs of Junior High School Students," Final Report, 1982, Alberta, Canada, Department of Education, Edmonton: Planning and Research Branch, Edmonton Public School Board, Reproduction supplied by ERIC, ED 225 946, SP 021 649.

59. Anderson, loc. cit.

60. Flummerfelt, loc. cit.

61. Goldman, loc. cit.

62. Williams, op. cit.

63. Sigurdson, op. cit.

64. Joseph M. Carroll, "The Copernican Plan: Restructuring the American High School," *Phi Delta Kappan,* January 1990, pp. 358–365.

4

Grouping for Instruction

Determining how students should be grouped for instruction has been debated for the past century. Teachers and administrators working in the same school may be divided on whether to group by ability, by performance, or whether to group at all. Parents, too, have strong feelings about grouping.

Currently many forms of grouping are practiced in public schools. Two of the more prominent types are between-class grouping and within-class grouping. *Between-class grouping* shifts children among teachers for instruction in various subjects. *Within-class grouping* places children in various instructional arrangements within the same class.

Homogeneous grouping is defined as "the classification of pupils for the purpose of forming instructional groups having a relatively high degree of similarity in regard to certain factors that affect learning."[1] This practice has generated considerable controversy. Three major questions related to homogeneous grouping are

1. Is achievement greater for students when they are grouped with students who are of similar ability?
2. Are placement processes fair, accurate, and a true reflection of past achievement?
3. Are teachers more likely to attend to individual differences in homogeneous groups than in heterogeneous groups?[2]

In this chapter, a review of the development of grouping for instructional purposes is presented. Subsequent sections examine the following dimensions of grouping: (1) equity, (2) the social-psychological factors related to the grouping, (3) grouping practices and the resegregation of schools, and (4) the impact of grouping on student achievement. At the end of the chapter, suggestions are offered to policymakers for use in formulating guidelines about this controversial issue.

THE EVOLUTION OF GROUPING PRACTICES

The practice of widespread ability grouping has its roots in the early 1900s. Between 1880 and 1920, America's population was growing rapidly and becoming quite diverse. Due to immigration, school populations swelled 700 percent between 1880 and 1918.[3]

Prior to this century, public schools were attended primarily by the children of white middle- and working-class parents. The lower classes needed their children at home, while upper-class parents sent their children to private schools. For these reasons, a relatively homogeneous population attended public schools, and grouping was not considered necessary.[4]

Compulsory-attendance legislation passed between 1865 and 1918 brought new problems to public schools. Thousands of children perceived as slow-witted and unruly, children who would once have dropped out during the early grades or never attended school at all, were suddenly the responsibility of the public schools. Many of these students had little use for a classical education. Consequently, the responsibility of compulsory attendance "really tended to force differentiation of school purposes and curricula in order that the many different educational needs of a heterogeneous population might be met."[5]

Public pressure for schools to serve better a wider range of students culminated in the institutionalization of the comprehensive high school—a school that offered "something for everyone."[6] Students who aspired to attend college took college preparatory classes, and students who wanted a general education took general academic classes. Vocational programs, which were also incorporated into the comprehensive school, had several objectives, including providing students with marketable skills to get jobs, supplying the nation with needed industrial workers, and meeting the needs of students for whom the academic program was inappropriate.[7]

Public schools, especially at the high school level, developed "educational tracks" to accommodate different sets of interests and abilities. By 1959, James Conant could report that "ability grouping of students subject by subject with special and rigorous attention accorded to the academically talented, was . . . the common sense means of shoring up American academic resources in the wake of Sputnik."[8] Many agreed with Conant that ability grouping was the best method for differentiating instruction, meeting the needs of all students, and still keeping up with the Soviet Union. With more than one-half of the nation's work force consisting of unskilled or semi-skilled workers, schools did not feel compelled to provide all students with a comparable level of academic preparation.[9]

By the late 1970s and 1980s, attitudes toward tracking were starting to change. Society was moving from an industrial-production emphasis to a service-technological emphasis, thereby changing the educational needs of American business.[10] Little room was left for unskilled laborers. Workers now had to be able to manipulate computers, handle sophisticated communications equipment, interpret data, and provide a range of services.

The 1970s and 1980s also witnessed growing concern over grouping practices at the elementary level. Research on school effects indicated that students achieved more in schools where expectations for all students were high. Grouping practices were criticized because of the tendency of many teachers to lower expectations for students in low-ability groups. That large numbers of these students were minorities raised additional concerns about de facto segregation and inequality of educational opportunity.

According to Jeannie Oakes, educators' reliance on grouping is based on the following beliefs: (1) that students learn better when grouped with students considered academically similar; (2) that low-ability students will develop more positive self-concepts when not forced to compete with students of far greater capacity; (3) that grouping decisions can be made fairly and accurately on the basis of ability or past achievement; and (4) that teachers are better able to accommodate individual differences in homogeneous groups.[11]

Although these assumptions are widely accepted by educators, some researchers report the arguments have limited validity. Dawson, for example, claims that much of the research "suggests not only that homogeneous grouping is ineffective in improving achievement . . . but that it may result in a quality of education inferior to that provided in heterogeneous classrooms, inferior with respect to instructional practices . . . classroom climate . . . and the resulting student attitudes."[12]

Finley claims that tracking often results from teacher initiative, without pressure by district, state, or national policies. In her study, she found that teachers created ability grouping for their own reasons—such as its effect on their job satisfaction and sense of competence. Finley stated: "The history of tracking in a suburban school's English department reveals that teachers' own needs structured the tracking system."[13] Many teachers organize their instructional programs around classroom management concerns.[14] The primary function of grouping for these teachers is to make the group more manageable. Homogeneous grouping is popular with these teachers because it fosters the belief that there are no individual differences among members of the class. Teachers can therefore presume to teach as if all learners were identical.[15] Perhaps Finley's study, though limited in scope, helps explain why grouping practices persist, despite a number of serious questions about their value.

THE EQUITY ISSUE

One damaging aspect of policies and practices that call for dividing students into ability groups is the tendency for such divisions to become permanent. Teachers often give more attention and better instruction to students who are labeled "most capable." Teachers also communicate higher expectations to these "bright" students.[16] Teachers pay less attention to low achievers, call on them less often, wait less time for them to answer questions, provide them with less accurate and detailed feedback about their responses, and require less work and less effort from them.[17]

In an ethnographic study on the social impact of grouping, researchers looked at mobility from group to group and compared groups as to the nature and type of tasks engaged in, teacher time and attention devoted, feedback, and the personal relationships developed between teachers and students. Some classes were labeled "white-collar" and others "blue-collar." The researchers reported that during the 5 months of the study, only 5 percent of the students changed groups. They also reported that the tasks engaged in by the groups varied considerably. Students in groups labeled "white-collar" were much more involved in self-directed activities than were students in blue-collar groups, and "high" white-collar groups engaged in even more self-directed activities than did "low" white-collar groups.[18]

There were also differences in feedback between high and low groups. In blue-collar classes, teachers tended to both praise and criticize more often. High groups did not receive any more praise than did low groups; however, low groups did receive more criticism. There were differences also in the frequency of qualitative comments between the two groups. Low groups often received praise like: "If you keep up the good work...." Such phrases, according to Bracey, carry implications that the students' problems won't be changed. In the high groups, however, teachers' comments often reflected the assumption that students' problems were temporary and would change.[19]

The issue of inequity in the classroom is somewhat counterintuitive. If educators acknowledge the individual needs of students based on their differing learning styles and paces of learning but still give all students an equal amount of time to learn, then inequity only grows further. *Equality* does not necessarily translate into "equity." The problem is magnified when one looks at the time for instruction and learning given to tracked students. Barr and Dreeben found that the curriculum often dictates instructional time and load.[20] Their studies of reading groups revealed that students in high groups read more pages and encountered more new words every day than did students in low groups. When districts adopted demanding textbooks for high groups, teachers taught more words and principles of phonics. Some groups of students received three times as much instruction as others, even others with similar ability, and the more students were taught, the more they learned. The researchers also reported that when children who had done poorly on word-learning tests were placed in higher groups, they were taught more than were similar students who remained in low-ability groups. They also learned more, nearly as much, in fact, as group mates with much higher measured ability. Barr and Dreeben claim that the discouraging level of achievement in low groups is not a result of low status of learners but is a result of the pace and depth of instruction which accompanies low grouping and classification of students.

The teacher who teaches lower-ability groups must also contend with discipline problems. These problems generally are not found in higher-ability groups. Mixed ability grouping allows lower achievers to watch and imitate high-achieving peer models. Kelly states that "the less able do better when working side by side with pupils of all abilities."[21]

In a study conducted at Banbury, a school in England, Kelly found little direct evidence to suggest that high ability pupils are disadvantaged as a result of heterogeneous grouping.[22] Oakes offers further support with the following: "The presence of a number of the brightest students in class may raise the quality of both the content presented and the kinds of learning opportunities available to students of all types."[23]

THE SOCIAL-PSYCHOLOGICAL FACTORS RELATED TO THE PROBLEM

Many educators believe that children in low groups come to see themselves as "stupid" and, therefore, achieve less because self-expectations are reduced. Adam

Gamoran, however, claims to have shown recently that there is no evidence that membership in low-ability groups results in feelings of inferiority.[24]

One of the arguments made by advocates of ability grouping is that the self-concept of low-ability students suffers when they are forced to compete against students of much higher ability. Dawson, however, reports that research fails to support this assumption: Self-concept scores are no higher for low-ability students placed in homogeneous classes than they are for low-ability students placed in heterogeneous classes.[25]

One of the largest studies of the impact of ability grouping on students' attitudes was conducted as part of the "Study of Schooling" and reported by Oakes. In her book *Keeping Track: How Schools Structure Inequality,* Oakes reported that students in high groups had significantly more positive attitudes about themselves than did students in low groups. She also found that "high" students had significantly higher educational aspirations than did "low" students. Low-track students were more likely to see themselves as not well-liked by others and were more likely to want to change things about themselves.[26]

According to Pomeroy and Johnson, the "remedial" or "slow" label is still unstable at the end of a child's first year of schooling. This is evident in the "across-the-board" choice of friends these children make during their first year. From the second year onward, however, the label is "institutionally and perceptually confirmed."[27] Children within the group indicate an acceptance of their previously unacknowledged grouping; they start to make most of their friendships within their own groups and begin to perpetuate the social impact of their grouping.[28]

Research data to the contrary, however, is offered by the High School and Beyond Study. Kulik and Kulik state that "students seemed to like their school subjects more when they studied them with peers of similar ability."[29] Data did not indicate, however, whether or not remedial-group placement led to poor self-concepts or poor attitudes toward school.[30]

Two prominent researchers calling for reform of grouping policies are John Goodlad and Robert Slavin. Goodlad states that "the continuation of this folly tempts me to urge its mandatory abolition so that ill-informed people will be forced to refrain from its use."[31] Slavin concludes, more cautiously, "He who groups best groups least but least may not be zero."[32]

THE ISSUE OF DEMOCRATIC VALUES

Ability grouping is challenged not only on the basis of equity and social-psychological factors but also in terms of democratic principles. At the turn of the century, policymakers and practitioners responsible for providing educational opportunities for a new population of students felt tracked schools made sense. Such schools solved the problem of educating diverse groups of students under one roof. Oakes states:

> This solution defined student differences and appropriate educational treatments in social as well as educational terms. At the same time, the use of standardized tests provided a seemingly scientific and meritocratic basis for the sorting process in schools. But surely tracking was more than a technical solution to an instructional problem. Tracking helped to institutionalize beliefs about race and class differences in

intellectual abilities and to erect structural obstacles to the future social, political, and economic opportunities of those who were not white and native-born.[33]

Extreme ability grouping focuses primarily on the sorting-and-selecting function of the school. Historically, schools have served many functions in society. The custodial, sorting-and-selecting, and teaching-and-learning functions have remained, but at different times throughout history, these functions have varied in perceived importance. During the 1980s, pressure increased for the schools to serve a greater custodial function, as evidenced by the increase in school-based day-care centers and after-school programs for "latchkey" children. Sorting and selecting gained ground as reformers placed greater emphasis on testing and graduation requirements. If schools are to serve lower-ability students, however, the teaching and learning function must be paramount.

Educators who argue for tracking assume that the practice promotes educational excellence because it enables teachers to provide the curriculum and instruction needed to "maximize the potential" of every student and it enables students to achieve a form of excellence at their own level. But there is growing evidence that tracking policies help widen, rather than narrow, the vast differences which students bring to school. The question is asked, Can schools—a major institution in a democratic society—continue to force students whom the schools judge to be inferior into separate classes and then provide them with a curriculum and opportunities to learn that are vastly different from those provided to students for whom the schools have higher expectations?

Related to the issue of democratic principles is the fact that grouping labels students, thus creating social stigma and decreasing self-esteem. Educators who practice grouping often contend that grouping is not harmful because most groupings are flexible and change from subject to subject and year to year. In practice, however, such flexibility exists for a very small percentage of the school population. Grouping labels do stick,[34] and, although labeling is practiced widely in the United States and in Europe, numerous researchers have concluded that superior students may benefit from ability grouping but that lower-ranking students may be hurt.[35]

We teach students that they live in a society that values democratic ideals, that professes to value individual differences. Tolerance for individual differences, in fact, may be one of the most important values educational policymakers can hope to instill. It is a challenge, however, that becomes increasingly difficult as students, because of growing economic disparities, become more separated by the communities they live in, the schools they attend, the classrooms in which they are placed, and the curriculum they are assigned. It can be argued that when policies separate students by ability, the very children schools should be working to integrate are the children who become isolated. Even if it could be shown by research that ability grouping produces significant results in terms of student achievement, policymakers who adopt homogeneous grouping policies may still be missing an opportunity to teach students the value of diversity, a lesson of tremendous importance in a society that says it values democratic principles.

THE IMPACT OF GROUPING ON STUDENT ACHIEVEMENT

The impact of ability grouping on student achievement, as indicated in Chapter 3, has been the focus of many studies. These studies vary greatly in quality, time, stu dent and group numbers, classes, and schools. Most of the research investigating ability grouping's impact on achievement has been quasi-experimental in design, often comparing the achievement of students in ability-grouped classes with that of students in heterogeneous classrooms. Some researchers conclude that "no consistent evidence of beneficial effects of ability grouping exists for any group of students, while considerable evidence exists that ability grouping may reduce achievement levels in average and low-ability groups."[36] Others reach different conclusions. Kulik, for example, found that homogeneous grouping for gifted and talented students did produce positive results.[37] Dawson notes that critics may have gone beyond the data when they claimed that experimental studies have shown that ability grouping has almost uniformly negative consequences on the achievement of low-ability students.[38]

Employing many of the same studies used by Kulik and Kulik,[39] Slavin conducted his own metaanalysis of ability grouping. From his studies, Slavin reported that the median effect size for ability-grouped classes is zero. He went further to state that research fails to support between-class ability grouping as a means to increase overall student achievement.[40] Slavin's research did support some other methods of ability grouping, however. The strongest support was for the Joplin plan—a means of ability grouping across grade levels for reading only. Within-class ability grouping for mathematics also received support. Slavin concluded that ability grouping is most effective when students are assigned to heterogeneous classes but regrouped on a homogeneous basis for one or two subjects. Slavin cautioned that the benefits of such grouping depend on the willingness of teachers to alter instruction according to students' needs.

DETERMINING GROUPING POLICIES

Local policymakers must ensure that school practices do not interfere with the opportunities of any student to obtain a sound education. To the extent that certain grouping practices limit these opportunities for certain groups of students, policymakers must reconsider such practices. Recent research supports the fact that grouping practices based on past performance tend to segregate students according to socioeconomic and racial factors and expose students in "low" groups to an inferior curriculum. Denying these students access to a quality curriculum in elementary school ultimately leads many into low tracks in high school. Escape is nearly impossible.

If grouping policies are to be used for the benefit of all students, the following guidelines should be adhered to:

- Grouping is most successful in terms of student outcomes in subjects where the content is presented primarily in a hierarchical format. Even then, however, there is no one placement procedure that can predict accurately in September how a student will perform in April. Constant assessment and reassessment need to occur.
- School policymakers should insist that the quality of instruction be constant across groups. Students in "low" groups should not be assigned to classes consumed by discipline problems and large amounts of routine paper-and-pencil tasks.

- Regardless of the group in which a student is placed, the assignment should be temporary and closely monitored. With effort, it should be possible for a student to move to another group.

Prince George's County (Maryland) Public Schools have made an effort to provide guidelines for within-class grouping that are responsive to research findings. In the Revised 1988 version of Prince George's "Elementary Instructional Guidelines" the following practices are encouraged:

Grouping

The instructional program should provide opportunities for:

a. grouping and regrouping of students through continued diagnosis of skill strengths and needs as demonstrated in daily work and on tests.
b. flexible grouping and instructional adjustments to meet the needs of students who learn at a different rate or with a different learning style.
c. flexible grouping and regrouping of students, according to individualized instructional needs and interests.
d. students to participate in large group, small group, and individualized activities.
e. students to move on a continuum of skills.
f. instruction which is differentiated on the basis of skill need.
g. students sharing information in groups of five or less.
h. total class instruction when appropriate.

No matter how carefully designed are grouping policies, ethical and administrative problems are likely to arise from time to time. For example, should students be placed in groups against their will? Should parents be considered in determining their child's group placement? How should grades be determined? Will students in "low" groups be unable to earn any grade above a C or D? Should students receive credit for effort? It may be necessary for policymakers to approve at least two forms of grades. Students in some groups may need to be evaluated and ultimately graded on the basis of their level of improvement and effort while other students are graded on individual achievement outcomes.

Regardless of the intent of grouping policies, a student's personal identity is developed, in part, from group membership. Labels assigned to students based on ability can lead to decreased motivation, reduced self-confidence, and social stigma. If grouping is used, it is important that students have choices and that problems of labeling be ameliorated by constant reassessment.

NOTES

1. Miriam L. Goldberg, A. Harry Passow, and Joseph Justman, *The Effects of Ability Grouping,* Teachers College Press, New York, 1968, p. 2.
2. Jeannie Oakes, *Keeping Track: How Schools Structure Inequality,* Yale University Press, New Haven, Conn., 1985, pp. 6–7.
3. Ibid., p. 19.
4. Ibid., pp. 16–20.
5. Freeman R. Butts and Lawrence Cremin, *A History of Education in American Culture,* Holt, Rinehart, and Winston, New York, 1953, p. 415.
6. Oakes, op. cit., p. 21.

7. Ibid., p. 32.
8. Ibid., p. 39.
9. Larry Cuban, "The 'At Risk' Label and the Problem of Urban School Reform," *Phi Delta Kappan,* June 1989, pp. 780–801.
10. Ibid.
11. Oakes, op. cit., pp. 6–7.
12. Margaret Dawson, "Beyond Ability Grouping: A Review of the Effectiveness of Ability Grouping and Its Alternatives," *School Psychology Review* 16, no. 3 (1987): 349.
13. Merrilee Finley, "Teachers and Tracking in a Comprehensive High School," *Sociology of Education* 54, no. 4(1984): 233–243, 242.
14. Victor Dupuis and Bernie Badialdi, "Classroom Climate and Teacher Expectations in Homogeneously Grouped Secondary Schools," *Journal of Classroom Interaction* 23, no. 1 (1987–1988): 28.
15. Ibid.
16. Thomas L. Good and Jere E. Brophy, *Looking in Classrooms,* 4th ed., Harper & Row, New York, 1987, pp. 128–134.
17. Dawson, op. cit., p. 356; also Good and Brophy, op. cit., pp. 128–129.
18. Gerald W. Bracey, "The Social Impact of Ability Grouping," *Phi Delta Kappan,* May 1987, pp. 701–702.
19. Ibid., p. 701.
20. Rebecca Barr and Robert Dreeben, *How Schools Work,* University of Chicago Press, Chicago, 1983, pp. 105–125.
21. A. V. Kelly, *Mixed Ability Grouping: Theory and Practice,* Harper and Row, London, 1978, p. 14.
22. Ibid.
23. Oakes, op. cit., p. 195.
24. Adam Gamoran, "Organization, Instruction, and the Effects of Ability Grouping: Comment on Slavin's 'Best Evidence Synthesis,'" *Review of Educational Research* 57, no. 3, Fall 1987.
25. Dawson, op. cit., p. 354.
26. Ibid., pp. 122–135; 145–146.
27. Richard Pomeroy and Trevor Johnson, "Friendship Choices and Self-Image: An Investigation of Group Cohesiveness and Perceptions of Remedial Children in Comprehensive School," *Educational Review* 35, no. 1 (1983): 56.
28. Ibid.
29. C. C. Kulik and J. Kulik, "Effects of Ability Grouping on Secondary Students: A Meta-Analysis of Evaluation Findings," *American Educational Research Journal* 19, no. 3 (1982): 426.
30. Ibid.
31. John I. Goodlad, *A Place Called School,* McGraw-Hill, New York, 1984, pp. 296–297.
32. Robert E. Slavin, Teleconference, ETV, April 1989.
33. Jeannie Oakes, "Keeping Track, Part 2: Curriculum Inequality and School Reform," *Phi Delta Kappan,* October 1986, p. 150.
34. Jill Rachlin, "The Label That Sticks," *U.S. News & World Report,* July 3, 1989, pp. 51–52.
35. Helen Abadzi, "Ability Grouping Effects on Academic Achievement and Self-Esteem: Who Performs in the Long Run as Expected?" *Journal of Educational Research,* September/October 1985, p. 36.
36. Dawson, op. cit., p. 350.
37. Ibid., p. 351.
38. Ibid.
39. J. Kulik and C. C. Kulik, "Effects of Ability Grouping on Student Achievement," *Equity and Excellence* 23, nos. 1–2 (1987): 22–30.
40. Dawson, loc. cit.
41. Robert E. Slavin, "Ability Grouping and Its Alternatives: Must We Track?" *American Educator,* Summer 1987.

5

Special Programs for At-Risk Students

The preceding chapter examined policy-related issues associated with the grouping of students for instruction. One set of grouping policies that deserves special attention pertains to the myriad of programs targeted especially for at-risk students. So extensive are these programs in some schools that they appear to constitute a system within a system. With increases in special programs for at-risk students have come an assortment of concerns for local policymakers.

The chapter opens with a brief description of the evolution of special programs, followed by a section describing the range of current programs serving at-risk students. Programs are grouped into four categories: those designed primarily for (1) remediation, (2) prevention, (3) nonacademic support, and (4) discipline. Specific policy issues are addressed in the next section. These issues include program goals, student identification and eligibility, resources, and program effectiveness. The concluding section provides guidance for local policymakers concerned about at-risk students.

THE EVOLUTION OF SPECIAL PROGRAMS

Once schools consisted of students, classrooms, classroom teachers, and a principal. Students partook of the program provided for them or they left school. And, of course, many students did leave school before graduating. The only alternatives were private schools for children from wealthy families. Today's school still consists of students, classrooms, classroom teachers, and a principal; but added to this list are a host of special programs, support staff, specialists, and assistant or quasi administrators. Much of the additional structure and staff resulted from mounting concern that the conventional program—what historian David Tyack calls "the one best system"—had failed to serve well the needs of specific groups of young people.

One of the first of these groups to receive special attention were students from "disadvantaged" homes. In the early sixties, *disadvantaged* referred to the student's cultural background. Gradually, negative views of minority cultures shifted, and *disadvantaged* came to refer to the student's economic circumstances.

Special programs for children of the poor were spawned by reform-minded politicians during the Kennedy-Johnson years. Title I (now Chapter 1) and Headstart are two of the most successful and long-lived of these programs.

In the seventies, non-English-speaking and handicapped students were targeted for special programs. Controversy swirled around the best way to assist non-English-speakers, with some favoring bilingual programs and others pressing for English-immersion or English-as-a-second-language programs. With the advent of P.L. 94-142 in 1975, most traditionally separate programs for handicapped students were revamped. Handicapped students began to be mainstreamed for all or part of the school day. Special education programs and resource rooms started to appear within the organizational structure of conventional public schools.

At the same time that public schools were expanding to accommodate special programs for disadvantaged, non-English-speaking, and handicapped students, a countertrend was developing that led to the formation of "alternative" schools and programs detached or totally separate from conventional schools. Some of these alternative schools were designed for alienated or underachieving middle-class youth, others for children of parents disenchanted with public education, and still others for poor inner-city youngsters unable to cope with the demands of conventional schools.[1]

Despite the proliferation of special programs and alternative schools during the last three decades, little evidence exists that the number of at-risk students has abated. Largely due to factors beyond the control of educators, the number of these students actually appears to be growing.[2] Among the reasons for the burgeoning at-risk population are increases in teenage pregnancies, in births to parent drug abusers, and in inner-city children living under the poverty line.[3] Contemporary educators are also more *aware* of at-risk students because of the spread of testing and early-identification programs. A primary purpose of these efforts has been to locate students in need of assistance. Once identified, these students become candidates for a plethora of special programs and services.

The eighties have been a time of great ferment in American education. The initial impetus for reform was a blue-ribbon commission report—*A Nation at Risk*—which argued that declining achievement among students in the United States jeopardized the country's ability to compete economically with foreign nations. In the wake of *A Nation at Risk,* published in 1983, came wave after wave of calls for educational change. Legislatures and boards of education responded to these challenges by pressing for higher standards, more graduation requirements, and greater academic rigor at all levels. Efforts so far to assess the impact of these reforms, however, indicate that many at-risk youth are failing to benefit.[4]

Some even suggest that the very attempt to raise the level of student achievement in the United States is contributing to the growth of the at-risk population and creating a greater need for special programs. One blue-ribbon commission concluded the following:

> Our schools . . . have become distracted from their main mission. Educators have become so preoccupied with those who go on to college that they have lost sight of those who do not. And more and more of the non-college-bound now fall between the cracks when they are in school, drop out, or graduate inadequately prepared for the requirements of the society and the workplace.[5]

As a result of the kind of concern expressed in the preceding passage, educators are being compelled to examine the impact of current reform policies and practices on at-risk students. Van Dougherty, writing for the Education Commission of the States, notes that recent research indicates "that schools must change some of their policies and practices to achieve greater success with some students."[6] It is interesting to note that while the push for higher standards and educational excellence has come from the White House and the State House, there has been surprisingly little high-level pressure to help at-risk students. The job of rallying support for these youngsters seems to have been left to local policymakers. Let us examine the variety of ways in which these individuals are responding to the challenge.

THE RANGE OF CURRENT PROGRAMS SERVING AT-RISK STUDENTS

To gain an appreciation for the variety of special programs available to at-risk students today, it may be instructive to look at one urban-suburban school district. The Mesa (Arizona) Unified School District serves more than 56,000 students.[7] As of 1988, Mesa spent roughly $3,200 per student. About four of every five students who graduate from Mesa enroll in 2- or 4-year colleges; however, one of every four ninth graders drops out of high school before graduating. The percentages of students who passed the state reading and mathematics tests in 1988 were 82 percent and 78 percent, respectively. The ratios of students to teachers in elementary and secondary grades are 28 to 1 and 26 to 1.

In 1989, the Mesa Unified School District published a comprehensive list of high-risk student programs that consisted of forty-five separate entries. Programs were classified as (1) academic, (2) general, or (3) "substance abuse, dropouts, related behavior." Programs for high-risk students included the following:

- *Migrant Project*
  Chapter 1: Migrant education was established to meet the special needs of the children of migratory workers. Services are provided in language, reading, and mathematics (K–12). The Migrant Project serves 700 students at a per-student cost of $400 (federal funds).
- *Study Skills*
  This program teaches study skills to teachers of high-risk students (district funds).
- *Mesa Vista*
  This is an alternative school for students who have difficulty adjusting to regular high school. Students attend Mesa Vista for one-half day and return to the regular high school once they can cope and be successful. Mesa Vista serves 600 students at a cost of $583 per student (district funds).
- *Mesa Vista Night School*
  This is an alternative school for students who have difficulty adjusting to regular high school. Students attend during the evening and work on computerized programs. The school serves 50 students at a cost of $200 per student (state and federal funds).

- *Taking Charge Program*
  This program is an alternative to long-term suspension of students removed from school for involvement with drugs and/or alcohol. The program includes an evaluation assessment by a community agency, parent involvement, and support group counseling at the home school. The program is run without special funds and serves about 200 students.
- *YES (Youth Experiencing Success)*
  The YES program is offered as an elective class at all secondary schools. At-risk students are selected for the class, which focuses on self-esteem, study skills, and the coping skills needed for success. The program serves 750 students at a cost of $147 per student (district funds).
- *Parent University*
  Offered throughout the year, Parent University workshops provide an opportunity for parents to learn how to help their youngsters strengthen basic skills, improve self-esteem, and develop a positive attitude toward learning. Approximately 1,500 parents are served at a cost of $3 per parent (district funds).

These examples indicate that Mesa's programs serve at-risk students of all ages, their parents, and their teachers. Funds for special programs are derived from local, state, and federal sources as well as private foundations. Some programs, such as D.A.R.E. (Drug Abuse Resistance Education) and P.O.P.S. (Power of Positive Students) are part of nationally coordinated efforts to assist at-risk students, while other programs derive solely from local initiative. Eight of the forty-five programs deal exclusively with handicapped students involved in special education.

Some districts, particularly the smaller ones, are unable to provide as great a selection of special programs as Mesa, but many—if not most—districts offer at least some at-risk programs in each of four categories—(1) remediation, (2) prevention, (3) nonacademic support, and (4) discipline. Let us briefly examine each.

REMEDIATION

The purpose of remedial/compensatory programs is to intervene in the regular educational program of at-risk students in order to correct learning deficiencies and increase the odds that students will improve their performance in conventional classroom settings. An illustration of a policy intended to promote remedial/compensatory programs comes from the Richardson (Texas) Intermediate School District (policy issued on July 31, 1985).

> The District shall provide to identified students remedial or compensatory instruction that focuses on areas of deficiency and provides additional time on task to enable the student to master the essential elements for a course or subject area. The regular teacher and any special teacher providing remediation shall coordinate their delivery and assessment procedures.

As the last sentence of the Richardson policy suggests, remedial/compensatory programs may be offered apart from a student's normal classroom activities. These so-called pullout programs—discussed in Chapters 2 and 3—range from special education resource rooms to individual tutorials with specialists or volunteers.

Some educators have begun to criticize "pullout programs" because so much instructional time is lost during transitions, class activities are disrupted, and students may be stigmatized. To respond to these concerns, many schools are creating programs that deliver remedial/compensatory services in the regular classroom or during non-school hours. In the latter category are found before- and after-school tutorials, clinics, homework-assistance centers, evening schools, and special summer programs.

In one of the largest efforts to provide non-pullout remedial assistance, the Houston Independent School District, in 1988, established a policy requiring students experiencing academic difficulties to devote nearly 2 hours a week of their free time to tutorial sessions in subjects they had failed to master.[8] In the first months of Houston's "Required Academic Proficiency" program, approximately 40,000 students were sent to 55-minute tutorials before and after school and on Saturdays. Tutorials are taught by certified teachers who are paid a supplement (equal to one-tenth of their normal salary). A maximum of fifteen students is permitted in each tutorial. The program's cost, in its initial semester of operation, was estimated to be $1.25 million.

PREVENTION

A second approach to helping at-risk students is to prevent them from encountering problems in the first place. Some preventive programs focus on intensive efforts to provide young children with the fundamental skills needed to experience success in school. Examples of such programs include Headstart, prekindergarten summer schools, and accelerated schools such as those initiated by Stanford professor Henry Levin. Other programs aim to prevent students from dropping out of school. These programs encompass alternative schools, schools for pregnant girls and teenage parents, street academies, and work-study programs. It is even conceivable that public boarding schools will be added to the list in the near future in an effort to prevent young people forced to grow up in unsafe and unstable environments from losing interest in school.

An example of district policy designed to promote preventive programs for potential dropouts comes from the Garland (Texas) Intermediate School District.

> By September 1, 1988, the District shall have a plan in place designed to retain students in a school setting. The District plan shall be the responsibility of the Superintendent or the designated at-risk-coordinator(s) and shall:
>
> 1. Emphasize a comprehensive team approach that includes the Superintendent, principal, parent/guardian, teacher, student, community service provider, business representative, or others.
> 2. Include objectives to meet the identified needs of at-risk students and to retain those students in school.
> 3. Be designed to use community resources that are available to serve at-risk youth.
> 4. Provide for parental involvement, such as participation in developing student academic plans and training programs for students.
> 5. Provide for review of individual student data and development of individual profiles for at-risk students.

The Garland policy suggests that preventive programs may encompass dimensions of remedial/compensatory programs, particularly when they serve older students. Preventive programs also may overlap the third type of at-risk program—that dealing with the nonacademic needs of students.

NONACADEMIC SUPPORT

Nonacademic programs address such areas of concern as student health, mental health, personal development, and self-esteem. Examples include school-based health clinics, peer counseling groups, day-care for the children of teenage parents, after-school care for "latchkey" children, and nutrition programs providing students with well-balanced meals. Besides nonacademic programs for students, schools may offer special training for parents and teachers of at-risk students.

DISCIPLINE

The final type of program is disciplinary in nature. The most common program of its kind is one that serves as an alternative to suspension or expulsion. In some school districts, student offenders involved in first-time drug- or alcohol-related incidents, for example, may choose to participate in awareness or rehabilitation programs. Utah's Jordan School District requires that the parents of the student offenders, as well as the students themselves, enroll in drug and alcohol awareness classes. In some districts, students who have been expelled for drug or alcohol offenses may be required to provide evidence of participation in an approved treatment program before applying for reinstatement. Other disciplinary options include in-school suspension, work detail, and community service. While programs such as these are not limited to at-risk students, the young people involved in them frequently can be described as at-risk.

Many districts have realized that no one type of program is likely to address the needs of all at-risk students. As a result, a growing number of comprehensive programs combining elements of several types of at-risk intervention are being developed. The SUCCESS program of Prince George's (Maryland) Public Schools is one nationally recognized example. In each school where SUCCESS has been implemented, a specially trained staff of teachers, an instructional aide, and a coordinator work with approximately 100 students selected during the last month of their eighth-grade year. The students selected for the program may have been retained for a year or more, possess low test scores, and/or have a grade-point average below 2.0.

When they begin the ninth grade, SUCCESS students are placed in classes of twenty or fewer students with four teachers responsible for English, mathematics, science, and social studies. The coordinator counsels the students, works with teachers and parents, and provides instruction in study and learning skills. The instructional aide handles attendance and maintains close contact with the students' families. Other special features of the SUCCESS program include a common planning period for the instructional team, a fifteen-station computer lab for computer-assisted instruction, a parent seminar program, regularly scheduled parent conferences, tutorial assistance provided by community volunteers, and monthly newsletters to parents.

Having reviewed the rich variety of programs available to many at-risk students, it is now necessary to investigate some of the policy-related issues associated with the creation and maintenance of these programs.

SPECIFIC POLICY ISSUES

PROGRAM GOALS

Determining the goal or goals of programs for at-risk students may not be as simple as it seems. Local policymakers must decide, for example, whether or not the intent of such special programs is to facilitate the integration of at-risk students into mainstream programs. Laurraine Landolt, principal of an alternative school for high school students in a northern Virginia school district, argues that graduation from high school should not be the only criterion used for judging the success of a student's experience in a special program. Her goal is to provide as positive an experience as possible for the students who choose to attend her school. For many of these students, dropping out of school altogether is the only other realistic choice. Landolt reasons that forcing her students to accumulate the required number of credits and to pass standardized tests may be counterproductive. She feels that students who leave her school feeling good about themselves can always attend night school later and earn a general equivalency diploma.

Those who regard special programs as *permanent* placements for at-risk students are sometimes accused of operating "safety valves" to relieve conventional schools of the pressure of trying to meet the needs of these youngsters. Special programs, the argument goes, should be integrated into the conventional school's regular offerings. This line of reasoning is similar to that of advocates of the Regular Education Initiative (R.E.I.), an effort launched during the eighties to eliminate many "pullout programs" for handicapped students. Advocates of R.E.I. claimed that handicapped students could be served best if regular classroom teachers worked closely with special educators to implement strategies for teaching all students.[9]

An issue underlying the debates over the appropriate locus of and focus for at-risk programs concerns expectations for students. Adherents of the so-called school-effectiveness research claim that the best way to help at-risk students is to expect the same of them as is expected of other students. While it is clear that many at-risk students benefit from elevated expectations, it is equally apparent that many others are unable or unwilling to meet the challenge. Policymakers must decide whether it is more important to maintain the integrity of the regular program by insisting that all students meet the same minimum expectations or to modify expectations for certain students in the hopes of providing them with successful school experiences.

In its grading guidelines, the Fairfax County Public Schools (Virginia) advise teachers to hold all students "to course objectives but use adopted or simplified materials and multi-level strategies and activities to meet objectives."[10] What is unclear about this policy is exactly how it applies to special programs. Can course objectives be different in these programs so long as all the students in them are held accountable for the same objectives? Or must the course objectives in at-risk programs be identical to those in regular programs?

This issue is not fully resolved in the list of "expected student outcomes" for students enrolled in the Murray Educational Center, an Albemarle County (Virginia) alternative school for students in grades eight through twelve, but at least a range of expectations is specified.

1. Students and teachers will expect successful achievement of course objectives and will recognize their power to significantly influence that achievement.
2. Student attendance will be 92 percent of the established individual instructional time.
3. Students will be actively involved in the instructional activities.
4. Student behavior will be supportive of learning for other students.
5. All students who attend regularly and are actively involved in instructional activities will master no less than 80 percent of their course objectives.

Another goal-related policy issue concerns the range of services to be provided for at-risk students. In recent years, educators and noneducators alike have decried the ever-expanding list of responsibilities laid at the schoolhouse steps. The case has been made that schools are unable to take on these new responsibilities and still meet their traditional obligation to foster competence in the basic skills and academic disciplines. Those who resist this position counter that student learning cannot be separated from student health, safety, and welfare. If other sectors of society are failing to ensure that at-risk students are fed, counseled, and helped to stay healthy, the schools must be willing to intervene.

School districts that decide to provide a full range of services for at-risk students frequently encounter strong resistance. For example, opponents of birth control fight efforts to locate health clinics in schools on the grounds that they may promote birth control and thus, by implication, sexual activity. Counseling programs that confront students' values and beliefs are attacked as an infringement on family rights. A basic issue for policymakers is whether or not the public schools are obliged to take whatever steps are necessary to educate all youngsters. Districts—especially urban districts—with large numbers of at-risk students seem to have decided that they are obliged to address any needs that might interfere with a student's ability to obtain an education. Rural and suburban districts have been more reluctant to provide comprehensive services, perhaps in part because of concerns expressed by parents of students not at risk.

STUDENT IDENTIFICATION AND ELIGIBILITY

Determining which students should participate in special programs is a second issue that must be dealt with by local policymakers. The issue has been deliberated most actively by advocates for so-called exceptional students. In this section, however, we will concentrate on students who do not qualify for special education or gifted programs. The guidelines for deciding who qualifies as "at risk" are far less clear than those governing selection for special and gifted education.

One reason for vagueness regarding the definition of *at risk* involves the politics of public education. The more students who fit under the "at-risk" rubric, the greater the likelihood of broad-based support and additional resources for special programs. Some educators go so far as to suggest that all students are potentially at risk. Such an all-inclusive view of at-risk status goes beyond economic disadvantagement and low achievement to encompass such factors as divorce, depression, stress, peer pressure, and substance abuse.

While all-inclusive definitions of *at risk* are useful for mobilizing public support and resources, they may become a hindrance when the time comes to select students for the special programs. As districts strive for greater precision in the selection process, the term *at risk* increasingly is being reserved for students with a relatively high likelihood of leaving school before graduation.

In a previous section, the criteria governing selection for Prince George's SUCCESS program for ninth graders were listed as low standardized test scores, a grade-point average below 2.0, and/or a year or more of retention at grade level. Prince George's schools serve large numbers of at-risk youth. Across the Potomac River, in a district with relatively few at-risk students, Fairfax County considers potential dropouts to be students who

- have extended absences unrelated to illness (10 or more consecutive days).
- have class grades that have dropped two letters or more in a majority of classes.
- show an extreme mood or attitude change, withdraw from participation, and so on.[11]

In the Garland (Texas) Intermediate School District, the policy governing which students qualify as being at risk is much more inclusive than the policy at either Prince George's County or Fairfax County. It states:

> In determining whether a student is at high risk of dropping out of school, the District shall consider the student's academic performance as well as whether the student is adjudged delinquent; abuses drugs or alcohol; is a student of limited English proficiency; receives compensatory or remedial education; is sexually, physically, or psychologically abused; is pregnant; is a slow learner; enrolls late in the school year; stops attending school before the end of the school year; is an underachiever; is unmotivated; or exhibits other characteristics that indicate the student is at high risk of dropping out of school.

It appears that students judged to be at risk by one school system may not be so judged by another school system. Eventually, differential criteria among school systems could lead to equity issues and possible litigation. Such action probably will not occur until a determination is made of the extent to which special programs for at-risk students are effective. This matter is addressed in an upcoming section.

Another issue involves when to identify at-risk students. Early identification has obvious benefits in terms of problem prevention, but critics point out that premature identification may lead to labeling and the self-fulfilling-prophecy effect. In other words, the fear exists that labeling a student at-risk or a potential dropout may lead to differential treatment that ensures the student will experience difficulties. Perhaps because of this concern, district policies calling for the identification of students who are at risk of dropping out frequently focus on secondary school students. Younger students may be selected for special programs, but these programs are likely to focus primarily on boosting their achievement in the basic skills. There is much to merit the development of different policies governing the selection of elementary and secondary students for special programs.

A third issue related to student identification and eligibility concerns the right of refusal. Should a student, or his parents, have the option of refusing placement in a special program even though the student has been identified as at-risk? Parents of students referred for special education services possess the right of refusal, but school districts can go to court to override the parents' decision. Currently, many districts have no policies or guidelines spelling out the options available to at-risk students who do not fall under special education provisions. Given the United States Supreme Court's reluctance to dictate school discipline policies, it appears that school districts have the authority to require student offenders to participate in special awareness and rehabilitation programs. Whether school districts can also compel students who are not experiencing, or are not likely to experience, success in conventional academic programs to participate in remedial/compensatory or preventive programs is yet to be determined.

RESOURCES

In many cases, the decision to provide or not to provide special programs for at-risk students hinges on the availability of resources. Funds may be needed to hire additional staff, reimburse existing staff for assuming extra duties, obtain special materials, rent or renovate space for extra classrooms, and provide training for teachers and parents. Currently these funds are derived from a variety of sources, including local school budgets, special state accounts, federal programs, foundations, and grants from businesses. Several issues related to resources must be addressed by local policymakers involved in creating or sustaining special programs for at-risk students.

One issue concerns the formula for funding special programs. Frequently school districts base funding on a dollar amount per student. In the case of special education, a weighted formula is used so that more dollars will be earmarked for each handicapped student than for each nonhandicapped student. This practice recognizes that staffing needs are greater, proportionately, for handicapped students. Weighted formulas for at-risk students, however, are not as prevalent. One reason may be the difficulty in determining how many students will actually be involved in at-risk programs. Budgets are built months in advance. At-risk students, however, do not represent a stable population. They may drop out of school or be forced, for economic reasons, to move frequently. State aid based on daily attendance is often lost because absenteeism among at-risk students is high. Local policymakers may be forced to decide whether local funding for special programs will be based on the projected number of eligible students or an estimate of the percentage of eligible students who will actually participate in such programs at any given time. They may also consider designating a maximum percentage of the student population that can qualify for at-risk status, as is done in federal guidelines for special education.

Problems, of course, may arise if estimates or maximum percentages are used as the basis for funding at-risk programs. For example, what are districts to do if they underestimate the number of eligible at-risk students or if they receive an influx of such youngsters after the budget has been approved? A key dimension of most special programs is a small student-teacher ratio. If these programs have not allocated sufficient personnel to handle the maximum number of eligible students, they must either make midyear adjustments in the student-teacher ratio or deny access to some students. Determining how to fund programs serving such an unpredictable population remains a major challenge for local policymakers.

A related challenge concerns the best way to use incentive funds. An increasing number of school districts are using incentive funds to encourage school-based initiatives. Should these funds be used to reward schools that reduce their dropout rate or to help schools with increasing numbers of dropouts? In districts experimenting with school-based management, dilemmas of this kind need not be resolved at the board level. The administration and staff of each school can decide how best to focus their efforts and use their discretionary budgets. The school board's role is to set the criteria by which to hold schools accountable for incentive funds and the consequences in the event schools fail to meet the criteria.

In an effort to increase services to at-risk students, many school districts offer extended day programs and summer programs. Funding these programs, however, can be a problem. If tuition is charged, the fear arises that many of the neediest students may not be able to participate. One solution, at least with regard to summer school, may be to switch to year-round schools. At-risk students could have access to free instructional services on a 12-month basis while other students are free to elect an off-quarter for vacation. Another strategy involves creating a district-based foundation capable of receiving donations and grants from local businesses. Foundation funds can be used to cover summer school and after-school program tuitions for needy students.

Ultimately, perhaps the greatest fiscal responsibility of local policymakers is to make the public aware of the costs of failing to help at-risk students. As countless national reports have stressed, it is far more expensive to deal with young people who fail to receive an education than it is to help them *before* they give up and drop out. Seeing that adequate funds are available for at-risk students is particularly crucial when school districts confront retrenchment or substantial loss of funding. As was discovered in California in the aftermath of Proposition 13, local policies that distribute budget cuts equally across all programs do not necessarily ensure that all students will share the impact of cuts equally. As might be expected, evidence exists that at-risk students are more likely than others to suffer from losses in services during belt tightening.[12] It is vital that local policymakers create policies to protect funds for special programs for at-risk students even during downturns in the economy or periods of declining enrollment.

PROGRAM EFFECTIVENESS

Local policymakers may initially support the creation of special programs despite the absence of data attesting to their effectiveness. Policymakers live in a political world where it is sometimes necessary to take action simply in order to signal top-level commitment to addressing a pressing concern.

Eventually, however, information on program effectiveness will be needed if policymakers are to continue providing support. It should be pointed out, of course, that evidence of program effectiveness is no guarantee of continued support. Effective programs are occasionally eliminated because of shifting priorities or scarce resources.

Local policymakers can play an important role in determining the basis or bases upon which judgments of program effectiveness are founded. As noted in the section on goals, they may decide, for example, whether to judge the progress of students in at-risk programs by the same criteria and standards used to judge mainstream students. They may choose to look for unintended costs associated with operating special programs. It is conceivable, for example, that special programs are achieving positive outcomes but not enough to justify periodically removing at-risk students from class and disrupting the flow of instruction. Policymakers need sufficient data to determine whether the outcomes of special programs justify their cost.

Research on special programs for at-risk students yields a mixed verdict on their effectiveness. Consider the case of remedial/compensatory programs. John Ralph, after reviewing two decades of evaluation data, noted that programs such as Chapter 1 consistently produce a modest positive effect on student achievement "which is mostly observable in the early grades, is strongest in mathematics, and does not endure once program services are ended."[13] He goes on to point out that

> One troubling finding about Chapter 1 is that its services are most effective with marginal students, who often make rapid improvements and are then promoted out of the program. Chapter 1 services are least effective with the weakest students, who continue to receive Chapter 1 services year-after-year.[14]

Research on the effectiveness of alternative schools reveals a similar mix of findings. The positive findings reported with greatest frequency concern improvements in students' attitudes toward school, relations with teachers, behavior in school, and attendance.[15] Evidence of improved academic performance is disappointingly infrequent. When Gold and Mann investigated the effectiveness of three alternative schools for at-risk adolescents, they drew conclusions similar to those reached by Ralph.[16] While the behavior of most students improved when they transferred to one of the three alternative schools, the students who demonstrated the most positive outcomes were those who were not overly anxious or depressed. Special programs may be most beneficial for the at-risk students who least need them.

A primary focus for many at-risk programs is dropout prevention. When Catterall and Stern investigated whether student participation in vocational education and other California alternative programs reduced the likelihood of dropping out, their findings were somewhat encouraging.[17] Nondropouts were more likely than were dropouts to have participated in alternative programs. Also, the students involved in alternative programs who went on to graduate were more likely to have secured employment than were dropouts. They also tended to earn more than the latter. On the other hand, in a subsequent study of a dropout prevention program based on intensive group counseling, Catterall failed to detect positive outcomes.[18] He speculated that substantial bonding occurred among the alienated young people in the group counseling program, providing reinforcement for negative attitudes and undermining efforts to encourage proactive behavior.

Despite the lack of evidence that at-risk programs are universally effective, two points can be made with relative certainty.

1. Evidence exists that *some* special programs succeed in providing *some* at-risk students with beneficial educational experiences.
2. More is being learned all the time about which instructional practices are most effective with at-risk students.

It would be impossible to describe all the special programs that have been effective for at least some at-risk youth. An illustration may help demonstrate the types of outcomes that can be achieved. Prince George's SUCCESS program was mentioned earlier. The profile for students entering the program was as follows:

- Group GPA of 1.46 (4.0 scale).
- Average attendance rate of 78 percent.
- 54 percent of students had been suspended at least once.
- 73 percent of students had a GPA below 2.0.[19]

After participating in SUCCESS for a year, the profile changed substantially.

- Group GPA of 1.85.
- Average attendance rate of 89 percent.
- 18 percent of students had been suspended during the year.
- 49 percent of students had a GPA above 2.0.
- 12 percent of students achieved honor roll.

Along with the proliferation of effective programs like SUCCESS has come increased awareness of the instructional strategies most likely to be effective with at-risk students. One recent review of research in this area reported consistent positive outcomes associated with the following strategies:

- Continuous progress models (such as mastery learning)
- Cooperative learning
- Remedial tutoring
- Computer-assisted instruction
- Intensive (one-on-one) instruction[20]

For local policymakers, the message from research seems to be that a key to effectiveness is comprehensiveness. No one type of program or instructional strategy will work for *all* at-risk students. The more policymakers encourage and support a diverse set of programs and strategies, the more likely they will be to promote productive learning for at-risk students.

DETERMINING POLICIES FOR AT-RISK STUDENTS

In the opening chapter, a *good policy* was described as "one that increases the likelihood that school goals will be achieved without adversely affecting any particular group of students." A case can be made that the cumulative impact of recent policies aimed at promoting educational excellence has been to reduce the likelihood that many at-risk students will derive benefit from their schooling. While there is no question that policies calling for higher standards and a more rigorous curriculum are needed, it is equally apparent that such policies must be accompanied by other policies assuring at-risk students access to various kinds of special assistance.

The initial chapters of this book suggested that some of the school policies in regard to scheduling, grouping practices, and special programs can inhibit the learning of at-risk students. Subsequent chapters will address other policies that can affect at-risk students. One point must be stressed, however: The failure of at-risk students to benefit from their schooling should not be blamed entirely on lack of personal motivation, poor parenting, negative peer influence, or economic disadvantagement. To some extent, the failure of at-risk students must also be regarded as a failure of local school policies.

A recent assessment by Joe and Nelson captures this position well:

> The key contention here is that conventional grading systems, the use of visible ability tracking, the reliance on curricula and teaching methods that respond to a limited range of learning styles, traditional discipline and suspension policies, existing eligibility rules for health and social services, and customary selection bias in job training and hiring—all of these accepted characteristics of contemporary youth-serving institutions contribute to, if not actually cause, failure among at-risk youth.[21]

The fact is that local policymakers—including board members, superintendents, school administrators, and teacher leaders—are not elected or selected to promote the interests of only the most able and advantaged young people. They are obliged to help all students. School systems must not be allowed to function as the educational equivalent of hospital triage units, channeling their services primarily to the youngsters judged most likely to benefit from them.

In their efforts to help at-risk students, local policymakers should also avoid the temptation to think of these students as a highly homogeneous group. At-risk students come from all racial and ethnic groups as well as from different socio-economic classes. While they may all be considered "at risk," the reasons vary greatly, as do the most appropriate intervention strategies. It is incumbent upon policymakers to see that a range of special programs are available to these young people and that no particular program is jeopardized simply because it fails to meet the needs of *all* at-risk students.

NOTES

1. Daniel L. Duke, *The Retransformation of the School,* Nelson-Hall, Chicago, 1978, pp. 24–37.
2. Aaron M. Pallas, Gary Natriello, and Edward L. McDill, "The Changing Nature of the Disadvantaged Population: Current Dimensions and Future Trends," *Educational Researcher,* June/July 1989, pp. 16–22.
3. Lisbeth B. Schorr, *Within Our Reach: Breaking the Cycle of Disadvantage,* Anchor Books, New York, 1988, pp. 23–32.
4. *Education Reform: Initial Effects in Four School Districts,* U.S. General Accounting Office, 1989; William A. Firestone, Susan H. Fuhrman, and Michael W. Kirst, *The Progress of Reform: An Appraisal of State Education Initiatives,* The Center for Policy Research in Education, New Brunswick, N.J., 1989; David D. Marsh and Allan Odden, "Key Factors Associated with the Effective Implementation and Impact of California's Educational Reform," unpublished paper.
5. *The Forgotten Half,* final report of the William T. Grant Foundation Commission on Work, Family and Citizenship, William T. Grant Foundation, Washington, 1988, p. 3.
6. Van Dougherty, *The First Step: Understanding the Data,* Education Commission of the States, Denver, 1987, p. 9.
7. Data on the Mesa Unified School District were taken from Charles Harrison, *Public Schools USA,* Williamson Publishing, Charlotte, Vt., 1988, p. 292.
8. William Snider, "Houston School Chief's 'Get Tough' Policy Will Send 40,000 to After-School Tutorials," *Education Week,* February 17, 1988, pp. 1, 25.
9. James M. Kauffman, Michael M. Gerber, and Melvyn I. Semmel, "Arguable Assumptions Underlying the Regular Education Initiative," *Journal of Learning Disabilities,* January 1988, pp. 6–11.
10. *Intermediate and Secondary Teacher's Guide: Grading and Reporting to Parents,* Fairfax County Public Schools, Fairfax, Va., 1987.

11. "Students-at-Risk," memo from the Fairfax County Public Schools, Department of Student Services and Special Education.
12. Daniel L. Duke and Jon Cohen, "Do Public Schools Have a Future? A Case Study of Retrenchment and Its Implications," *The Urban Review* 15, no. 2 (1983): 89–105.
13. John Ralph, "Improving Education for the Disadvantaged: Do We Know Whom to Help?" *Phi Delta Kappan,* January 1989, p. 396.
14. Ibid.
15. Daniel L. Duke and Irene Muzio, "How Effective Are Alternative Schools?—A Review of Recent Evaluations and Reports," *Teachers College Record,* February 1978, pp. 461–484; Daniel L. Duke, "School Organization, Leadership, and Student Behavior," in Oliver Moles (ed.), *Strategies to Reduce Student Misbehavior,* U.S. Department of Education, 1989.
16. Martin Gold and David W. Mann, *Expelled to a Friendlier Place,* University of Michigan Press, Ann Arbor, 1984.
17. James S. Catterall and David Stern, "The Effects of Alternative School Programs on High School Completion and Labor Market Outcomes," *Educational Evaluation and Policy Analysis* 8, no. 1 (1986): 77–88.
18. James S. Catterall, "An Intensive Group Counseling Dropout Prevention Intervention: Some Cautions on Isolating At-Risk Adolescents Within High Schools," *American Educational Research Journal* 24, no. 4 (1987): 521–540.
19. These data were provided by Donald Murphy, supervisor of the SUCCESS program, Upper Marlboro, Md.
20. Robert E. Slavin and Nancy A. Madden, "What Works for Students at Risk: A Research Synthesis," *Educational Leadership,* February 1989, pp. 4–13.
21. Tom Joe and Douglas W. Nelson, "New Futures for America's Children," in Frank I. Macchiarola and Alan Gartner (eds.), *Caring for America's Children,* Academy of Political Science, New York, 1989, p. 217.

6

Evaluating Student Performance

Among the local school policies most likely to affect the lives of students and parents are those related to evaluation and grading. Many parents can recall at least a few miserable dinners on the evenings when report cards came home, and most teachers can recall agonizing moments trying to decide a grade for a particular student. Grades take on even greater meaning when used to make decisions regarding promotion or retention. It has been reported, for example, that students rank the stress that accompanies being retained at grade level only slightly less stressful than losing a parent or going blind.[1]

Grading, evaluating, and reporting student performance are integral components of the teaching/learning process, and all three acts involve the weighing of options. There is evidence that considerable subjectivity exists in any grading process. Rinne stated the issue as follows:

> Letter grades are nothing more than a shorthand device to communicate to a student the teacher's biases, goals, performance expectations, standards, call them what you will. Some people decry letter grade standards as "subjective." Precisely the case: All performance standards are subjective.[2]

Marshall asserts that "Grading is the act of assigning value within an ordered (usually small) set of labeled categories, the order corresponding to merit, [for example] A–F for letter grading."[3] A grade serves as a symbol that something has come to an end. It is usually assigned or at least determined by someone other than the person receiving the grade.[4]

Students have another view of grades and the grading process. Generally speaking, students—male and female, older and younger, high-achieving and low-achieving—do not understand grades.[5] Much of what they learn about grades they learn informally—from other students, elder siblings, friends, and the school grapevine. When students do not understand the grading process, grades likely are being used more for comparing, evaluating, and sorting the students than for communicating with and motivating them.[6] In his study of student perceptions of grading, Evans found that (1) there is an increasing tendency for many students to perceive grades as arbitrary and often unfair; (2) lower-achieving students feel that getting good grades is something beyond their control or influence; and (3) students interpret grades according to their individual needs, fears, motivations, and understandings.[7]

In evaluating grading procedures, policymakers need to consider a variety of issues including the following:

1. What purpose or purposes is to be served by grades?
2. What factors should be considered in determining a grade?
3. What role should grades play in deciding whether or not a student must repeat a grade or subject?
4. Do alternatives to current grading practices exist?
5. Under what conditions can grades motivate students?

To help answer these questions, this chapter will address (1) the evolution of grading practices in American schools, (2) current grading practices, (3) policy issues associated with grading practices, and (4) recommendations for policymakers.

THE EVOLUTION OF GRADING PRACTICES

Grades are part of our daily life. We grade meat, eggs, pencils, houses, and students; grades are an established American tradition. The demise of the one-room schoolhouse in the early 1900s was accompanied by a push for efficient educational institutions modeled after bureaucratic organizations. Neatly printed report cards became a hallmark of this trend. The graded report card took root so firmly, states Bellanca, "that by 1911 the first major research project's negative conclusions could not destroy it."[8]

In the years from 1911 to 1960, schools experimented with various reporting systems. Although research continued to show that grades were damaging to the teaching and learning process, only superficial changes were made. As an example of the types of changes that were made, Bellanca cites the Philadelphia schools. "Between 1910 and 1960, the Philadelphia elementary schools tried a 1 to 10 number system to denote all-around progress and letter grades for conduct (1913–22), a five-letter code by subjects (1922–34), a three-symbol approach (1934–54), a two-letter approach (1940–48), a four-letter approach (1948–54) and a five-letter approach (1954–60)."[9] Through the years, however, the typical grades of A, B, C, D, and F remained in most schools, though the numerical scales they represented varied substantially.

In the struggle to reform schools during the 1960s and early 1970s, grading systems were altered. Pass/fail options were permitted, along with written evaluations. Parent-teacher conferences took on greater importance in the evaluation process.[10] In the 1960s, personalized instruction was stressed, along with an integration of subjects into units and core areas of study. During this time, there was also a search for a different way of reporting student progress.

The advent of individualized instruction during this time compelled educators to seek new ways to organize and to administer student evaluation. Many elected continuous-progress systems guided by behavioral objectives and the precepts of people such as Bloom[11] and Mager.[12] Policymakers supported behavioral objectives because of their perceived efficiency and greater accountability. The idea of specific objectives with corresponding mastery units was also a boost to the idea of continuous-progress, which developed in the United States as an outgrowth of the open classroom approach and admiration for British infant schools. Behavioral objectives were seen as a way of "managing" nongradedness and sequencing instruction for large groups of students.[13] Related reporting systems, illustrated by the following example, were developed:

> The student will add and subtract up to four place numbers.
> Mastered_____;
> Needs additional teaching and practice_____;
> Needs to drop to a lower level of the objective_____.

Other challenges to traditional grading practices were raised in William Glasser's book entitled *Schools Without Failure*;[14] Rosenthal and Jacobson's studies of teacher expectations and pupils' achievement;[15] and the book *Wad-ja-get?* by Kirschenbaum, Napier, and Simon,[16] which led to the Conference on Grading Alternatives and then to the organization of the National Center for Grading/Learning Alternatives.[17] At the college level, Pollio and his associates at the University of Tennessee Learning Research Center reported their extensive nationwide survey showing that commonly used testing and grading procedures do not promote learning and may even distort the value of a college education for many students.[18]

Despite various efforts to reform grading practices, the grading systems in most schools remained the same. Those concerned about at-risk youth indicted grades as a tool for sorting and selecting students into various groups.[19] The spread of mastery learning in the 1980s brought with it some revisions of grading practices at the elementary level,[20] but grading at the secondary level remained largely unchanged.

CURRENT GRADING PRACTICES

Most current evaluation practices can be grouped into one or more of the following three categories: group-referenced, self-referenced, and task-referenced. *Group-referenced practices,* or norm-referenced, as they are sometimes known, call for "grading on a curve." This practice is based on a frequency distribution corresponding to a normal curve.[21] *Self-referenced practices* are based on the idea of allowing each student to compete against himself by focusing on the progress made from one point to another point in time. In this way, each student's achievement can be measured in terms of his own rate of learning. *Task-referenced practices* focus on distinct student learning outcomes, usually stated as behavioral objectives. Task-referenced evaluation resulted primarily from the rise of criterion-referenced testing and the move toward mastery learning.[22]

In determining grading practices, it appears that, at least in high schools, teachers enjoy considerable discretion. For example, some teachers will count homework as part of a final grade; other teachers will not. Some teachers will drop one or two of the lowest grades for each student during a particular grading period, while other teachers believe all grades must be counted. Agnew insists, though, that administrators can still affect grading practices within an individual school.[23]

In Agnew's study of high school grading practices, he found much agreement among teachers of all grades and subject areas regarding teacher control over grading. Teacher subject area seemed to influence how grades were awarded, as did the school from which the grade was issued. There were differences in the policies implemented by department heads and principals concerning the amount of autonomy given teachers to make their own grading decisions and determine grading criteria.

Agnew found that among almost all teachers, class discussion was not an important grading criterion. This finding implies that the quality and quantity of student oral expression may make little or no difference in the determination of students' grades. With some trepidation, Agnew also reported that the school in his study that placed the least emphasis on actual learning when assigning grades was also the school with the greatest percentage of minority students and the lowest levels of parent education. Teachers at this school used attendance, behavior, and effort to a much greater degree than other performance criteria in determining grades. In all the other schools in his sample, the reverse occurred.

Another finding of Agnew's study was that while teachers reported virtual total control over grading policies, they also indicated a high degree of dissatisfaction with grading standards. If teachers control this phase of their professional responsibilities, then why such dissatisfaction? There is some evidence that when teachers talk about low standards and poor grading practices, they really are talking about other teachers and not themselves. There is also evidence that teachers feel they have control over grading practices only so long as they never fail a student.

Canady and Hotchkiss describe several grading practices which, they contend, decrease the odds for student success. They suggest that these practices relate less to teaching and learning than to the need to sort and select students to satisfy various administrative functions of schools.[24] One of the major concerns about grades is that they serve as the basis for homogeneous grouping. Large numbers of students may be denied access to a full curriculum because the content of low-ability groups is modified so more students can clear the grading hurdles.[25]

For example, some school systems select basal reading programs that introduce a large vocabulary during grade 1, while other school districts select basal programs which introduce a smaller vocabulary at grade 1. A study reported by Barr and Dreeben revealed that there was a relationship between selected basal reading programs, the first-grade vocabulary, and the socioeconomic factors of the school district. Lower-achieving students, who often have lower socioeconomic status, are placed in basal reading programs having smaller vocabularies than higher-achieving and higher SES students. Barr and Dreeben reported that even teachers in the same school district made distinctions according to ability groups which often correlated to the students' socioeconomic conditions. They found one basal program introduced 716 words, while another reading program introduced 388 vocabulary words at grade 1.[26]

If students in each of the two basal groups master 75 to 80 percent of the words expected of their group, students in both groups will probably be promoted to the next grade; individual students in the groups may conceivably receive similar grades on report cards; and teachers, administrators, and parents will be satisfied that the school is doing a good job and that the students are doing well. However, we must ask: What if both groups were allowed to participate in the basal program having 716, words even if some students mastered only 50 percent of the vocabulary words? They would still be mastering more than 75 to 80 percent of the 388-word list. The problem is that 50-percent mastery, in many schools, would result in the students being retained at grade level or promoted to a "transition class."

Other grading practices which Canady and Hotchkiss found decreased the odds for student success included the following:

1. Using varying grading scales within the same department, grade level, school and school district
2. Using grade averaging to arrive at a final grade for a particular grading period or school term
3. Using zeros indiscriminately in determining a final grade
4. Failing to maintain teaching/testing congruency
5. Using pop quizzes
6. Grading the initial efforts of students in a new subject area
7. Using grading practices that penalize students for taking risks.[27]

Grade averaging may be one of the worst ways to determine a grade for lower-ability students. If a scale of 0–100 is used for purposes of averaging, and passing is 75, these students always have 75 points (including 0) working against them, with only 25 points working for them. They can become frustrated over perennially low grades, despite evidence of learning and growth.

Averaging zeros can also be a discouraging policy. Students who, for whatever reason, receive zeros must work much harder to raise their average. Many may choose to give up instead. If averaging is to be used, and if passing is 75, all grades below 50 could be brought to 50 for purposes of averaging. In this way, students would have as many points averaged for them as they have averaged against them.

If you go into a hospital with a temperature of 105°F, the doctors will probably start medication very quickly to help bring your temperature down. During the period of medication, your temperature will be taken every hour or two, but the various thermometer readings will not be averaged to see if medication should be continued. Most likely, the medication will be continued until your temperature reaches 98.6°F! This story reveals another basic problem with grade averaging. Averaging permits extreme scores to carry excessive weight in the final outcome. Two zeros during a grading period can just about assure students of a failing mark. The question is: Is it reasonable to have a grading policy that allows a student's performance during 2 days to cancel out any progress made for the remainder of the grading period?

A further problem with grade averaging is that the intervals between grades do not represent the same value in some systems. For example, an A may represent 95–100, while a C represents 81–88. In the A range, students have 6 points to work with, while the C grade includes a range of 8 points. Such a scale means that a grade of C, when used to determine a final grade, works against a student more than a grade of A works for the student.

Grading scales vary widely among school systems. In some districts, 59 is a passing grade; in other systems, 75 is a passing grade. In some, 80 percent is a grade of D; in others, 80 percent is a C; and in still others, 80 percent earns the student a grade of B. Students who transfer from one school system to another can be adversely affected or assisted, depending on differences in the two grade scales.

To deal with the problem of varying intervals, some school districts ask teachers to assign weights to grades and then average the weights to arrive at a final grade for the grading period. For example, A equals a weight of 5 points for purposes of averaging to determine a final grade, and F equals a weight of 1 point. The scale is as follows:

$$A = 5$$
$$B = 4$$
$$C = 3$$
$$D = 2$$
$$F = 1$$

The reason for allowing a grade of F to be given any weight for purposes of averaging is because it can be argued that learning occurs even when a student earns a grade of F. When school districts use pluses and minuses on grades, A^+ might carry a weight of 13 points, while F counts for 1 point, as shown below:

$$A^+ = 13$$
$$A\ \ = 12$$
$$A^- = 11$$
$$B^+ = 10$$
$$B\ \ = 9$$
$$B^- = 8$$
$$C^+ = 7$$
$$C\ \ = 6$$
$$C^- = 5$$
$$D^+ = 4$$
$$D\ \ = 3$$
$$D^- = 2$$
$$F\ \ = 1$$

In school systems where averaging is the primary method for determining a grade, there are often policies requiring teachers to give a certain number of graded assignments during a particular grading period. Such a policy may compel teachers to grade students prematurely, before they are prepared to be evaluated. Low-achieving students are more likely to be successful in school systems that base grades on final outcomes. Recall that in the hospital example, once the patient's temperature had reached 98.6°F, the previous readings were not averaged in order to decide what to do. If a student continues to work on a paper until it is acceptable, why should all the grades received during the process of improving the paper be averaged to determine the final grade?

Canady and Hotchkiss observed that grading systems in secondary schools often penalize students for taking risks.[28] There are cases in which students, with the support of their parents, have opted for lower-level classes in order to protect their Grade Point Average (G.P.A.). Thomas suggests two ways to handle this problem. One is to grade high-level classes strictly on a pass/fail basis; a second is to assure all students in high-level classes that they will receive As and Bs if they do acceptable work.[29] A third possibility is to give greater weight to a grade in a high-level course than to the same grade in a less rigorous course. A further option is to permit students to drop to a lower-level class anytime during the school year and receive the final grade for the course based on the grade earned in the lower-level class.

Thomas states that ability grouping can create difficulties when it comes to school grading practices. Grouping students into classes on the basis of their ability complicates the problem of assigning fair and representative marks because a student doing high-caliber work in a regular class may appear to be "just average" when placed in a class of high achievers.[30] Some educators in the reform movement of the late 1980s have asked if it might not be better for some students to learn 50 percent of truly challenging content than to learn 80 percent of watered-down material.[31]

Recognizing that between-class ability grouping is a common practice in most high schools, it may be necessary for schools to develop policies to encourage students to tackle more difficult courses. One solution, according to Thomas, is the following policy: "Inasmuch as the marks for courses, regardless of the level of the class, are considered from the transcript without any consideration of the level of the class, it is strongly recommended that . . . where homogeneous grouping by ability is used, the mark (grade) a student receives in a 'grouped' class should reflect his or her relation to all students in all levels of the same course."[32] It is Thomas's contention that such a policy should be applied to all courses using the same course title on transcripts and official records. A problem may develop, however, in classes for slower students. If a teacher feels that this policy compels him or her to assign low marks only to less-able students, it prevents marks from being used to motivate students.

Thomas recommends that the course title be changed for classes designed for slower students and that the school catalog specify that these courses are non-college preparatory. In this way, teachers would be able to issue marks that, in their judgment, enhanced the instructional process for these students without being unfair to students working at higher levels.[33] A problem with such a policy, however, is that it encourages the use of homogeneous groups and adds to the complexity of scheduling.

A major problem with grading is that grades may not accurately reflect student ability. Grades may be artificially depressed, for example, if (1) students panic during tests, (2) there is little congruency between what the teacher covered in class and what is presented on the test, or (3) the test material is much more difficult than the material presented in class. If class time was spent primarily on low-level skills and simple recall of material, for instance, and then the test requires students to synthesize and apply information, some students will not be able to perform at a passing level. If the test were an objective item test requiring only recall, on the other hand, their grades might be considerably higher.

Despite these and other problems associated with assessing student performance, teachers spend a major portion of their time involved in the process. Stiggins reports that teachers may spend as much as 40 percent of their teaching time directly involved in assessment-related activities. Yet teachers, he maintains, are neither trained nor prepared to do this job.[34]

Stiggins observes that grades may be motivators for only a small segment of the students who receive Ds and Fs. "Until we understand the true complexity of the relationship of grades, motivation, and achievement and until we reflect that complexity in classroom practices," he contends, "we will have difficulty addressing the needs of those students who are in danger of failing."[35]

POLICY ISSUES ASSOCIATED WITH GRADING PRACTICES

A major policy issue that must be addressed, therefore, is how to devise an evaluation system that will stimulate and challenge brighter students and, at the same time, not inhibit the academic growth and development of slower students by making them feel that academic success is out of their reach.[36] This issue becomes particularly important as schools grow more diverse and classes become more heterogeneously grouped. Beady and Slavin offer an alternative grading system called Individual Learning Expectations (ILE) to help deal with this problem.

> In ILE students receive points based on a comparison of their weekly quiz scores with an individually determined "base score," derived from a pretest. Students are told that their base scores are the minimum scores they should receive on a quiz, and that they will earn points for exceeding their base scores. The students earn zero points if their quiz scores are at or below their base scores, and they earn one point for each point they exceed their base score, up to a maximum of 10. Students always receive 10 points if they get perfect papers, regardless of their base scores, so that no student can earn more points than someone who got a perfect paper. This avoids placing an unfair ceiling on the possible scores of high-performing students. Base scores are adjusted every two weeks to reflect actual performance and to correct gradually the level of expectations for each student.[37]

Although ILE points and certificates are emphasized as indications of week-to-week improvements or increments in performance, students may still receive individual grades based on their actual (unadjusted) performance.[38] The researchers suggest that the ILE approach may be an effective motivational strategy. There is evidence to suggest ILE is especially effective in increasing minority students' achievement.[39]

How to assess and report unsatisfactory student performance poses a second challenge for local policymakers. Thomas argues that school personnel need policies guiding the use of F as a grade. Such a policy should specify a uniform basis for determining a failing mark that (1) minimizes the negative effect an F can have on a student's self-image and (2) maintains standards. A sample of such a policy, according to Thomas, is as follows:

> In required courses a student who, in the judgment of the teacher, has made his or her best effort should not receive an "F" mark. In elective courses a student failing to meet the minimum passing standards for the course should receive an "F" mark.[40]

This policy, according to Thomas, provides a student who is required to take a course that exceeds his or her academic ability with an incentive for making an effort, thereby gaining maximum value from the course material while avoiding the negative effects of a failing mark. The student in an elective class would be required to meet minimum standards in order to pass.[41]

An alternative approach involves a dual reporting system. Under this system—which is sometimes referred to as a *dual progress plan*—the grade is considered to be a combination of two marks. One mark reflects what the student has mastered in terms of the content presented; the other mark indicates what the teacher believes about the student's efforts. The second mark legitimizes the teacher's professional judgment, while recognizing that it may not correspond to the student's actual achievement. In a dual progress plan, the mark related to mastery (the more objective part of the grade) is the mark considered for purposes of instructional grouping and admission to advanced classes. This system reduces the penalty for students who pass all their tests but get low grades because they do not complete their assignments or attend class regularly. An example of a dual progress plan is found in Appendix B.

Dual progress systems are used most commonly in middle, junior, and senior high schools where students are assigned to a team, department, or grade level; are exposed to the same units of study and/or content; and are tested in the same skills and content. A modification of a dual progress plan for elementary school involves the use of a mark as a point of reference. For example, in reading and mathematics the actual level of performance might be shown by one mark, while another is used to show the teacher's opinion of the student's performance. The second mark may be based on data collected at the local school or district level or on state and national data.

As more schools use cooperative learning, policymakers will be faced with the issue of how to grade team efforts by students. For example, to what extent should overall team performance affect the individual grade of a student? If the essence of cooperative learning is interdependence, rewarding students for group effort seems appropriate. The risk is that grading on group performance may conceal the inadequacies of individual students. Among the possible ways in which to award grades for team effort are the following:

Average team members' individual scores.

Total team members' individual scores.

Designate a group score on a single product.

Randomly select one member's paper or exam to score.

Give an individual score plus the group average.

Calculate the average of an academic score plus a "collaborative skills performance score."[42]

Generally speaking, we believe team performance should help a student's individual grade, but policymakers must be careful about practices that allow team performance to reduce an individual student's grade; such practices may be subject to legal challenge.

Establishing policies related to grading demands careful consideration, especially if the grades will affect a student's promotion or graduation. The courts take an interest in grading practices when there is evidence that a student's rights may be in jeopardy. Sendor reports, for example, that a Pennsylvania court refused to allow a student's grade to be lowered as punishment for misconduct unrelated to the student's academic performance. The particular case involved a student who drank a glass of wine while on a field trip. Following the incident, the student was suspended from school for 5 days, and, in accordance with school rules, the student's grades were reduced in each class by 10 percentage points—2 points for each day of suspension. In this ruling, the court pointed out that use of nonacademic criteria in assigning grades misrepresents a student's academic achievement.[43]

On the matter of whether schools can impose academic sanctions for excessive absences, the jury is still out. Liggett, after citing several court cases, concludes that "a school board can prescribe that a student may miss only a certain number of classes before that student would not receive credit." Should the student appeal the decision, the board may, on testimony from the teachers involved, reverse the policy and award the student credit.[44]

DETERMINING EVALUATION POLICIES

Local policymakers are expected to protect the educational interests of all students. This obligation may compel these individuals to review on a regular basis district evaluation and grading policies and practices. The preceding discussion has suggested possible problems related to grading scales, the calculation of final grades, and the use of grades as a basis for student grouping. Policymakers must clarify the purposes of their grading system before they can address these issues productively.

When policymakers in the Jackson (Mississippi) Public School District developed guidelines for evaluating and reporting student progress, they determined that there were six purposes of the grading system:

- To monitor each student's progress in mastering Common Body of Knowledge objectives.
- To evaluate student performance.
- To provide a uniform method of determining numerical grades.
- To provide a uniform method of converting numerical values to letter grades.
- To report student progress to parents.
- To identify the basis for student promotion and retention.

Whenever multiple purposes must be served by the same system, the possibility exists for confusion and coordination problems. It is therefore essential that policymakers continually ask whether evaluation, grading, and reporting practices actually are serving the purposes for which they were intended. If, for example, failures increase substantially after the introduction of a policy requiring a minimum number of days of attendance to pass a course, questions must be raised regarding the merits of the policy. A more prudent course of action might be to investigate why students are absent so frequently.

It does not appear that any one evaluation, grading, or reporting system is uniformly best for all types of schools and districts. Policies and guidelines likely should vary depending on the numbers of at-risk students served, the aspirations of students, and the expectations of the community. In all cases, however, policymakers should be guided by the conception of "good policy" we present in

Chapter 1—a good policy is one that facilitates the achievement of school goals without adversely affecting the welfare of any particular group of students.

As a precaution, all districts need a policy governing appeals related to evaluation and grading. Educators, like other individuals, are capable of making mistakes or overlooking special circumstances. Rather than trying to compose policies that anticipate every possible exception and error in judgment, it makes more sense to develop procedures for the review of grades and other evaluation decisions. Too much is at stake to deny students the right of appeal.

NOTES

1. Lorrie A. Shepard and Mary Lee Smith, "Synthesis of Research on Grade Retention," *Educational Leadership,* May 1990, p. 85.
2. Carl H. Rinne, "Grading and Growth: Answer to an Editorial," *Educational Leadership,* January 1975, p. 248.
3. John D. Marshall, "Teaching's Most Taxing Traditions: Reflections on Evaluation and Grading," occasional paper, Spring 1983, The University of Texas at Austin, SP 025 945, p. 4.
4. Ibid.
5. Ellis D. Evans, "A Developmental Study of Student Perceptions of School Grading," paper presented at the biennial meeting of the Society for Research in Child Development, Toronto, Ontario, Canada, April 25–28, 1985. ED 256 482 PS 015 078.
6. Ibid.
7. Ibid.
8. James A. Bellanca, *Grading,* National Education Association, Washington, 1977, p. 9.
9. Ibid., p. 10.
10. Robert Lynn Canady and John T. Seyfarth, *How Parent-Teacher Conferences Build Partnerships,* Phi Delta Kappa Educational Foundation, Bloomington, Ind., Fastback 132, 1979.
11. Benjamin S. Bloom et al., *Taxonomy of Educational Objectives: The Classroom of Educational Goals by a Committee of College and University Examiners,* 1st ed., Longmans, Green, New York, 1956.
12. Robert Frank Mager, *Preparing Instructional Objectives,* rev. 2d ed., Lake Management and Training, Belmont, Calif., 1984.
13. For example, see Sidney P. Rollins, *Developing Nongraded Schools,* F. E. Peacock Publisher, Itasca, Ill., 1968, pp. 23–24; and Lee L. Smith, *A Practical Approach to the Nongraded Elementary School,* Parker Publisher, West Nyack, N.Y., 1969, pp. 13–30.
14. William Glasser, *Schools Without Failure,* 1st ed., Harper & Row, New York, 1968.
15. Robert Rosenthal and Lenore Jacobson, *Pygmalion in the Classroom; Teacher Expectation and Pupils' Intellectual Development,* Holt, Rinehart and Winston, New York, 1968.
16. Howard Kirschenbaum, Rodney Napier, and Sidney B. Simon, *Wad-ja-get? The Grading Game in American Education,* Hart Pub. Co., New York, 1971.
17. Bellanca, op. cit., p. 12.
18. "Is the A to F Grading Scale Obsolete?" *Torchbearer,* The University of Tennessee, Knoxville (Summer/Fall 1987): 26, no. 3.
19. Robert Lynn Canady and Phyllis R. Hotchkiss, "It's a Good Score: It's Just a Bad Grade," *Phi Delta Kappan,* September 1989, pp. 68–71.
20. David U. Levine (ed.), *Improving Student Achievement Through Mastery Learning Programs,* Jossey-Bass, San Francisco, 1985, preface ix; Jackson F. Lele, Jr., and K. Wayne Pruitt, *Providing for Individual Difference in Student Learning: A Mastery Learning Approach,* Charles C. Thomas, Springfield, Ill., 1984.
21. Richard J. Stiggins, David A. Frisbie, and Phillip A. Griswold, "Inside High School Grading Practices: Building a Research Agenda," *Educational Measurement: Issues and Practice* 8, no. 2 (Summer 1989): 10.
22. Robert I. Wise and Betty Newman, "The Responsibilities of Grading," *Educational Leadership,* January 1975, pp. 253–256.

23. E. John Agnew, "The Grading Policies and Practices of High School Teachers," paper presented at the 1985 annual meeting of the American Educational Research Association (AERA), Chicago, Ill., March 31–April 4, 1985, ED259022.
24. Canady and Hotchkiss, loc. cit.
25. Ibid.; for additional information related to this issue, see: Jeannie Oakes, *Keeping Track: How Schools Structure Inequality,* Yale University Press, New Haven, Conn., 1985.
26. Rebecca Barr and Robert Dreeben, *How Schools Work,* University of Chicago Press, Chicago, 1983, pp. 105–125.
27. Canady and Hotchkiss, loc. cit.
28. Canady and Hotchkiss, loc. cit.
29. William C. Thomas, "Grading—Why Are School Policies Necessary? What Are the Issues?", *NASSP Bulletin,* February 1986, pp. 24–25.
30. Ibid.
31. Discussion with educators at Effective School Conference, Farmington, Conn., July 17–19, 1989.
32. Thomas, op. cit., pp. 25–26.
33. Ibid.
34. Richard J. Stiggins, "Revitalizing Classroom Assessment: The Highest Instructional Priority," *Phi Delta Kappan,* January 1988, p. 363.
35. Ibid., p. 365.
36. Charles Beady and Robert Slavin, "Making Success Available to All Students in Desegregated Schools," *Integrated Education,* September/December 1980, p. 28.
37. Ibid. (For more information on ILE, see: Robert E. Slavin, "Effects of Individual Learning Expectations on Student Achievement," *Journal of Educational Psychology* 72, no. 4 (1980): 520–524.
38. Ibid.
39. Ibid., p. 31.
40. Thomas, op. cit., p. 25.
41. Ibid.
42. David Johnson, R. Johnson, and E. Holubec, *Circles of Learning: Cooperation in the Classroom,* Interaction Book Company, Edina, Minn., 1986.
43. Benjamin Sendor, "You May Discipline Kids for 'Acting Up' Outside of School, But Don't Lower Their Grades," *The American School Board Journal,* March 1985, p. 23.
44. Lee B. Liggett, "Discipline by Grade Reduction and Grade Denial Based on Attendance," *School Law in Contemporary Society,* National Organization on Legal Problems of Education, 1980, p. 10.

7

Homework

Homework has emerged in recent years as a major focus of concern for local policymakers. It has been viewed as a key to academic improvement and an inexpensive way to extend learning time. Reactions to homework, however, have not always been favorable. It humbles parents, frustrates students, and causes debate among teachers. Equity issues are also raised by homework. Does the high school student who has $2,000 worth of computer equipment, for example, have a significant advantage in completing homework assignments over the student who is not so fortunate? What if one student has greater access to homework assistance than another?

The general effectiveness of homework is yet to be proven. Basic questions remain unanswered. How essential is homework in the effort to raise student achievement? Is it more important at some grade levels than at others? Is homework more valuable for some disciplines than for others? Should all students be assigned the same homework? How much homework is too much? Should homework be graded? How should teachers deal with students who do not complete homework assignments? What role should homework play in determining a student's overall grade?

In this chapter, we will address many of these questions and try to assess the role that local policy can play in answering them. The chapter opens with a brief review of the evolution of homework policies. The discussion then turns to research on homework and specific policy issues, such as the purposes of homework, the evaluation of homework, and equity. The chapter closes with recommendations for local policymakers.

THE EVOLUTION OF HOMEWORK POLICIES

Homework is a school tradition that has experienced waves of both enthusiasm and disenchantment. Historically, the stress placed upon homework has varied according to the prevailing educational philosophy. When school was viewed primarily as a place where information was dispersed, practices governing study at home or homework were a simple matter. "Students were given at-home tasks that involved practice in skills learned in school; or they were expected to prepare, usually by reading, for the next day's lessons. Assignments often involved substantial amounts of memorization—names, dates, sequences of events, passages of literature—and practice drills, particularly in mathematics."[1] Homework was viewed simply as a means of disciplining students' minds. The only issues to be decided, therefore, were the length of assignments, their age appropriateness, and how they would be evaluated.[2]

Teachers and parents in the United States questioned the value of homework during the forties and the seventies. During these periods, the popularity of homework as an instructional strategy decreased.[3] Cooper states: "When the 20th century began, the mind was viewed as a muscle that could benefit from mental exercise, or memorization. Since memorization could be done at home, homework was viewed as good. During the 1940s, the emphasis in education shifted from drill to problem solving. Thus . . . homework fell out of favor."[4] This new educational philosophy, which emerged during the second quarter of the twentieth century, stressed problem solving as a basic educational activity and, consequently, the concept of homework as an activity of memorization and drill began to be questioned.[5]

When advocates of the life-adjustment curriculum began to examine the role of the school after World War II, they suggested that homework was an unwarranted intrusion into the private lives of students.[6] If students spent 7 to 8 hours at school, was it realistic to expect them to spend additional time on homework? Would not students profit more from spending time with family members and friends, and engaging in sports?

During the 1980s, the escalating school dropout rate caused a reexamination of the homework question. Some researchers found correlations between students' success in school and the amount of homework they completed. Increased homework was therefore recommended as one way of improving student achievement.[7] Other researchers, however, speculated that the students who did well on homework assignments probably would succeed even without homework. Some students lacked home environments and support systems conducive to the completion of homework. Schools began to develop alternatives to conventional homework, including more time for guided practice during school hours and at after school or Saturday tutorials.

In spite of unresolved questions regarding the value of homework, many parents believe that homework is a valuable school experience. "The seventeenth annual Gallup Poll of attitudes toward the public schools revealed that 40% of adults sampled believed that elementary school children should be assigned more homework, while 38% felt that present levels were adequate. For high school students, 47% felt more homework was in order, while 31% disagreed."[8] The parents of public school students were not as enthusiastic about homework as were the parents of private school students.[9]

Teachers also vary in their beliefs about the value of homework. High school teachers tend to place more stress on homework than do elementary teachers; however, most teachers assign some homework, partly because they believe it is expected. When asked why they assign homework, teachers offer as additional reasons the following: homework improves students' academic discipline; it fosters responsibility; it reinforces and supplements school learning experiences; and it promotes closer home-school relationships.[10]

Recent calls for educational reform have included a call for more homework as a means of expanding academic learning time. Reformers cite data suggesting

that American students do less homework than their counterparts in other indus-
trialized nations and point out that these foreign students score higher on standardized tests. Walberg, Paschal, and Weinstein claim that the "superior achievement of Japanese students appears attributable not only to study time in
school . . . but extraordinary effort outside school, both totaling to perhaps twice
the typical American student's time."[11] Strother reports that some groups of educators currently believe that American elementary school students should be assigned a minimum of 1 hour of homework each evening.[12] Policymakers in many
school systems have felt compelled, as a result of the pressure to improve the performance of American students, to develop homework policies.

RESEARCH ON HOMEWORK

Is it reasonable to associate homework with higher student achievement? Recent
research findings on this question have been mixed. A Maryland study of elementary school students in sixteen school districts found that:

> A negative relationship was revealed between homework time and achievement
> in math and reading. Epstein reported that low achievement was associated with more
> time spent doing homework, teachers' frequent requests for parental help at home,
> and resultantly more minutes of parental assistance. Also associated with more home-
> work were children's negative attitudes toward it and more discipline problems. High
> achievement, on the other hand, was associated with reduced need for homework and
> parental assistance, more positive attitudes toward homework, and fewer discipline
> problems. Epstein therefore concluded that it was not clear that increasing home study
> time improved the achievement, attitudes, or behaviors of low-achieving elementary
> students.[13]

Natriello and McDill cite several studies in which modest academic gains
were made by students who completed regular homework assignments. They also
reported studies offering conflicting evidence. While only affective changes were
noted for some students completing homework assignments, several researchers
reported a negative correlation between hours spent on homework and achievement in reading and math.[14]

Walberg, Paschal, and Weinstein synthesized fifteen empirical studies of
homework and found "large and consistent" effects of homework on learning by
elementary and secondary school students.[15] "When homework is merely assigned
without feedback from teachers," they reported, "it appears to raise, on average,
the typical student at the 50th percentile to the 60th percentile. But when it is
graded or commented upon, homework appears to raise learning from the 50th to
the 79th percentile."[16] This effect represents one of the largest in the educational
research literature, according to the authors.

Cooper's survey of the literature revealed that in general, homework had a
positive effect on student achievement at the junior and senior high school levels.
"When homework and in-class study were compared in elementary schools, in-
class study proved superior," he wrote, but "within reason, the more homework
high school students do, the better their achievement." He also found that "it is
better to distribute material across several assignments than to have homework
concentrate only on material covered in class that day."[17]

Cooper concluded that:

> Homework has a positive effect on achievement, but the effect varies dramatically with grade level. For high school students, homework has substantial positive effects. Junior high school students also benefit from homework, but only about half as much. For elementary school students, the effect of homework on achievement is negligible.
>
> The optimum amount of homework also varies with grade level. For elementary students, no amount of homework—large or small—affects achievement. For junior high school students, achievement continues to improve with more homework until assignments last between one and two hours a night. For high school students, the more homework, the better achievement—within reason, of course.[18]

While Cooper found no clear pattern of homework being more effective in some subjects than in others, he did find that the beneficial effects of homework are greater when the material is neither too complex nor completely unfamiliar.[19] Walberg, Paschal, and Weinstein, however, reported that the beneficial effects of homework were of longer duration in reading and social studies than they were in other areas of the curriculum.[20]

One major problem with research on homework is that the students who complete their homework assignments on a regular basis tend to be those students who are more motivated to achieve.[21] They are also more likely to have adequate places to study, appropriate materials, and supportive parents or adults to assist them. Are these factors, rather than the completion of homework, per se, the real keys to student success in school?

Epstein cites recent research on nonpublic education that concludes "homework and discipline were two characteristics of private schools that contributed to successful learning environments over public schools. The implication is that if public schools would assign more homework, their students would learn more and the schools would be more effective."[22] The question that arises, however, is: Are the findings relative to homework for students in private schools applicable to students in public schools?

Epstein found that the assignment of homework by teachers and the completion of homework by students were associated positively with student academic performance and school behavior at the secondary level. Student outcomes also were associated with more frequent and longer homework assignments.[23] Epstein added, though, that cross-sectional data were reported only as zero-order correlations and could mean that schools with good, hard-working students had diligent teachers who assigned more homework more often."[24]

A national study of homework practices and television viewing among 10,000 seventeen-year-old students reported that higher-achieving students in mathematics completed about 10 hours of homework and watched about 5 hours of television per week. Lower-achieving students often were assigned no homework, and they varied in the amount of television they watched.[25] Could it be that teachers of lower-achieving students do not assign homework because they do not expect their students to do it?

Using data collected in the High School and Beyond study, Keith reported modest positive effects of homework on high school grades. While controlling for race, family background, ability, and school group, he showed a linear relationship between hours of homework completed per week and school grades. Low-ability students who did 10 hours of homework or more per week earned grades equal to high-ability students who did no homework.[26]

It is difficult to draw policy-oriented conclusions based on contemporary homework research. What can be said at this point is that a positive relationship between homework and student outcomes appears to exist, but it is least apparent at the elementary level. As students mature, the benefits of homework seem to increase—but not necessarily for all students. It is likely that the effects of homework are related, in part, to the purposes for which homework is intended.

SPECIFIC POLICY ISSUES

THE PURPOSES OF HOMEWORK

One of the most important issues for local policymakers to consider is the purpose, or purposes, of homework. A variety of possibilities exist. Nottingham, for example, maintains that homework is "a form of directed practice, designed to review concepts taught."[27] Students often hope that homework will help them do better on tests and examinations.[28] In its *What Works* series, the U.S. Department of Education contends that one purpose of assigning challenging homework is to "instill habits of persistence and self-control."[29] Additional purposes for homework include diagnosis of student learning problems, enrichment, individualization of instruction, punishment for students who have misbehaved, and assurance for parents that students are working hard in school.

Some purposes for homework are more defensible than others. For example, if the goal is to have students regard homework as helpful, it is hard to justify using it as a form of punishment. The effectiveness of homework for certain purposes also depends on factors such as teacher monitoring. Unless teachers check homework regularly and adjust their instruction according to how well the homework was done, it has little value as a diagnostic tool or as a source of guided practice. Also, if homework assignments are so difficult that students must obtain assistance, fulfilling the purpose for which the homework was assigned will depend on students' access to help outside of school.

The homework policy of the Florence (South Carolina) School District suggests that some local policymakers want homework to address a variety of purposes.

Florence School District One—Rationale and Guidelines for the District Homework Policy

I. Rationale

It is the position of the Board and administration of Florence School District One that learning should go beyond the limitations of the school building and school day, and extend into the home and community. In order to insure this extension, a coherent policy for out of school assignments is required. This policy is based on several assumptions: to wit—

1. Effective use of homework helps students to be more effective learners and high achievers.

2. Effective use of homework helps to set the tone of school as having a serious attitude towards learning.

3. Effective homework can extend formal learning time.
4. Homework can make the difference between a program which is merely basic and one which is enriched.
5. Students need to develop responsibility for their own work. Responsibility, therefore, must be introduced in a systematic manner.
6. Parental support can add a powerful dimension to school learning and homework experiences.
7. Homework can and should go beyond drill and preparation. Some assignments should involve application of knowledge, critical thinking, creativity, problem solving and investigation.
8. Effective use of homework can serve as preparation for the extensive study requirements demanded in higher education and the dependability required in the world of work.
9. Homework can provide students with opportunities to learn using different learning styles.

Many districts prefer to leave the determination of homework purposes up to each school. Illustrative of this approach is the homework policy of the Henrico County (Virginia) Public Schools.

> Homework is an integral extension of classroom experiences. It will be assigned and enhanced by cooperation and communication among pupil, teacher and parents. Individual schools will have specific written guidelines governing time allotment for homework, grading of homework, and parent involvement.

Once the purposes of homework have been decided, either at the school or district level, local policymakers can focus on the best ways to achieve these purposes. In the course of doing so, they must determine the appropriate role of evaluation in homework assignments.

EVALUATION OF HOMEWORK

Should homework be graded? To answer this question, a distinction must be made between "providing feedback" and grading. While little evidence exists to support the practice of assigning grades to homework, there is considerable evidence that students benefit from feedback on homework assignments.[30] Nottingham recommends that completed homework be reviewed in class by the teacher, with students scoring their own papers.[31] After the review, the teacher should collect the papers for additional review and decide what material needs further emphasis or what concepts are giving students the most trouble.

Madgic argues that in determining summative grades, assessment of the most significant learnings of the course should be based on actual performance. Students should be told that other activities, such as homework, are secondary in importance. The major purpose of instruction should be to prepare students to achieve the stated learning objectives.[32] Teachers should be discouraged from giving a student a low grade because of incomplete homework assignments. If the student can demonstrate mastery of the course content, a passing grade should be awarded regardless of the quality of homework assignments.

In his synthesis of the literature, Cooper offers additional advice concerning the evaluation of homework.

> The existing research indicates that different strategies for providing feedback differ little in their influence on homework. Realistically, it seems that students might not take assignments seriously or might not complete them at all if they are not going to be monitored, either through grading or some penalty for failure to turn the work in. The evidence suggests, however, that intermittent grading and comments is no less effective than providing continuous feedback. I suggest, therefore, that the practice of grading homework be kept to a minimum, especially if the assignment's purpose is to foster positive attitudes toward the subject matter. Grading might provide external reasons for doing homework that detract from students' appreciation of the intrinsic value of the exercise.
>
> This does not mean that some homework assignments should go unmonitored. All homework should be collected, and teachers should use it in the diagnosis of learning difficulties. If a teacher notices a student falling behind in class, homework assignments can be carefully scrutinized to determine where the difficulty lies. When errors or misunderstandings on homework are found, the teacher should more assiduously go over the student's other assignments. Problems that the teacher finds should be communicated directly to the student. In a sense, then, homework can help teachers individualize instruction. I see no more reason to treat each homework assignment as if it were a test than I see reason to grade students for their performance on each class lesson.[33]

Grading homework can be harmful in several ways. Students may feel compelled to copy others' work rather than complete assignments on their own. Grading homework can also work to the disadvantage of at-risk students. If they are unable to do homework, for whatever reasons, then policies calling for homework to be graded can lead to frustration and avoidance. Stiggins notes that the threat of low grades tends mostly to motivate high-achieving students.[34] Low-achieving students do not need another reminder of their low-achieving status. The question of whether to grade homework leads directly to the most important policy issue—equity.

EQUITY

In considering the factors that affect a student's opportunity to complete homework assignments successfully, local policymakers must confront the issue of equity. If we were to visit the neighborhoods and homes of American students, we would find vast differences in the quality of domestic environments. Some students have warm, quiet places to study; others are homeless. Some students have adults in the home who will read *to* them and *with* them and who can and will assist them with their homework assignments. Some students have parents who will obtain art supplies, equipment for science-fair projects, and library books for them. Other students have no access to out-of-school assistance at all. Still others have outside responsibilities that prevent them from doing homework.

The school reformers who equate homework with achievement and recommend additional homework as a way to improve American education seem to overlook the changing demographics of American education. While homework may benefit many students, there are others for whom homework can be a barrier to success. Physical or mental abuse, drug or alcohol addiction, or simply lack of adequate domestic supervision can rob the at-risk student, for example, of the discipline needed to concentrate on homework assignments.

To minimize the likelihood that homework policies will place some students at a disadvantage, local policymakers may need to develop supporting policies that provide assistance for students having difficulty completing homework assignments. Supporting policies may require the establishment of school-based homework centers where students can go for assistance before, during, and after school. Such centers can be staffed by teacher "coaches" or honors students serving as peer tutors. Provisions may also be needed for late transportation home, homework hot lines manned by teachers and volunteers, and parent training. Several middle schools in Baltimore, Maryland, for example, recently established a phone service for parents desiring to find out their children's homework assignments. To prevent students from being overwhelmed with homework on some occasions, policies designating specific days of the week for homework in particular subjects can be useful. A special type of homework assistance is required for students preparing for tests and examinations. Local policymakers can encourage the use of study groups, in-class review sessions, and special study halls as a means of assisting students who are unlikely to benefit from home-based preparation.

DETERMINING HOMEWORK POLICIES

We have seen that the value of homework depends on a variety of factors, including the care with which it is assigned and evaluated, the purposes for which it is intended, and the extent to which assistance is available for students having difficulty completing assignments. As has been demonstrated elsewhere in this book, it is often difficult to develop effective policies in one domain without considering policies in other domains. In determining homework policies, local policymakers must also review curriculum, scheduling, grouping, grading, and related policies.

Walberg, Paschal, and Weinstein illustrate the interrelatedness of policies by focusing on written homework.[35] Noting the recent concern for improving students' writing, they point out some problems associated with giving students homework designed to encourage writing practice. One major problem involves the number of students assigned to most secondary teachers. The time required to comment on 120 to 150 written assignments would discourage many teachers from giving these assignments. The researchers therefore urge policymakers either to rearrange the work schedules of writing teachers or to provide assistants to help mark writing assignments. Their point is that homework policy cannot be considered apart from policies governing class size and supplemental staffing.

The set of homework guidelines developed by the Fairfax County (Virginia) Public Schools recognizes that there is unlikely to be one best homework policy for all situations. Rather than prescribe the kinds of homework that will and will not be accepted, the guidelines focus on the conditions associated with effective homework practices. The guidelines read as follows:

A. There should be flexibility in and differences among the assignments to individual students. These should stem from real needs and the consideration of the total educational background of the individual students.

B. Homework should serve a definite purpose.

C. Homework should be used as a technique for learning. "Busy work" turned in by the pupil and discarded by the teacher does not further learning; it merely inspires resentment and lessens the effectiveness of the teacher.

D. Homework should not be assigned as punishment under any circumstances.

E. Homework should be reasonable in view of the pupil's situation. Health, housing conditions, outside work or responsibility, leisure-time activity, and conflicting demands of home and school should not be allowed to become a frustrating and damaging combination for the pupil.

F. Homework should not be used to replace or reduce supervised study, which should take place during school hours. This type of study usually achieves better results than homework.

G. Homework for elementary students is more effective if a conference with the parent results in understanding of purpose and ways in which help at home can best be offered.

H. Responsibility for homework in the elementary school should gradually increase for grades 1–6. Elementary teachers should explain that parents can supplement school instruction by helping pupils drill on their spelling words and number combinations, encouraging them to read at home, and working with other assigned activities. Homework in the junior high school grades usually increases from approximately one to one and one-half hours per night until, at the senior high school level, two hours of homework per night are expected.

I. There should be a cooperative effort on the part of teachers to coordinate homework assignments so that students are not overburdened with excessive quantities of homework.

J. Teachers should teach pupils what to study and how to study.

K. Homework should be checked by the teacher and mistakes of pupils indicated for correction with individual comments wherever indicated or possible.

L. Homework should serve valid purposes to:
  1. Provide drill or practice on a principle or skill already taught
  2. Provide real-life application of the matter at hand
  3. Develop appreciation for or knowledge of community resources
  4. Develop the personal culture of the student
  5. Enrich, enhance, and extend school experience

M. Desirable outcomes of good homework include:
  1. Growth in responsibility
  2. Training in good work habits
  3. Opportunities for increasing self-direction
  4. Assistance in learning to budget time
  5. Contact with out-of-school learning resources
  6. Acquisition of additional information.[37]

Based on the research reviewed in this chapter, homework policies probably should vary according to student age and grade level.

For elementary school students, homework assignments probably should be short, no more than 15 or 20 minutes per night. Ample independent reading for pleasure should be stressed. The level of reading and math should be considered in assigning homework, and these subjects should be assigned on alternate nights,

COMPARISON OF HOMEWORK ACROSS GRADES (Florence School District One)

	Elementary	*Middle school*	*High school*
Frequency of assignments	Twice each week in each subject	No minimum requirement, but must be "frequent"	Once each week (averaged over 9 weeks)
Limits	Grade 1—30 minutes Grades 2–3—no more than 15 minutes for each academic subject, not to exceed a total of 45 minutes Grades 4–6—No more than 20 minutes for each academic subject, not to exceed a total of 1 hour	25 minutes for each academic class Not to exceed 1½ hours total	35 minutes for each academic class
Weekends and holidays	No assignments over weekends and holidays	Assignments permissible when necessary over weekends but not over holidays	Assignments permissible when necessary over weekends but not over holidays
Types of assignments	A minimum of 4 assignments that go beyond practice drill or recall questions required each 9 weeks	At least 1 assignment per week per class should go beyond drill/practice or answering recall questions	At least 1 assignment every other week should go beyond drill/practice or answering recall questions

with weekends and holidays kept assignment-free. The purpose of these assignments should be to build student self-confidence and a positive self-image; therefore, the assignments should be motivating and at a level of difficulty where students can feel confident and successful.

Middle and secondary school teachers should coordinate their long-term, rigorous assignments so that last-minute pressure will not be placed on students. Most students should be able to do 2 hours of homework a day if accommodations are made for those who have unavoidable conflicts. If, for instance, the editor of the yearbook is facing a printer's deadline, an assignment may be waived or postponed. The same may hold for the athlete who is in a championship play-off. Teacher-student contracts can be developed to accommodate these special circumstances and ensure that students complete homework on a regularly scheduled basis.

An illustration of how a homework policy can differentiate by grade level comes from Florence, South Carolina. The above table specifies the frequency of assignments, time limits, special restrictions, and acceptable types of assignments for elementary, middle, and high school students.

Reformers probably will continue to urge educators to increase homework assignments. Our analysis suggests that simply assigning more homework is unlikely to foster greater learning, and it can actually have an adverse effect on both students and teachers. Before promulgating homework policies, local policymakers must be clear about the purposes homework is intended to accomplish. They must also consider ways to ensure that at-risk students receive the encouragement and assistance necessary to complete homework assignments.

NOTES

1. Ronald T. LaConte and Mary Anne Doyle, *Homework as a Learning Experience,* National Education Association, Washington, 1986, p. 7.
2. Ibid.
3. Holly O'Donnell, "ERIC/RCS: Homework in the Elementary School," *Reading Teacher,* November 1989, pp. 220–222.
4. Harris Cooper, "Synthesis of Research on Homework," *Educational Leadership,* November 1989, p. 85.
5. LaConte et al., loc. cit.
6. Ibid., pp. 7–8.
7. Joyce L. Epstein, "Homework Practices, Achievements, and Behaviors of Elementary School Students," The Johns Hopkins University: Center for Research on Elementary & Middle Schools, Report no. 26, July 1988, p. 1.
8. Harris Cooper, *Homework,* Longman, New York, 1989, p. 4.
9. Ibid., pp. 4–5.
10. LaConte et al., op. cit., pp. 12–13.
11. Herbert J. Walberg, Rosanne A. Paschal, and Thomas Weinstein, "Homework's Powerful Effects on Learning," *Educational Leadership,* April 1985, p. 79.
12. Deborah Burnett Strother, "Homework: Too Much, Just Right, or Not Enough?" *Phi Delta Kappan,* February 1984, pp. 423–426.
13. LaConte et al., op. cit., p. 16.
14. Gary Natriello and Edward L. McDill, "Performance Standards, Student Effort on Homework, and Achievement," *Sociology of Education,* January 1986, pp. 18–31.
15. Walberg et al., op. cit., p. 76.
16. Ibid.
17. Cooper, "Synthesis of Research on Homework," pp. 85–89.
18. Ibid, p. 88.
19. Ibid.
20. Walberg et al., op. cit., p. 77.
21. Natriello et al., loc. cit.; also Epstein, loc. cit.
22. Epstein, loc. cit.
23. Ibid.
24. Ibid., pp. 1–2.
25. Yeary, E. E., "What About Homework?" *Today's Education,* September/October 1978, pp. 80–82.
26. Keith, T. Z., "Time Spent on Homework and High School Grades: A Large-Sample Path Analysis," *Journal of Educational Psychology,* 1982, pp. 248–258.
27. Marv Nottingham, "Grading Practices—Watching Out for Land Mines," *NAASP Bulletin,* April 1988, p. 27.
28. Ruth Strang, *Guided Study and Homework,* National Education Association, Washington, 1968, p. 16.
29. "Schools That Work: Educating Disadvantaged Children," *What Works,* U.S. Department of Education, 1987, p. 23.
30. For example, see: Cooper, *Homework,* op. cit., p. 183.
31. Nottingham, loc. cit.
32. Robert F. Madgic, "The Point System of Grading: A Critical Appraisal," *NASSP Bulletin,* April 1988.
33. Cooper, loc. cit.
34. Richard J. Stiggins, "Revitalizing Classroom Assessment: The Highest Instructional Priority," *Phi Delta Kappan,* January 1988, p. 365.
35. Walberg et al., op. cit., pp. 78–79.
36. Fairfax County (Va.) Public Schools, Regulation 2450, July 1, 1986.

8

Discipline and Attendance

Student conduct has long been a focus of attention for those involved in local-school policymaking. This chapter examines schoolwide, as opposed to classroom, efforts to deal with attendance problems and inappropriate student behavior—an area popularly referred to as *school discipline*. Two questions guide our inquiry.

1. To what extent can between-school differences in discipline be attributed to differences in school policies? In other words, can school discipline policies actually contribute to, as well as alleviate, student behavior problems?
2. What is the range of local policy options facing educators concerned about school discipline? This second question represents a theme throughout the book and relates closely to the first question.

Chapter 8 begins with a brief account of the evolution of school discipline policies. The body of the chapter deals with the major organizational strategies designed to control and manage student conduct: rules, punishments, disciplinary procedures, and comprehensive discipline plans. For each set of strategies, pertinent research and professional commentary is reviewed. The chapter closes with a discussion of some of the factors that educators should take into account when developing and assessing local policies related to student behavior.

THE EVOLUTION OF SCHOOL DISCIPLINE POLICY

The tendency for each generation to express concern over the behavior of the succeeding generation reflects the fact that the conduct of young people is hardly a new problem. Doyle, for example, compared student behavior in the 1890s and the 1970s and concluded that the variety of ways in which students test and circumvent rules has remained "remarkably consistent" over the years.[1] Duke and Jones maintain that school discipline has been a constant focus of attention for two decades, though perceptions of the most troublesome acts of misconduct shift periodically.[2] It is safe to say, however, that the overall incidence of inappropriate behavior has probably increased in recent years as schools have hosted larger and more diverse numbers of young people and as constraints on the ability of school officials to expel difficult students have tightened.

In the past, the traditional response of local policymakers to an increase in student behavior problems was to promulgate more rules and increase the severity of punishments. Educators were regarded as surrogate parents and accorded in loco parentis status to handle student behavior problems with relatively little fear of external review or intervention.

The sixties brought dramatic changes in the ways educators handled school discipline. The rights of individual students and groups such as minorities and females became a major focus of political, judicial, and educational concern. Educators lost their immunity from legal review of their discipline policies. Certain practices, such as suspension and expulsion, were indicted as discriminatory, and the due process rights of all students accused of serious behavior problems were proclaimed. In a very brief period of time, school discipline shifted from a relatively informal process to a highly complex enterprise, involving considerable paperwork and the ever-present threat of litigation. With students and their parents raising legal challenges to school discipline policies and practices to an unprecedented degree, school policymakers were compelled to develop discipline codes and carefully worded descriptions of their disciplinary procedures. Disciplinary action could no longer be left to professional discretion.

The eighties, however, were marked by another shift, as the number of federal lawsuits involving school policies declined.[3] Courts became more conservative, and judges grew reluctant to intervene in matters of school discipline. In areas such as corporal punishment, student dress, and student freedom of speech, the judgment of school officials has been upheld by the courts. Despite this shift, it is unlikely that we will ever return to the days when educators could deal with misbehaving students however they pleased. While many bemoan the red tape associated with contemporary discipline, agreement seems to exist that clearly worded and communicated policies regarding student conduct and the handling of unacceptable behavior are in the best interests of students and educators alike.

RULES

School rules have been defined as "formal statements of expected behavior ... for which consequences exist if the expectations are not met."[4] The statements may be in the form of "you shall not" or "you shall." One school, for example, may direct students to "refrain from damaging school property," while another school may encourage students to "respect the property of others." Whether expressed as injunctions or as positive expectations, rules are meant to protect the interests of everyone and are based on the presumption that certain individuals may choose to pursue their own self-interests even if doing so interferes with the self-interests of others.

Various categories of rules have been created by educators concerned about student conduct. One team of researchers found that school rules tended to cluster around behavior involving talk, movement, time, the teacher-student relationship, and the student-student relationship.[5] Duke offers a somewhat different framework for classifying rules:[6]

I. Attendance-related rules
  A. Absence from school without permission (*truancy*)
  B. Absence from class without permission (*skipping, cutting*)
  C. Late arrival to school or class (*tardiness*)
  D.Leaving school or class without permission
II. Rules related to general student behavior
  A. Criminal conduct
   1. Physical assault or battery
   2. Extortion; intimidation
   3. Theft
   4. Possession or use of weapons
   5. Possession, use, or distribution of controlled substances
   6. Destruction or abuse of property (*vandalism*)
   7. Bomb threats
   8. Setting false fire alarms
  B. Noncriminal conduct
   1. Fighting (without sustained injury)
   2. Cigarette smoking (outside of designated smoking areas, where they exist)
   3. Possession or use of "nuisance" equipment (such as radios, skateboards, "beepers," and so on)
   4. Littering
   5. Loitering
   6. Public displays of affection
   7. Improper attire
   8. Disruptive behavior outside of class (school bus, cafeteria, playground, extracurricular activities)
III. Rules related specifically to classroom behavior
  A. Classroom deportment
   1. Talking or answering out of turn
   2. Disrespect toward the teacher
   3. Disruptive behavior
   4. Chewing gum or eating
   5. Moving around the room without permission
  B. Conduct related to academic work
   1. Failure to complete assignments
   2. Turning work in late
   3. Forgetting equipment or materials
   4. Cheating
   5. Copying or plagiarizing

The rules covered in this chapter are those pertaining to general noncriminal student behavior and attendance. Rules involving criminal conduct will not be addressed because policymakers have relatively little discretion with regard to such behavior. It is in the area of noncriminal conduct that policymakers have the greatest number of options.

In determining general rules governing student conduct in school, going to and from school, and at school-sponsored activities, there are several key issues which school policymakers must consider. These include the reasons for establishing the rules, the number of rules, and the nature of the rules. Each of these issues will be examined, and relevant research will be reviewed in order to assist educators faced with the task of setting rules.

School rules may be created for two basic reasons: (1) to forestall misconduct before it occurs and (2) to reduce unacceptably high levels of misconduct. The first reason is oriented toward prevention and requires school policymakers to anticipate possible problem behaviors *before* they become problems. An example may be a rule forbidding students from wearing expensive gold jewelry to school. The intention of this rule is to remove the temptation to steal before a rash of thefts necessitates some action. The second reason is more reactive than the first. It assumes unacceptable behavior has already generated sufficient concern to justify official action. The creation of a "no expensive jewelry" rule after a series of thefts is designed to curb stealing by punishing the students who provided the incentive for the thefts.

On the surface, rules based on a desire to forestall problems seem to be preferable to those promulgated after the fact. An important issue arises, however. An almost infinite number of rules can be generated in anticipation of possible behavior problems. Does it make sense to create more rules than individuals are able to remember or educators are able to enforce? A second concern is the possibility that lengthy lists of rules and proscribed behaviors may communicate distrust and invite rule avoidance by students. Overly restrictive learning environments are often perceived as oppressive by those subject to the rules, and those who must enforce the rules can lose sight of the fact that their first obligation is to help students learn, not act as disciplinarians.

A third issue involves the nature of the rules themselves. Legal scholar Ronald Dworkin observes that "compliance with the rule book is plainly not sufficient for justice; full compliance will achieve very great injustice if the rules are unjust."[7] The legal system in the United States is based on the presumption of innocence until guilt is proven. A system of rules based on the *anticipation* of misconduct appears to contradict this presumption. School rules restricting symbolic expression (student arm bands, for example) or lawful assembly have been challenged successfully in the courts on the grounds that the "fear or apprehension of disturbance" is an insufficient basis for denying individual rights guaranteed under the Constitution.[8] The challenge to those faced with developing school rules is to protect the collective welfare and security of the school community without violating the basic rights of students as citizens.

Research on school discipline, while limited, provides some guidance for those confronting the issues discussed above. Three University of Wisconsin researchers took an interdisciplinary approach to the study of discipline in five public junior and senior high schools in a city of about 100,000 and one rural secondary school.[9] Data collection involved surveys of school personnel and students, structured interviews, and examination of discipline records and school reports. While four of the urban schools were characterized as orderly, one was found to be "troubled." Based on their findings, the researchers concluded that schools can invite problems by fostering a "self-destructive disciplinary culture."[10] The troubled school manifested some disruptive behavior, but the reaction to this behavior was judged to be excessive. The proliferation of rules and punishments led the students to feel "mistrusted and rebellious" and to "misbehave somewhat more than students in nontroubled schools."[11]

A somewhat different conclusion was drawn by researchers from the National Opinion Research Center. In a large-scale study of longitudinal survey data gathered in the High School and Beyond Study,[12] school administrators' reports of rule enforcement were analyzed to determine the relationship between misconduct and the number of rules enforced. The findings indicated that the rate of misbehavior tended to decrease as the number of enforced rules increased.[13] Correlational studies of this kind, of course, do not prove that more rules "cause" better student behavior, and reliance solely on the judgments of school administrators presents a further limitation. The study, however, does suggest that perceptions of rule enforcement (or lack thereof) may be an important factor in accounting for variations in school discipline.

Gary and Denise Gottfredson provide support for this claim in an extensive reanalysis of data from the Safe School Study, a project commissioned by Congress to provide information about the nature and extent of violence and vandalism in American schools and to recommend strategies for reducing these problems.[14] In the concluding chapter of their book, the Gottfredsons advise policymakers to:

> formulate explicit rules and disciplinary policies, to make these rules and policies known, and to ensure that these policies are adhered to. The rules must not only be clear, firmly enforced, and equitably administered, but *they must also appear to be so to students.* [italics added][15]

The findings of one further study should be noted. Duke and Perry studied student behavior in eighteen California alternative high schools and an equal number of nearby conventional high schools.[16] Discipline was rarely a major concern in the alternative schools, despite the fact that they enrolled large percentages of students who had been regarded as "discipline problems" in conventional high schools. The researchers discovered that most of the alternative schools functioned with very few rules. They concluded that rules may be less useful, and perhaps even counterproductive, in settings characterized by relatively small numbers of students and teachers, attitudes of tolerance and understanding, close relations between teachers and students, and substantial student involvement in school decision making. The study serves as a reminder to policymakers that appropriate student behavior can be achieved by strategies other than increasing the number of school rules.

*P*UNISHMENTS

It is impossible to discuss rules without addressing the consequences of failure to obey the rules. Agreement regarding the nature, purposes, and effectiveness of punishment in educational settings is elusive, however. For example, some educators regard punishment as exposure to an unpleasant experience for the purpose of behavior adjustment. Others believe that punishment should vindicate the victim of wrongdoing as well as alter the wrongdoer's conduct. Still others reject the idea of punishment altogether, preferring to think in terms of the "logical consequences" of inappropriate action.[17] Perhaps the only statement on which most educators agree is that "education is best conducted in a world in which both the costs of virtue and the benefits of evil are slight."[18]

Besides the nature and intended purposes of punishment, school policy-makers must be concerned with three central issues: (1) the range of possible punishments, (2) their effectiveness, and (3) the appropriate level of discretion for those authorized to mete out punishment. Each of these issues will be examined more closely.

The past two decades have witnessed a steady increase in the variety of punishments employed for disciplinary purposes. It is difficult to isolate a single reason for this trend. The diversification of punishments probably derives from factors such as the public's perception that schools are not doing enough to combat misconduct, the willingness of the courts to review school discipline cases, the proliferation of formal school discipline codes and plans, and the decreasing acceptability of suspension and expulsion as punishments. Some appreciation for the range of punishment options currently available can be gained by reviewing the "1988–1989 Student/Parent Handbook" for Albemarle High School in Charlottesville, Virginia. The handbook indicates that "violation of any regulation may result in one or more of the following actions:"

1. Student-teacher conference
2. Office conference
3. Teacher- or office-assigned detention (during or after school)
4. Work detail (in cafeteria or parking lot)
5. Notification of parent/guardian
6. Loss of certain school privileges. Continued disciplinary problems may result in a student being placed on probationary status (restricted from school activities, from areas of the building, and so on)
7. Overnight suspension (parents must report with student for readmission conference)
8. In-school suspension
9. Suspension for one to three days. In the case of a drug violation, at least five days but not more than thirty days
10. Expulsion for remainder of school year

The range of options available to teachers and administrators at Albemarle High School, as well as other schools throughout the country, reveals several interesting features of contemporary school discipline. Punishment, for example, may involve teachers, administrators, and parents. The locus of punishment can vary from the classroom to another school setting to home (in the case of suspension or expulsion). Corporal punishment is not listed as an option at Albemarle High School; but its use has been upheld by the Supreme Court, and many schools in the United States use some form of it. Suspension has been divided into three separate categories (overnight, in-school, and one to three days), presumably to provide additional alternatives for school officials.

With so many options, how does the educator select a suitable punishment? A review of the pertinent research and legal opinion on the subject is a good way to begin to search for an answer.

Research on ways to ensure good student behavior reflects a preference for the reinforcement of appropriate behavior rather than the punishment of misconduct. For example, in one extensive study of fifty primary schools in England, researchers found the following:

> In schools where the headteachers emphasized punishments rather more than rewards, pupils' progress tended to be inhibited; the greater the number of punishments listed, the more negative were the effects. In contrast, whenever the number of rewards exceeded the number of punishments, progress in reading was greater.[19]

Some researchers, however, acknowledge what many educators have come to believe—that certain situations require some form of punishment or negative consequence.[20] Where punishment is necessitated, Good and Brophy offer a set of research-based guidelines for its application.[21] They find little to justify, for example, abusive verbal attacks, corporal punishment, or extra schoolwork. In fact, they maintain that these punishments may actually be counterproductive, resulting in student resentment and avoidance of those who administered the punishment. Physical punishment tends to be ineffective because it (1) focuses student attention on the punishment itself rather than on the misbehavior that led to it and (2) ends quickly, thereby failing to induce sustained reflection and guilt. Good and Brophy add, however, that how punishment is presented to students is often more important than the type of punishment administered.

Duke stresses that effective punishments are those that students *perceive* to be punishing.[22] Suspending a student for chronic truancy may be perceived by the student to be more of a reward than a punishment. In fact, a number of school systems have adopted in-school suspension and Saturday detention programs in lieu of suspension for this very reason. When Duke reviewed a variety of district-sponsored evaluations of these alternative sanctions, he found that they generally were perceived to be effective in reducing discipline problems and encouraging greater student self-control.[23] Added benefits of in-school suspension and Saturday detention include the opportunities they afford for supervised study and the savings in state aid that otherwise would be lost when students are suspended from school. Some of this money can be used to reimburse school personnel for supervising detention centers.

Emmer, in a comprehensive review of research on classroom management and discipline, provides additional advice for those faced with the task of selecting appropriate forms of punishment.

1. Whenever possible, the punishment should relate logically to the misbehavior.
2. Severe punishment is frequently no more effective than moderate punishment and, at times, less so.
3. Punishment procedures should be focused on helping the student understand the problem and make a commitment to change to more acceptable behavior.
4. Punishment should not be overused with respect to either time or frequency.[24]

Guidance in the determination and administration of punishment can be derived from legal opinion as well as educational research. Among the points emphasized by legal experts are that punishments must not (1) deprive students of their constitutional right to an education without due process of law, (2) be cruel or unusual, (3) be applied in an arbitrary or capricious manner, or (4) be applied in ways that discriminate against certain groups of students. The courts have been most concerned about the last point. A recent study by the National Coalition of

Advocates for Students, in fact, indicates that disparities in student discipline persist despite a decade of efforts to eliminate them.[25] The study found, for example, that black students were involved in twice as many incidents of corporal punishment and suspension as were white students, despite the fact they make up only 16 percent of the total school population.

The courts have refrained from challenging the authority of school personnel to punish students so long as the punishment was judged to be reasonable and fair. In fact, the Supreme Court even upheld the use of corporal punishment, claiming it was a matter reserved for the states to decide. The courts have also supported the punishment of students for out-of-school misconduct so long as the students' actions could be shown to have a "direct and immediate effect either on school discipline or on the general safety and welfare of students and staff."[26] A recent study of state and federal court cases involving the suspension and expulsion of students noted a decline in the number of such cases since 1970.[27] Furthermore, school officials have won more than half of these cases since 1965 and 66.7 percent of them between 1985 and 1987. Despite claims to the contrary, the courts do not appear to have seriously hampered the ability of local educators to administer school discipline.

A third punishment-related issue for school policymakers to consider is the appropriate level of discretion for those responsible for meting out punishment. Should policy specify which punishments must be used for which offenses, or should teachers and administrators be free to choose?

One argument for individual discretion in the administering of punishment is that no two disciplinary cases are likely to be identical. One student may be a repeat offender with no respect for school rules while another student may possess a good record and simply have experienced a momentary lapse in discipline. In addition, two students may view the same punishment quite differently. Loss of eligibility for a sport can be a qualitatively different experience for a first-string athlete and a perpetual bench warmer.

An argument against individual discretion is that sanctioned inconsistency can mask discriminatory treatment. Teachers and administrators may not intend to apply punishment in a biased manner but may simply hold different expectations for different types of students. For example, sharing answers to homework assignments may be tacitly condoned for very able students but punished when found among less able students.

Except in cases involving the most serious offenses, school districts appear to favor individual discretion. When researchers studied the implementation of Chicago's Uniform Discipline Code (UDC) in 1981, they found that the UDC provided for schools to exercise "broad discretion in many areas, since the code's purpose is to 'codify the penalties that should be applicable systemwide, yet retain administrative flexibility in application.'"[28] Perhaps this preference for discretion and flexibility helps account for the persistence of discrepancies in the punishment of nonwhite and white students.

ATTENDANCE BEHAVIOR: A SPECIAL CASE

So frequent and so complicated have problems related to student attendance become that many school systems consider them to be separate from other discipline problems. This fact may be explained, in part, by the relationship between school attendance and state aid to education and the link between attendance and a student's constitutional right to an education. Attendance rules include those pertaining to unexcused absence (*truancy*) from school and class, tardiness, and leaving school without permission. Since, by law, students must attend school up to the state-dictated school-leaving age, attendance-related issues for local policymakers do not concern rules so much as the consequences for absenteeism and attendance practices.

Among the consequences for absenteeism that require the most careful consideration by policymakers are suspension, denial of course credit, and parent prosecution. Each of these issues will be examined briefly.

The wisdom of suspending students for truancy was questioned earlier in this chapter. Such a punishment can actually constitute a reward for certain students. Because of this, many school systems have introduced alternatives, such as in-school suspension and Saturday school. Some researchers, however, urge educators to approach such alternatives with caution. As one group concludes, "the use of in-school suspensions does not have a substantial likelihood of success in keeping students in school unless the approach is carefully tailored to address the problems of student disengagement."[29] Rather than serving as "holding tanks," in-school suspension and Saturday detention centers must focus on helping students to identify the causes of their attendance problems and to develop better self-discipline. For such assistance to be provided, these centers should be staffed by trained personnel.

In recent years, school policymakers concerned about the relationship between the time spent in school and student learning have begun to condone denying course credit and awarding failing grades for chronic absenteeism. The number of absences resulting in denial of credit or a failing grade usually ranges from 10 to 24 in a semester. School systems vary in terms of how they define *absence,* however. In some cases, they count only unexcused absences; in others, they count *all* absences. Questions have been raised about what to do with students who exceed the maximum number of absences before the end of the semester. Clearly they will have little incentive to attend class or keep up with their studies, if they automatically fail or are denied credit. Where absenteeism can result in denial of credit or a failing grade, therefore, an appeal or review procedure is a necessity.

A third issue concerns the extent to which school officials should seek to punish parents for a young person's absenteeism. Many states treat chronic absence from school as a form of parental neglect and allow for the prosecution of parents. Understandably, school systems are often reluctant to exercise this option. The role of parents in ensuring school attendance has grown less clear with the increase in single-parent families and families in which both parents work. The situation is made even more complex by the advent of state laws permitting home instruction and other exceptions to compulsory school attendance.[30] A 1980 case in Chesapeake, Virginia, however, upheld the school system's challenge to home instruction when neither parent meets the state requirements of a qualified teacher. As a rule, though, parent prosecution is not used by school districts to enforce attendance laws.

The procedures for monitoring attendance are another focus of concern for local policymakers. In the past, the first line of defense against absenteeism was the truant officer, an individual hired to roam neighborhoods and commercial areas during school hours looking for minors. Today, the task of monitoring student attendance falls on the shoulders of various individuals, including teachers, counselors, administrators, school social workers, and attendance clerks. Policies that have been developed to guide these individuals deal with matters such as what constitutes an attendance offense, how attendance data are to be collected, and parent notification.

Deciding what constitutes an attendance offense is not as simple as it sounds. School officials used to distinguish between excused and unexcused absences. An *excused absence* was an absence due to illness, an appointment with a doctor, or a college visit. A note from a parent was enough to verify the reason for the absence. School personnel frankly admit, however, that it is virtually impossible to be sure that the parent wrote the note or that the parent is telling the truth. Students may forge notes, and parents often cover up for their children. The increasing number of legally emancipated minors creates additional problems for those charged with monitoring attendance. As a result, some schools no longer attempt to differentiate between excused and unexcused absences. Instead, these schools —mostly at the secondary level—merely specify that a certain number of absences, excused or unexcused, will result in sanctions.

Related to the definition of an attendance offense is the matter of double standards. Many school systems, in an attempt to prevent students from dropping out, have created alternative schools and programs. These alternatives often operate with fewer rules, and the rules they have may not be enforced as rigorously as they would be in a conventional school. Similar discrepancies can sometimes be found when examining how attendance problems are handled at elementary and secondary schools in the same district. School officials should provide clear reasons for any officially recognized differences in attendance policies.

A second procedural issue involves the collection of attendance data. Traditionally, the policy at many schools has been to call the roll once a day, usually first thing in the morning. As instances of late arrival, class cutting, and leaving school without permission have grown, however, school officials have been forced to collect attendance data more frequently. It is not unusual for high schools with computerized attendance systems to collect and distribute lists of absent students each period of the day. Such efforts consume a great amount of time and usually necessitate hiring at least one full-time attendance clerk.

Even when attendance data are collected every period, it is still difficult to get accurate information on student absenteeism. Some teachers may be unaware that certain students are still enrolled in their classes, a result of poor communications between counselors and teachers. It has also been suggested that some educators may not take roll calls seriously because they do not view absenteeism as a problem.[31] In fact, in cases where classrooms are overcrowded or there are many troublesome students, they may even view absenteeism as a benefit!

Parent notification is a third area where school policies may be needed. With increased numbers of working parents, parental awareness of student absenteeism cannot be assumed. Some school officials feel that a policy calling for immediate notification of parents is an effective deterrent to attendance problems. Some school districts even have automatic phone-dialing systems with pretaped messages for the parents of absent students. When parents cannot be reached, written notices may be sent home via certified mail.

A variation on the theme of parent notification is a system where parents are required to phone the school when their children are unable to attend. This provision reduces the work load for attendance clerks, who phone only those parents from whom messages were not received.

It is difficult to judge the effectiveness of these and other attendance procedures because few controlled studies have been conducted. In a review of the research on elementary school absenteeism, Barth recommends a battery of interventions based on the various causes of student absence.[32] These interventions include direct contact with students, family counseling, coordination with child welfare agencies, staff development for teachers, and peer involvement. A yearlong case study of efforts to improve attendance at two secondary schools found that various disciplinary innovations, such as an independent study program for chronic truants and a midyear amnesty agreement, seemed to work only for brief periods of time.[33] The failure of these interventions to produce a lasting improvement in attendance was attributed (1) to poor coordination among the various school employees charged with the task of monitoring attendance and (2) to overreliance on punishment when much of the absenteeism was caused by a lack of student engagement and academic problems. In the concluding section of this chapter, more will be written about nondisciplinary strategies for improving attendance.

DISCIPLINARY PROCEDURES

The preceding section indicated several local policy concerns related to school procedures for dealing with attendance problems. In this section, additional concerns with disciplinary procedures will be addressed. These can be clustered into four categories: (1) procedures to protect student rights, (2) procedures to build awareness of school discipline, (3) procedures to increase involvement in school discipline, and (4) investigatory procedures.

Two developments have provided impetus for policies designed to protect the rights of students facing disciplinary action. The first involved a growing awareness by advocates for minority students that school discipline was often discriminatory. The second derived from Public Law 94-142 and the move to protect the rights of handicapped students. Together, these developments forced school officials to institute a variety of procedures, including disciplinary hearings and appeal processes. These procedures constitute a recognition by school officials that students cannot be denied access to education, as occurs in the case of suspension or expulsion, without due process of law.

An example of a discipline policy that stresses the due process rights of students is this one from the Henrico County (Virginia) Public Schools:

> Pupils may be expelled from attendance at school after written notice to the pupil and his parent or guardian of the proposed action and the reasons therefor and of the right to a hearing before the school board or a committee thereof in accordance with the regulations of the school board. If the regulations provide for a hearing by a committee of the school board, the regulations shall also provide for an appeal of the committee's decision to the full school board, which appeal, if requested, shall be decided by the school board within thirty days. (Policy 6-06-003)

The critical elements of this policy are the requirement that written notice of the charges be given, the provision for a hearing at which the charges can be heard and challenged, and the right of appeal in cases where the full school board is not present for the hearing. In addition, students are permitted to have access to pertinent school records and to be represented by legal counsel.

The fact that these due-process procedures consume a considerable amount of time causes many school officials to worry about reaching a point where school personnel will be spending more time on discipline than on school programs. In light of this concern, school policymakers need to determine the circumstances under which due-process procedures must be followed. Should they be used only in cases involving suspension or expulsion, or should they be used in all cases where students feel falsely accused or where a record of misconduct is kept? When disciplinary cases involve handicapped students, many school systems automatically provide for hearings and appeals, even if suspension or expulsion are not possible consequences.

A second set of concerns relates to informing students and parents of disciplinary procedures. It is indefensible to punish students for behavior which they did not realize was prohibited. School policies may call for copies of school rules and procedures to be displayed publicly, sent home to parents, and given to students. While teachers often review class rules with students, little is done in many schools to ensure that students know and understand school rules and procedures. For this reason, some school policies now call for students to be tested on their knowledge of the school discipline system. Awareness of rules may not ensure compliance, but it is an important step in that direction.

One way schools may try to increase compliance is to involve students and parents in the development and operation of the school discipline system. Their involvement may range all the way from helping to determine rules and consequences to participation in student courts. There is little research to indicate the effectiveness of any of these efforts. Student courts enjoyed some popularity two decades ago but are rarely found today. McPartland and McDill reanalyzed data collected from 900 principals and found that attitudes opposing violence and vandalism were positively correlated with student involvement in school decision making.[34] The Gottfredsons, on the other hand, reanalyzed data collected a decade later, in the late seventies, and found that teacher preference for student involvement in school decision making was related to *larger* numbers of reported victimizations.[35] A 1986 poll of 1,712 high school seniors across the United States found that less than 42 percent felt that students in their school were given enough responsibility in establishing rules of conduct.[36]

A fourth area of disciplinary procedures which school policymakers may need to address concerns investigatory activities. As violence, theft, and drug-related crime on campus increase, school officials feel the need to search students and their lockers for weapons, drugs, and other contraband. The school system in Baltimore, Maryland, for example, adopted a policy in 1988 requiring school police to search students with portable metal detectors when there is a "reasonable belief" that weapons may be present.[37] Since these preventive measures may be seen by some as infringements on a student's right to privacy, school policies governing such activities are necessary. Currently, school policies requiring drug testing for student athletes are undergoing a variety of legal challenges. The courts, however, have yet to agree on the constitutionality of such investigatory practices.[38]

The rise in criminal activity on campus has forced school policymakers to acknowledge that teachers and administrators are neither trained nor prepared to deal with acts of violence, drug dealing, and armed robbery. As schools come to rely more on police officers and security personnel, policies are needed specifying where the responsibilities of educators end and those of district or local police begin. One thing seems clear, however: School personnel must be prepared to keep accurate and accessible records of serious disciplinary incidents in order to support subsequent litigation. The days when principals or assistant principals could keep such information "in their head" are over.

COMPREHENSIVE DISCIPLINE PLANS

Given the growing concern over and the complexity of school discipline problems, it was probably inevitable that local disciplinary practices would be codified into formal district and school discipline plans. These plans, estimated to exist in three-fourths of the school systems in the United States, constitute official policy. While the plans vary considerably, most include expectations for student conduct, consequences for disobedience, a statement of philosophy or purpose, and a description of general disciplinary procedures.[39]

One impetus to the development of school discipline plans was the effort to desegregate large urban school districts. Fearful that desegregation might result in large-scale student unrest, federal judges in cities like Chicago and Cleveland actually ordered school officials to create discipline plans. A group of University of Illinois researchers studied the implementation of the Chicago Uniform Discipline Code (CUDC) in four inner-city elementary schools.[40] The philosophy and purpose of the CUDC is reflected in the following statement from the document:

> This code is designed to ensure that each classroom will have a climate or order, discipline, control and learning as well as a climate that brings out the best qualities in both the teacher and the student, allowing for individual growth and differences. Foremost, this code is a tool to reduce misconduct and thereby increase the educational benefits to which all students have a right.

The CUDC further seeks to ensure a measure of consistency in the establishment and enforcement of school rules while providing for considerable discretion on the part of school personnel. Local schools are encouraged to develop written plans within the framework of the CUDC, but the researchers found that none of the four schools studied had done so. The principals indicated that they had done little to apprise teachers and students of the contents of the CUDC and that they viewed it primarily as an "administrative convenience"—a de facto source of legitimation for their disciplinary decisions. In the four elementary schools studied, researchers concluded that the CUDC had made "little impact" on the improvement of school discipline. This study should not be regarded as a justification for rejecting district and school discipline plans as instruments of policy but, rather, as a warning to school policymakers of the need to invest energy and resources in policy implementation and enforcement as well as development.

An illustration of some of the contents of a district discipline plan is contained on the following page in the summary of "offenses" and "dispositions" from the DeKalb County (Georgia) School System. The complete discipline plan is contained in Appendix C.

Of particular interest is the wide range of offenses, the availability, in most cases, of punishment options, and the provisions for involving police or special resource personnel. Elsewhere in the DeKalb discipline plan, a glossary of terms is provided to help students and parents understand disciplinary procedures. This list of terms reveals how complex has become the management of student behavior.

- Informal hearing
- Formal hearing
- Waiver of attending formal hearing
- Hearing officer
- Detention
- Alternative instruction
- *Super program* (mandatory drug education program for first-time offenders)
- Short-term suspension
- Long-term suspension
- Student Evidentiary Hearing Committee
- Disciplinary Action Review Committee
- Expulsion
- Probation

In an article detailing the emergence and current state of discipline plans in the United States, Duke identifies several issues which should be considered by policymakers involved in developing or modifying discipline plans.[41] One issue concerns the extent to which some discipline plans reflect the interests of school employees rather than students. To be effective, plans need to be perceived by students, as well as teachers and administrators, as sensible and fair. A second issue involves the possibility of increased buck-passing. The rise of discipline plans has been accompanied by a proliferation in the number of people involved in discipline and by greater specialization of their functions. As a result, some school employees have begun to expect other individuals to handle student behavior problems they would once have tried to resolve themselves. The National Education Association, in fact, recommends that local school boards adopt policy language such as the following statement to acknowledge the expanding need for discipline-related resource people:[42]

> The Board recognizes the responsibility to give all reasonable support and assistance to teachers with respect to the maintenance of control and discipline in the classroom. Whenever it appears that a particular pupil requires the attention of special counselors, social workers, law enforcement personnel, physicians or other professional persons, the Board will take reasonable steps to relieve the teacher of responsibilities with respect to such pupil.

A problem with increasing the number of individuals involved in administering and supporting school discipline policies is that it is often hard to find one person willing to assume overall responsibility for correcting a student's behavior. Discipline plans should specify which school personnel are ultimately responsible for supervising discipline.

DeKalb County School System Summary Offense and Disposition Chart

Violation	Disposition Range	Comments
1. Tobacco	(a) 1st Offense—conference (b) 2nd Offense—suspension/probation *(c) 3rd Offense—possible expulsion	
*2. Alcohol		
*(a) sale/distribution	Suspension to expulsion	Police may be contacted
*(b)possession	Suspension to expulsion	Police may be contacted
*(c)use/influence	Suspension to expulsion	
*3. Weapons	Suspension to expulsion	Police may be contacted
*4. Threatening staff	Suspension to expulsion	Police may be contacted
*5. Drugs		
*(a) sale/distribution	Suspension to expulsion	Police may be contacted
*(b) possession	Suspension to expulsion	Police may be contacted
*(c) use/influence	Suspension to expulsion	
*(d) paraphernalia	Suspension to expulsion	
6. Property destruction	Detention to expulsion plus restitution	
7. Violence		
*(a) extreme violence	Suspension to expulsion	Police may be contacted
(b) fighting	Detention to expulsion	
8. Rude and disrespectful/refusal to follow instructions	Verbal reprimand to expulsion	
9. Unlawful absences/truancy	Detention to expulsion	Resource personnel
10. Skipping class	Detention to expulsion	
11. Classroom disturbances	Detention to expulsion	
12. School disturbance	Detention to expulsion	
13. Profanity/vulgar gestures/ indecent exposure/obscene material	Detention to expulsion	
14. Failure to accept disciplinary action	Detention to expulsion	
15. Chronic tardiness	Detention to expulsion	Resource personnel
16. Misbehavior on bus	Conference to suspension	
17. Threatening (without physical contact)	Detention to suspension	
18. Gambling	Detention to suspension	
19. Repeated violations		
(a) repeated misbehavior	Suspension to expulsion	Resource personnel
(b) violation of probation	Suspension to expulsion	
20. Parking/traffic violation	Loss of permit to expulsion	
21. Loitering/trespassing	Suspension to expulsion	Police may be contacted
22. False information	Suspension to expulsion	
23. Inappropriate bodily contact	Conference to expulsion	
24. Criminal law violation	Suspension to expulsion	
25. Behavior not otherwise in brochure	Conference to expulsion	
26. Conduct outside of school hours/away from school	Suspension to expulsion	
27. Student identification card violation	Warning to expulsion	Student pays for new card

*Offenses preceded by an asterisk carry a mandatory requirement that the area superintendent be consulted before charging the student.

A third issue identified by Duke concerns the possibility that school personnel will regard the creation of discipline plans as the extent of their commitment to school order. Discipline plans alone are unlikely to ensure appropriate student behavior. Good behavior is a function of various initiatives. Only concerted action on a variety of fronts is likely to create the ethos necessary for teaching and learning. This theme is addressed in the next section.

DETERMINING DISCIPLINARY POLICIES

Having examined various dimensions of school discipline, it is now necessary to consider the foregoing discussion in the aggregate and extract major themes of importance for school policymakers.

One theme concerns the possibility of confusion over the purposes of school discipline. Policies benefit from clear purposes that are understood and accepted by those subject to and responsible for enforcing them. Students, parents, and educators do not always agree as to the purpose of disciplinary policies. Schisms exist between advocates of prevention and advocates of intervention, advocates of risk avoidance and advocates of risk management, advocates of student rights and advocates of student responsibilities. Some see the primary purpose of school discipline as educative; others stress the goal of organizational control. Some maintain that school policies should protect the welfare of individuals; others contend that group welfare is paramount.

The aim here is not to prescribe one particular purpose for school discipline but to urge school policymakers to devote attention to the matter. It should not be assumed that agreement exists locally. For example, many disciplinary policies are motivated by a fear of risk and concern over legal liability. Students are ordered not to run in the halls, use skateboards on campus, or play unsupervised. An argument can be made, however, that an environment totally free of risk is not conducive to learning and development. Another example concerns differences between those who seek to minimize irresponsible student behavior and those committed to maximizing responsible student behavior. Policies for the former group stress tight control, limits on student options, pervasive supervision, and harsh punishments. The latter group is apt to prefer policies that encourage students to assume responsibility and provide corrective instruction for those who fail to do so.

Since school discipline policies should be designed to address a variety of purposes, policymakers must ensure that these purposes are compatible. As the preceding examples suggest, it may be counterproductive to strive both to eliminate risk and enhance learning or to reduce irresponsible behavior and encourage responsible behavior.

A second theme involves constraints on local disciplinary policymaking. School and district policies exist within legal and governmental frameworks. As a result, policymakers are expected to acknowledge the constitutional rights of all citizens and guard against the possibility that certain policies will adversely affect particular groups. Considerable evidence exists that some school discipline policies may be discriminatory toward minority students and handicapped students. In many cases, though, it is the selective *enforcement* of the policies, rather than the policies themselves, that is discriminatory. In other cases the policies themselves are the source of the problem. For example, attendance policies that punish students from impoverished homes because they must stay home to baby-sit younger siblings appear insensitive and potentially harmful. An alternative may be the creation of school-based day-care centers. Policies that require, as punishment, suspension from extra-curricular activities may place an unfair burden on students involved in athletics and other student activities. School policymakers must constantly grapple with the professional expectation that each client (student) should be treated as an individual and the bureaucratic norm that insists all clients be treated the same.

A third theme that emerges from the preceding analysis concerns the relative effectiveness of various discipline policies. Policymakers should consider the possibility that the purpose for which the policy was conceived might be better achieved by other means. For example, if student behavior problems are, in part, a result of inadequate instruction or course content that seems irrelevant to the students, policymakers might be wise to concentrate on improving teaching and the curriculum rather than conceiving of more rules, harsher punishments, and more innovative disciplinary procedures. If some misconduct can be traced to the fact that certain students never learned how to behave in school in the first place, a prudent strategy might be to provide instruction in deportment and increased opportunities for character development. Most important, rules are no substitute for relationships. If teachers do not have the time to build productive relationships with their students, it may be because their classes are too large or their work load is too great. Under such circumstances, policymakers should consider smaller classes and regularly scheduled teacher advisory periods as alternatives to new discipline policies.

This analysis of school discipline policies suggests that the variations in student behavior across different schools may be a function, to some extent, of variations in the policies designed to achieve and preserve order. It is clear that those responsible for determining district and school discipline policies confront a rich array of options. The development of these policies should not be regarded simply as a matter of composing rules and selecting punishments. Policymakers must debate the purposes of school discipline, alternative ways to achieve these purposes, and external constraints on their actions.

NOTES

1. Walter Doyle, "Are Students Behaving Worse than They Used to Behave?" *Journal of Research and Development in Education* 2, no. 4 (Summer 1978): 14.
2. Daniel L. Duke and Vernon F. Jones, "Two Decades of Discipline—Assessing the Development of an Educational Specialization," *Journal of Research and Development in Education* 17, no. 4 (Summer 1984): 26.
3. Tom Mirga, "Explosion in School Lawsuits Has Ended, 2 Unpublished Studies Find," *Education Week,* November 30, 1988, p. 1.
4. Daniel L. Duke, "Looking at the School as a Rule-Governed Organization," *Journal of Research and Development in Education* 11, no. 4 (Summer 1978): 118.
5. D. H. Hargreaves, S. K. Hester, and F. J. Mellor, *Deviance in Classrooms,* Routledge & Kegan Paul, London, 1975.
6. Duke, "Looking at the School as a Rule-Governed Organization," op. cit., pp. 118–119.
7. Ronald Dworkin, *A Matter of Principle,* Harvard University Press, Cambridge, Mass., 1985, p. 12.
8. H. C. Hudgins, Jr., and Richard S. Vacca, *Law and Education,* 2d ed., The Michie Company, Charlottesville, Va., 1985, pp. 319–363.
9. Ellen Jane Hollingsworth, Henry S. Lufler, Jr., and William H. Clune, III, *School Discipline: Order and Autonomy,* Praeger, New York, 1984.

10. Ibid., p. 20.
11. Ibid.
12. Thomas A. DiPrete, *Discipline and Order in American High Schools,* National Center for Education Statistics, Washington, 1981.
13. Ibid., p. 162.
14. Gary D. Gottfredson and Denise C. Gottfredson, *Victimization in Schools,* Plenum Press, New York, 1985.
15. Ibid., p. 174.
16. Daniel L. Duke and Cheryl Perry, "Can Alternative Schools Succeed Where Benjamin Spock, Spiro Agnew, and B. F. Skinner Have Failed?" *Adolescence* 13, no. 51 (Fall 1978): 375–392.
17. For a review of the concept of punishment, see Daniel L. Duke, "Punishment," *International Encyclopedia of Education,* Pergamon Press, London, 1985, pp. 4150–4153.
18. Thomas F. Green, "The Economy of Virtue and the Primacy of Prudence," *American Journal of Education,* February 1988, p. 132.
19. Peter Mortimore et al., *School Matters,* University of California Press, Berkeley, 1988, p. 225.
20. Jere E. Brophy and Joyce G. Putnam, "Classroom Management in the Elementary Grades," in Daniel L. Duke (ed.), *Classroom Management,* NSSE Yearbook, 1979, pp. 200–207.
21. Thomas L. Good and Jere E. Brophy, *Looking in Classrooms,* 4th ed., Harper & Row, New York, 1987, pp. 235–340.
22. Duke, "Punishment," op. cit., p. 4151.
23. Daniel L. Duke, "School Organization, Leadership, and Student Behavior," a paper commissioned by the Office of Educational Research and Improvement, U.S. Department of Education, 1986, pp. 27–32.
24. Edmund T. Emmer, "Classroom Management and Discipline," in Virginia Richardson-Koehler (ed.), *Educators' Handbook,* Longman, New York, 1987, pp. 247–250.
25. Lisa Jennings, "Disparities in Pupils' Treatment Persist, Rights Study Finds," *Education Week,* December 14, 1988, p. 5; "A Special Analysis of 1986 Elementary and Secondary School Civil Rights Survey Data," National Coalition of Advocates for Students, 1988.
26. Ann Majestic, "Disciplining Students for Out-of-School Misconduct," *School Law Bulletin* 19, no. 2 (Spring 1988): 6–11.
27. Mirga, op. cit., p. 17.
28. Julius C. Menacker, Emanuel Horwitz, and Ward Weldon, "Legislating School Discipline: The Application of a Systemwide Discipline Code to Schools in a Large Urban District," *Urban Education,* April 1988, p. 16.
29. Michael W. Sedlak, Christopher W. Wheeler, Diana C. Pullin, and Philip A. Cusick, *Selling Students Short,* Teachers College Press, New York, 1986, p. 94.
30. Hudgins et al., op. cit., pp. 247–248.
31. Richard P. Barth, "Reducing Nonattendance in Elementary Schools," *Social Work in Education* 30, no. 4 (Spring 1984): 153.
32. Ibid., pp. 156–163.
33. Daniel L. Duke and Adrienne M. Meckel, "Student Attendance Problems and School Organization: A Case Study," *Urban Education,* October 1980, pp. 325–358.
34. James M. McPartland and Edward L. McDill, "The Unique Role of Schools in the Causes of Youthful Crime," Report No. 216, Center for Social Organization of Schools, The Johns Hopkins University, Baltimore, 1976.
35. Gottfredson et al., op. cit., p. 173.
36. David L. Clark, "High School Seniors React to Their Teachers and Their Schools," *Phi Delta Kappan,* March 1987, p. 506.
37. *Education Week,* December 14, 1988, p. 3.
38. *Education Week,* January 11, 1989, p. 5.
39. Daniel L. Duke, "School Discipline Plans and the Quest for Order in American Schools," in Delwyn P. Tattum (ed.), *Management of Disruptive Pupil Behaviour in Schools,* John Wiley & Sons, Ltd., London, 1986, p. 223.
40. Julius C. Menacker, Emanuel Hurwitz, and Ward Weldon, "Legislating School Discipline . . . ," *Urban Education,* April 1988, pp. 12–23.
41. Daniel L. Duke, "School Discipline Plans and the Quest for Order in American Schools," op. cit., pp. 230–234.
42. John Dunlop, "Negotiating Student Discipline Policy," *Today's Education* 68, no. 2 (1979): 29.

9

Personnel Policies

We would be hard-pressed to find an area of local policymaking that is more central to good instruction than personnel. By personnel, we specifically refer to teachers, though policies obviously exist for other school employees, including administrators, specialists, and classified employees. Personnel policies cover a wide range of subjects, including selection, evaluation, and development. While federal and state laws constrain certain aspects of personnel policy—such as affirmative action—the discretionary authority available to local policymakers in this area is considerable.

Chapter 9 opens with a review of the development of personnel policies and the crucial watershed created by the advent of collective bargaining. Subsequent sections examine important topics frequently addressed by local personnel policies—teacher recruitment and selection, assignment and induction, supervision and evaluation, professional and staff development, teacher assistance and discipline, rewards and incentives, and teacher empowerment. The concluding section reviews major themes from the chapter in the hopes of helping local policymakers assess the adequacy of their policies.

THE EVOLUTION OF PERSONNEL POLICIES

Local personnel policies date back to the last century, when the major focus of concern was teacher conduct and propriety. Many school systems, for example, required women teachers to remain unmarried and limited the activities in which they might engage outside as well as within school. As long as the supply of teachers exceeded the demand, there was little incentive for local policymakers to address issues of teacher welfare or quality. Uncooperative or incompetent teachers were simply dismissed.

As teachers began to recognize their vulnerability, they tried to form professional associations and unions. Not until the advent of collective bargaining, however, did there emerge systematically negotiated sets of local personnel policies focusing on the welfare and working conditions of teachers. This development was facilitated by an increasing demand for teachers and the passage of laws protecting the civil rights of all public employees.

The sixties marked the beginning of collective bargaining between teachers and local school boards. By 1974, thirty-seven states had passed some form of legislation regulating bargaining by public employees.[1] While a number of states still do not require collective bargaining, the personnel policies of their local school systems suggest that the national collective bargaining movement has exerted an influence everywhere.

Mitchell and Kerchner report that relations between teachers and school districts seem to go through three distinct phases.[2] First there is general acceptance of the fact that ultimate authority in all school policy matters rests with the board of education. Phase 2 begins when the local teacher organization is accepted as a "legitimate interpreter of teacher interests." Teachers participate in "good faith bargaining" over issues pertinent to their welfare. During this phase, teacher "wins" are seen as management "losses." Phase 3 begins when teachers become involved in the creation of "negotiated policy" for the school district. School boards and administrators acknowledge that the teachers' working conditions are an important focus of local policy and need to be developed collaboratively with teachers. The transitions between phases are generally characterized by conflict and turmoil. By phase 3, the desire to avoid rancor has become so all-consuming that negotiations between teachers and management may focus more on coalition building than on improving school effectiveness.

The growth of teacher organizations and collective bargaining has meant that teachers have come to play a key role in the development of personnel policies as well as the other policies discussed in previous chapters. Initially, the teachers' goals may have been their own welfare and protection. While these bread-and-butter goals remain, they have been joined by a variety of professional aims. Kerchner detects a fundamental transformation, in fact, in the agendas of most teacher organizations.[3] Practices once considered heretical by teachers are receiving support. These include peer evaluation, differentiated staffing, standards setting, and self-management. The American Federation of Teachers, in fact, has endorsed the idea of teacher-initiated and teacher-run "charter schools" for students who are not being well served by conventional public schools.[4]

School boards and administrators are also displaying unprecedented receptivity to reforms in the personnel area. Ideas such as career ladders, merit pay, staff and professional development, teacher centers, shared decision making, and site-based management are being considered and implemented around the country. While teacher accountability continues to be a central concern for policymakers, good working conditions and teacher growth are also receiving attention.

TEACHER RECRUITMENT AND SELECTION

In his textbook on personnel administration, Rebore includes a compilation of sample personnel policies derived from the Educational Policies Service of the National School Boards Association. In the section devoted to personnel policy goals, he lists as the first aim of a district's personnel program

> to develop and implement those strategies and procedures for personnel recruitment, screening, and selection which will result in employing the best available candidates, i.e., those with highest capabilities, strongest commitment to quality education, and greatest probability of effectively implementing the district's learning program.[5]

It is important to note that this goal statement includes not only a commitment to finding "the best available" teachers but language describing what is meant by the "best." Without a clear conception of the kinds of teachers needed to implement a district's learning program, recruitment and selection practices are of little value. In this section, we look at ways that school districts can determine the kinds of teachers they want to hire and the procedures by which they can recruit and select these individuals.

Teacher recruitment and selection can be guided by several types of "vision." Some school districts develop checklists of desirable teacher attributes, based on research on teaching effectiveness. Others generate performance standards and indicators. These attributes and standards are usually intended as criteria for evaluating teachers, but they can also be used during the hiring process. For example, if one attribute of an effective teacher is good organizational skills, applicants can be screened for this quality.

Criteria for use in teacher recruitment and selection may be developed by consultants, administrators, or teams of teachers and administrators. One earmark of professionalism is the authority wielded by members of the profession when it comes to determining the criteria by which they will be selected and evaluated.[6] In many states, these criteria must be agreed upon at the bargaining table, where teachers are guaranteed a voice.

Selection and evaluation criteria vary greatly in their quality. Duke notes, for example, that performance standards for teachers are most likely to be useful when they are (1) clearly stated, (2) based on the latest research, (3) developed with teacher involvement, (4) widely publicized, and (5) reviewed on a regular basis.[7] It is also prudent for performance standards and lists of desired teacher attributes to be linked closely to teachers' job descriptions. It makes little sense to look for skills and qualities that teachers will not be expected to use on the job.

Assuming that district administrators have a clear idea of the kinds of teachers they want to hire, they must then develop a set of recruitment and selection policies and practices that will help them to secure these individuals. This task is no simple one given the shortage of prospective teachers in many localities and the lack of adequate incentives. When a team of Rand researchers studied teacher recruitment and selection in selected districts around the United States, they drew seven basic conclusions.

1. State and local policies can enhance or reduce the efficacy of wide-ranging recruitment efforts.
2. Tight coupling between recruitment and hiring decisions promotes more effective teacher selection.
3. Operational definitions of the "good teacher" vary across and within school districts.
4. In screening candidates, school districts inevitably balance high scores on objective measures of academic qualifications with assessments of other characteristics deemed important for teaching.
5. A school district's treatment of candidates during the selection process may cause some teachers to screen themselves into or out of the applicant pool.
6. The process and logistics of teacher hiring may have at least as much influence on the quality of staff hired as do formal screening mechanisms.
7. Initial hiring processes tend to screen candidates on the basis of their qualifications; later hiring processes screen candidates on the basis of the characteristics of the vacancy.[8]

Some of the above conclusions are more appropriately addressed through local policies than others. For example, enhancing the "logistics" of teacher hiring is probably a matter best left to administrator discretion. We shall focus our discussion on recruitment efforts and candidate screening—two areas for which policies can be helpful.

Attracting the best candidates to fill district teaching positions is not easy. The likelihood of finding talented teachers is related, in part, to the size of the applicant pool. Various factors act to diminish the applicant pool, however. State certification requirements, for instance, can make it difficult to recruit out-of-state teachers. Within-district transfer policies also can limit applicants. By the time all district transfer requests have been reviewed and acted upon, many of the most promising outside candidates may have accepted positions elsewhere. Other policy-related factors that can affect recruitment include starting salary, relocation incentives, fringe benefits, working conditions, and teaching assignments for newcomers.

To enhance recruiting efforts, local policymakers should consider doing the following:

- Establish a competitive starting salary.
- Create salary differentials or signing bonuses for individuals in subject-matter areas where shortages exist.
- Cover the costs of relocation.
- Create a line item in the budget to cover costs associated with recruitment.
- Guarantee new teachers attractive initial assignments with plenty of on-site support and mentoring.
- Devise ways to limit the size of the transfer pool.

In some cases, despite careful recruitment, no suitable candidates can be found. Rather than hiring marginal teachers to fill these positions, school administrators should have the option of hiring interim or part-time instructors while the search for suitable candidates continues. Hiring a tenure-track teacher can mean a commitment of over a million dollars if the teacher remains in the system for twenty-five years or more. Such a commitment of district resources should not be made hastily.

The process by which candidates are screened can be affected by confusion over definitions of the "good teacher," by invalid tests and interview instruments, and by lack of involvement by teachers and principals. School policymakers are advised by the aforementioned Rand researchers to ensure that school personnel help determine screening criteria and that these criteria are closely tied to the district's conception of a "good teacher."[9] Larger school districts tend to be characterized by more bureaucratic and impersonal screening practices. As a result, many talented applicants withdraw their applications and go elsewhere. The Rand study found that applicants preferred situations where screening occurred at the school site and involved teachers and principals.[10]

INDUCTION AND ASSIGNMENT

There was a time when teacher induction meant a day-long orientation before the opening of school in August or September. New teachers would meet the superintendent and other school administrators, receive a copy of the teachers' handbook, and be informed of key policies. A growing number of school districts are recognizing, however, that new teachers need continuing support and opportunities to learn and share. In the previously cited Rand study, researchers concluded that beginning teachers "value supervised induction, which helps them learn to teach and to learn the expectations of the school district" and that supervised induction "enhances a teacher's feeling of efficacy and reported propensity to remain in teaching."[11] State and local policymakers are beginning to create policies that provide new teachers with a formal, structured induction experience. Rebore suggests that all induction programs should have the following seven objectives:

1. To make the employee feel welcome and secure
2. To help the employee become a member of the "team"
3. To inspire the employee toward excellence in performance
4. To help the employee adjust to the work environment
5. To provide information about the community, school system, school building, faculty, and students
6. To acquaint the individual with other employees with whom he or she will become acquainted
7. To facilitate the opening of school each year[12]

What options are available to policymakers concerned about the induction of new teachers? Some systems assign a senior teacher or department chair to serve as mentor to new teachers. Others require new teachers to participate in special classes taught by district personnel and devoted to local policies and practices. Many school districts specify in their policies governing teacher evaluation that new teachers will be observed more often than veterans and receive more frequent feedback on their performance.

In determining policies to guide teacher induction, policymakers may have to deal with several problems. Funding can be a central issue. It may cost money to release senior teachers to mentor novices and to offer special induction classes. The Rand researchers reported that districts with inadequate financial resources encountered class-scheduling conflicts when trying to free senior teachers to mentor. In addition, principals were often so burdened with other responsibilities that they had little time to meet with new teachers, leaving the latter feeling as if they had been "thrown to the wolves."[13]

Another issue may be eligibility for induction programs. Is a "new" teacher only a person freshly graduated from a teacher preparation program? What about experienced teachers who transfer within the district, move to a new grade level, or transfer from another district? Do they qualify for the program? In many instances these individuals, also, are in need of support and guidance.

McLaughlin and her colleagues raise another issue that should be addressed in any induction policy: initial teaching assignments. They feel that no induction process, however thorough and well intentioned, is likely to offset the negative impact of an "impossible" first teaching assignment.

> Teachers whose initial assignments are frustrating or stressful seem more likely to experience decreased commitment, confidence, and satisfaction in later years than those whose initial assignments are supportive and satisfying.[14]

Policies designed to ensure new teachers reasonable assignments with relatively small classes and motivated students make sense professionally because these teachers are the least equipped to meet the challenges of large classes and troubled students. Unfortunately, such policies may clash with other policies—either formal or informal—that provide senior teachers with the least-challenging assignments. The key policy question is: Should favorable teaching assignments be used as a mechanism to increase the likelihood of retaining new teachers or to reward senior teachers? In the case of a conflict, which objective is more critical? In terms of the welfare of students, it hardly seems defensible to argue that those with the greatest needs are served best by inexperienced teachers. There are few matters more central to the mission of public education than how school districts decide which teachers will teach the neediest students.

To maximize district options with regard to the placement of teachers, Rebore advises policies that regard teachers as district resources rather than as occupants of a specific position in a particular school. The policy statement that he offers as an illustration begins as follows:

> The placement of employees within the school system is the responsibility of the superintendent of schools. The superintendent may delegate the implementation of the placement process to other appropriate administrators, but he or she ultimately retains the responsibility for placement. In determining assignments, the wishes of the employee are taken into consideration if these do not conflict with the requirements of the district's programming, staff balancing, and the welfare of students. Other factors that will be taken into consideration in making assignments are educational preparation and training, certification, experience, working relationships, and seniority within the school system.[15]

It is not uncommon for schools with large percentages of at-risk students to have high faculty turnover rates. As a result, these schools often have relatively large numbers of inexperienced teachers. Under such circumstances, districts may need either to reassess their policies governing within-district transfers or provide high-turnover schools with additional personnel to guide and support new teachers. The Rand researchers offer the following recommendation in this regard:

> School districts should establish supervised induction programs. They can do so by dispersing teachers so that the supervisory resources available in each school are adequate. Or they can create mentor teacher programs to increase the district's capacity for supervised induction; or they can establish specially staffed induction schools where senior teachers supervise beginning teachers.[16]

It is impossible in a brief section such as this to cover all the policy-related issues concerning teacher induction and assignment. Districts may have policies, for example, covering the misassignment of teachers (teaching outside of a teacher's areas of certification), within-district transfers, grievances related to assignments, itinerant teaching, and the use of part-time teachers. In all aspects of induction and assignment, however, the central challenge is how to strike a balance between the needs of students and the welfare of teachers.

SUPERVISION AND EVALUATION

School districts, like other organizations, require a control structure to ensure that systemwide goals are achieved and to prevent organizational entropy. The need for control is based on the assumption that the self-interests of individuals are always competing with organizational concerns. Four basic mechanisms characterize most control structures—supervision, evaluation, rewards, and sanctions. This section addresses the first two.

Great confusion often surrounds policy-level discussions of teacher supervision and evaluation. The confusion can be traced in many instances to the purposes of these time-consuming and anxiety-producing activities. Besides the control—or accountability—purpose, supervision and evaluation are also supposed to promote professional development. Research suggests, however, that relatively few teachers perceive this latter purpose to be well served by current supervision practices and evaluation systems.[17] Local policymakers must determine how best to hold teachers accountable for competent practice while also encouraging experimentation and growth. The "graying" of the teaching profession has made the second concern paramount.

The main focus in this section is supervision and evaluation for the purpose of accountability. The succeeding section is devoted to policies promoting the professional development of teachers.

No one disputes the need for teacher supervision and evaluation systems that monitor competence. The real issues for local policymakers involve how and by whom *competence* is defined, who is assigned the responsibility for supervision and evaluation, the types of data upon which evaluation decisions are made, and the frequency with which teachers are monitored.

The matter of how and by whom *teaching competence* is defined was addressed in the section on recruitment and selection. The case was made that every district needs a conception of "good teaching" as a guide in the recruitment, selection, and evaluation of teachers. While the form taken by such a conception may vary, many districts prefer policies that specify performance standards and give specific indicators of performance for each standard. The exhibit on page 118 is part of the evaluation form used for nontenured teachers in the Beaverton (Oregon) School District. Standards 9 through 15 deal with student performance, communication, and school relationships.

In developing evaluation criteria of the kind used in the Beaverton School District, policymakers must consider how performance for each standard will be rated. The system in the exhibit has only two ratings—"Meets District Standards" and "Does Not Meet District Standards." Some districts prefer a more complex rating system that differentiates between teachers who meet and teachers who exceed the standards. The more complicated the system, the more difficult it is for evaluators to justify and defend their ratings. Another question that policymakers must consider in setting performance standards is whether all teachers, from novices to seasoned veterans, will be held to the same level of performance or standards. Most systems of performance standards are easier to defend as criteria for judging minimum competence than as flexible bases for evaluating a range of professional competence.

While the problems identified above do not have clear-cut solutions, there is one aspect of teacher evaluation about which there is little debate. Teacher representatives should participate in the development and periodic adjustment of the criteria by which teachers are evaluated. To do otherwise is to deny the professional status of teachers.

Policymakers must also decide who is to have responsibility for teacher su-

PROBATIONARY TEACHER

Assessment Sheet

Teacher

Principal

| diagnosing |
| prescribing |
| facilitating |
| STUDENT PERFORMANCE |
| COMMUNICATION |
| SCHOOL RELATIONSHIPS |

Focus:
STUDENT PERFORMANCE
COMMUNICATION
SCHOOL RELATIONSHIPS

Meets District Standards / Does Not Meet District Standards

AREA: STUDENT PERFORMANCE EVALUATION

STANDARD 9: The competent teacher establishes procedures for assessing student performance by:
INDICATORS:
a. selecting means of evaluation which are appropriate to the objectives;
b. planning measurement procedures for specific purposes;
c. utilizing procedures whereby students receive feedback on their individual performance;
d. presenting information that indicates evaluation has taken place for each student.

STANDARD 10: The competent teacher interprets the results of student performance assessment by:
INDICATORS:
a. identifying the reasons why students have or have not met the performance objectives.

STANDARD 11: The competent teacher utilizes the results of student performance assessment by:
INDICATORS:
a. using objective data to arrive at a grade or indicator of student progress to be reported to parents;
b. providing feedback that facilitates the student accomplishment of goals;
c. planning changes in teaching strategies based on the results of the evaluation.

AREA: COMMUNICATION

STANDARD 12: The competent teacher communicates effectively with students by:
INDICATORS:
a. listening to and considering student comments and suggestions;
b. being open to suggestions about ways in which to present material;
c. conveying an attitude that promotes participation in activities.

STANDARD 13: The competent teacher communicates effectively with fellow colleagues and staff by:
INDICATORS:
a. participating in the group decision-making process;
b. listening to and considering suggestions from the staff;
c. sharing ideas and resources with others.

STANDARD 14: The competent teacher communicates responsibly to the public the significance of the school program by:
INDICATORS:
a. answering parents' inquiries promptly, honestly, and with discretion;
b. initiating when necessary, communication with parents;
c. having available or locating information to relate District philosophy to the community-at-large.

AREA: SCHOOL RELATIONSHIPS

STANDARD 15: The competent teacher has a consistent and professional attitude toward the accomplishment of building goals by:
INDICATORS:
a. contributing to the decision-making process and abiding by group decisions;
b. accepting shared responsibilities in and out of the classroom during the school day;
c. maintaining consistency in record keeping as defined by building or District administrative regulations and procedures;
d. using adopted courses of study or adjusting teaching objectives to include such adoptions;
e. carrying out reasonable requests given by proper authority.

EXHIBIT A Evaluation Form for Nontenured Teachers (Beaverton, Ore., School District).

pervision and evaluation. Ultimate authority for these activities, of course, rests with the school principal, but it is difficult for one individual to possess the expertise or time to supervise and evaluate all members of a faculty equally well. For this reason, many districts have policies calling for the involvement of assistant principals, department heads, district supervisors, curriculum coordinators, and master teachers. In some cases, contracts prevent nonadministrators from actually evaluating teachers, but recent years have found teacher organizations more receptive to the idea of peer involvement in certain parts of the supervision process. The Toledo (Ohio) School System attracted national attention when it inaugurated a union-approved system in which senior teachers actually evaluated new teachers and made recommendations regarding whether they should be tenured.[18]

The quality of teacher supervision and evaluation is dependent not only on the expertise of supervisors and other evaluators but on their sources of data. Research strongly suggests, for example, that policymakers should insist that teacher evaluations be based on multiple sources of data.[19] The reasons are obvious. The more sources of data, the greater the likelihood of drawing an accurate picture of teaching performance. Greater accuracy, in turn, protects teachers from arbitrary judgments and provides them with a reasonable basis for improvement. This means that school districts which require only that teachers be observed several times a year should consider supplementing formal observation data with student evaluations, parent feedback, informal drop-in observations, reviews of lesson plans and class assignments, and so on. The quality of observation data itself can be enhanced by using specially designed instruments and by observing the same teacher several days in a row.[20]

High-quality data from multiple sources does not ensure, of course, that teachers will benefit from supervision and evaluation. The data collected must be analyzed, interpreted, translated into suggestions for improvement, and communicated clearly to teachers. To do this, supervisors and evaluators need continuous training on data analysis, how to recognize effective teaching, and conferencing skills. And even this training will not be enough if the school administrators responsible for supervision and evaluation are so burdened with other responsibilities that they lack sufficient time to devote to these key activities.

Local policymakers can help school administrators function as instructional leaders. Stiggins and Duke, for example, feel there is little justification for requiring administrators to observe and evaluate every teacher every year, as many district and state policies now mandate.[21] Such policies ensure that supervision and evaluation will be relatively superficial operations, especially at the secondary level, where an administrator may be responsible for forty or more teachers.

The evidence strongly suggests that most tenured teachers are reasonably competent. To observe and evaluate them annually is to squander the precious time of teachers and administrators for little or no benefit. To use the time available for supervision and evaluation more effectively, some school districts are altering their policies to require that tenured (or continuing-contract) teachers be formally observed and evaluated only every 2, 3, or 4 years, while novice teachers and teachers in the process of correcting deficiencies continue to be monitored annually. Such a policy change means that (1) administrators are relieved of a substantial part of their supervisory and evaluation duties, thereby freeing them to focus their time and energy on a subset of the faculty each year, and (2) teachers who are not subject to standard supervision and evaluation every year can concentrate on professional and staff development. The ultimate benefits to a school system of teacher participation in these latter activities is likely to exceed by far those accruing from routine supervision and evaluation conducted by overworked administrators.

PROFESSIONAL AND STAFF DEVELOPMENT

Continuing growth and development is a fundamental dimension of all professions. Few dispute the need for veteran teachers to refine their skills, acquire new skills, and deepen their knowledge of subject matter and students. The major issue for policymakers is how best to promote and pay for the ongoing development of busy professionals.

A distinction needs to be made between professional and staff development. *Professional development* means the "process or processes by which minimally competent teachers achieve higher levels of professional competence and expand their understanding of self, role, context, and career."[22] *Staff development* means "efforts to help groups of teachers meet the organizational needs of their schools and school systems."[23] The purpose of the former is individual growth, while the latter is aimed at organizational improvement. One encourages diversity, the other collective development in a common direction. Both are necessary if schools are to be dynamic, responsive organizations.

A variety of strategies and activities are used by school systems to promote professional and staff development. They include the following:

- Job enlargement and promotion
- Career ladders
- Merit pay and special incentives
- Released time
- Peer coaching
- Sabbaticals and leaves of absence
- Teacher transfers
- In-service workshops
- Conferences
- Graduate courses
- Goal setting
- Visits to other classrooms and schools

These strategies and activities involve varying levels of financial commitment on the part of school systems. No single strategy or activity appears to work best for all teachers or even the same teacher at different times in his or her career. In thinking about how best to promote the continued growth of teachers, local policymakers are advised to

- refrain from expecting routine supervision and teacher evaluation to be effective sources of growth for most experienced teachers.
- provide teachers with a variety of professional development options from which to choose.
- ensure that resources for professional and staff development are protected as line items in the budget.

Let us examine each of these recommendations more closely. First, previously cited research indicates that experienced teachers are unlikely to find conventional supervision and evaluation practices very growth-producing. In part, this is due to lack of time and training on the part of many school administrators. The problem is also structural, however. Professional growth often entails risk, and many teachers are unwilling to take risks when the results may be a poor evaluation.[24] Evaluation—or external judgment—is, nonetheless, an important dimension of growth. Without such judgment, teachers are limited in their ability to examine critically their own performance. For this reason, Stiggins and Duke recommend decoupling evaluation for the purpose of accountability and evaluation for the purpose of professional development.[25] Teachers who demonstrate competence in the former process qualify themselves to participate in the latter for a period of time. It is essential that teachers who are subject to evaluation for the purpose of professional development be free from any threat of sanction or discipline. Such punitive measures only encourage them to select "safe," and often less meaningful, professional growth goals.

McLaughlin and Pfeifer take issue with the Stiggins and Duke recommendation. They argue that both accountability and growth can be well served by the same evaluation system.[26] Given appropriate incentives and well-trained administrators, a single-evaluation system can stimulate, they contend, the "necessary conditions for improvement—reflection, motivation, and integration."[27] The single-evaluation system they endorse goes well beyond the evaluation and supervision practices found in most districts, however.

Teacher growth can be stimulated in various ways, depending on available resources, teacher motivation and experience, and district needs. Veteran teachers may benefit, for example, from teaching a new subject or grade level, transferring to a different school, or otherwise shifting perspective; encountering new ideas from speakers and written material; and breaking established routines. Most teachers also seem to benefit from informal contact with other teachers. Opportunities for growth-oriented collegiality are provided by conferences, workshops, teacher center activities, and peer coaching. Policymakers should acknowledge that there is no one best way to promote professional development. Rather than relying solely on district-sponsored in-service workshops or salary incentives linked to graduate work, school districts need to offer teachers a variety of professional-development options from which to choose.

To support professional-development options, policymakers must secure adequate funds. Just as corporations often designate a percentage of their operating budgets for training and development, some school systems have created permanent lines in their annual budgets for these activities. When Fielding and Schalock studied the financing of staff development in Oregon, they found that districts spent between 2 and 5 percent of their budgets for teacher development.[28] Further, they discovered that teachers paid for roughly 20 percent of their own professional-growth activities. Some districts set aside a specific amount of money to support teachers' growth during the years when they are participating in professional development. Teachers are free to choose how to spend these funds.

TEACHER ASSISTANCE AND DISCIPLINE

In comparison to other personnel matters, there are relatively few options for local policymakers concerned about the remediation of deficient teachers and teacher discipline. In most states, for example, school officials are required to give just cause for dismissing tenured teachers, to observe due process, and to make a good-faith effort to help teachers correct their deficiencies. It is in this last area that local policymakers can exercise some discretion. The key question is: How far should a school district be prepared to go to assist a deficient teacher before pressing for dismissal?

In Salt Lake City, a system has been set up for dealing with deficient teachers.[29] When informal efforts by a principal have been unsuccessful in correcting a deficiency in teaching practice, the principal files a "referral for remediation" form with the superintendent. The superintendent then designates a central-office administrator to assemble and chair a "remediation team." This team consists of the referring principal, a teacher whose subject-matter area or grade level matches that of the teacher needing assistance, another teacher whose specific duty is to ensure the protection of due process rights, and the chair of the team. This team approach both decreases the likelihood of arbitrary judgments by a single supervisor and increases the amount of assistance available to the teacher in trouble. For a 2-month period, the remediation team works closely with the teacher. If, at the end of this time, the problem remains, the remediation team can ask a retired teacher or a teacher on leave to spend every day with the teacher in question. After 3 months of this intensive assistance, the referring principal must determine whether or not the deficiency has been satisfactorily corrected. The Salt Lake City system is one of the few that specifies a maximum length of time for the delivery of assistance to marginal teachers.

An agreement between school officials and the teachers' union in Toledo, Ohio, produced another model for remediating teacher deficiencies.[30] Under this system, teachers are placed in an intervention program only if the building committee (consisting entirely of teachers) and the principal agree that such action is necessary. Either the committee or the principal can initiate the process. Intervention entails the assignment of a *consulting teacher*—a teacher selected by a review board to serve for 3 years as a full-time resource person—to the teacher in need of assistance. While the intervention process carries no time limit, progress is monitored constantly by the review board. The board, made up of teachers and administrators, determines whether to continue or stop intervention and makes recommendations regarding contract renewal.

In providing assistance to teachers, school administrators are expected to specify the types of resources available as well as the specific targets for improvement. It is helpful if district policy requires these items to be recorded in a formal, written "plan of assistance." Such a plan, as represented by Exhibit B on page 123, constitutes a safeguard for both teacher and school system.

When an assistance program does not work, the consequence can be dismissal. Any teacher subject to such a penalty has "a right to know the standards by which his or her conduct will be judged."[31] When a study was conducted of 191 New York dismissal cases involving conduct unbecoming a teacher, it was discovered, however, that "no precise and useful standard of conduct has been developed [at least in New York] for teachers."[32] For this reason, it is essential that local policymakers agree on a uniform set of performance standards against which teacher conduct can be judged.

REWARDS AND INCENTIVES

If the preceding section involved the stick, this section deals with the carrot. What options are available to local policymakers who want to use rewards and incentives to encourage effective teaching? To answer this question, we must first know what teachers find rewarding.

Lortie divides rewards into three categories[33] *Extrinsic rewards* exist independently of the individual and are attached directly to a role. Earnings, prestige, and power over others are examples of extrinsic rewards. *Intrinsic rewards* are subjective in nature and, therefore, vary from person to person. *Ancillary rewards* are simultaneously objective and subjective and include aspects of work that are valued by certain groups. For example, teachers with families or those who enjoy travel may find long summer breaks to be a reward of teaching.

SAMPLE PLAN OF ASSISTANCE

I. Statement of Area Needing Improvement

The teacher fails to adequately plan and facilitate instruction so that students receive instruction appropriate to their pre-existing skill level, so that students receive individual help with concepts they do not understand, and so that students receive adequate feedback concerning their progress in mastering the material.

II. Program to be Followed:

1. By _____ , the teacher will have reviewed with Counselor _____ the results of the entrance math exam given to all 9th-graders the previous spring and will have developed a record keeping system showing each of her students' progress in meeting the District minimal competencies in math.

   This record-keeping system will be submitted to the principal by _____ .

2. Following _____ , weekly lesson plans will be developed for both the 9th and 10th-grade classes, listing for each day:
   — The math skill(s) to be taught.
   — Number of students functioning below competency level in that skill, according to the spring exams.
   — Specific activities, demonstrations, illustrations that will be used to teach the concept.
   — Supplementary work that will be assigned to those students who have already mastered this particular concept.
   — How mastery of the skill will be evaluated (in-class paper checking, assignment handed in, chalk board performance, etc.).

   Lesson plan will be submitted to the principal each Friday at or before 8 a.m. for the following week. The principal and teacher will meet each Friday at 2:45 p.m. to review the lesson plans, unless another time is arranged with the approval of the principal. The principal will observe to determine if the lesson plans for that particular day are being carried out as planned, and will provide feedback as to the effectiveness of the planned teaching activities, demonstrations, etc.

3. The teacher will develop a system for feedback and evaluation of student performance that includes the following components:
   — Completion of sample exercises in class as each skill is being taught so that students can determine if they are completing the problems correctly.
   — Teacher observation through board work, calling for answers, observing papers as students work so that teacher can identify those students who do not understand a concept.
   — Assigned daily work either graded in class (by student himself, fellow students, or volunteer helpers) or returned within two class days.
   — Review exercises assigned and reviewed in class prior to each major exam.
   — Program reports home to parents of any student who receives grades of D or F on any major exam.

   The principal, through review of lesson plans and through observation, will check to determine if this system is being followed.

   The teacher will keep a grade book that lists each daily assignment, how corrected, grades reported, and the date when papers were returned.

   The teacher will keep a file of review exercises assigned and progress reports sent home to students.

III. Monitoring System

The teacher's progress in meeting expectations listed above will be monitored by (1) principal review of weekly lesson plans, (2) principal review of teacher's grade book and file, as required in #3 above, (3) principal review of teacher's competency record keeping, and (4) at two formal and two informal observations prior to _____ .

An interim progress conference will be held by _____ .

IV. Final Evaluation

A final evaluation of the teacher's progress in making the required improvements will be made by _____
_____ .

EXHIBIT B   Sample Plan of Assistance. (Reprinted with permission of Nancy Hungerford, Attorney, Oregon City, Ore.)

In his early studies, Lortie observed that the traditions of teaching make teachers who seek extrinsic rewards suspect.[34] He found that the teachers he studied derived their primary satisfactions from intrinsic factors such as achieving desirable results with students and influencing students. While not necessarily contradicting Lortie's finding, a large-scale survey of former teachers and teachers seriously considering leaving teaching indicated that low salary was, by far, the most frequently cited source of discontent (60 percent and 62 percent respectively).[35] Other reasons given by the two groups included poor working conditions (36 percent; 41 percent), difficult students (30 percent; 31 percent), and problems with school administrators (30 percent; 25 percent).

The only conclusion that can safely be drawn from these and other studies of teacher motivation is that no single reward is likely to work for all teachers. A reward for some teachers may be the opportunity to exercise school leadership, while for others time to concentrate on classroom matters may be more important. Among the recent innovations that have been found effective as rewards for at least some teachers are career ladders, merit pay, special bonuses, job enlargement (adding new responsibilities to a teacher's role), and opportunities for professional development. In trying to determine which rewards to endorse, local policymakers should be clear about the purpose or purposes for which the rewards are intended.

Frequently mentioned reasons for introducing, augmenting, and enhancing rewards for teachers include improved productivity (as measured by student achievement on standardized tests), greater job satisfaction, and greater ability to attract and retain teachers. At present, there is little empirical data to indicate that increased job satisfaction leads to greater teacher productivity. In fact, Bacharach and Mitchell suggest that it is more likely that greater productivity yields increased job satisfaction than the reverse.[36] If their conjecture is valid, the primary reason for improving the rewards available to teachers would be to increase the capacity of a school system to attract and retain talented teachers.

Among the most hotly debated reward programs for teachers is merit pay. A recent Gallup Poll found that 84 percent of those surveyed favored an increased pay scale for teachers who prove themselves particularly capable.[37] The question for policymakers is: How is teacher accomplishment to be judged? Problems arise, for example, when student outcomes are used as a basis for determining merit. Teachers may not be assigned students in a random fashion—a procedure that would guard against the claim that some teachers get disproportionately large numbers of higher-or lower-ability students. Other problems occur when performance observation is used to judge merit. Questions can be raised about how many observations constitute a representative sampling of teacher performance and the criteria guiding the observation process.

Other problems related to merit pay concern the form of payment and teacher eligibility. The Fairfax County, Virginia, school board recently attracted national attention when it reversed a prior commitment to provide merit raises and opted instead for bonuses.[38] Claiming it could not afford raises, the board decided to give teachers judged to be meritorious one-time-only bonuses. A difficulty with merit raises relates to eligibility. If a district determines that only a certain number or percentage of teachers can earn merit raises, it invites challenges based on the teachers' Fourteenth Amendment rights.[39] If, however, a scheme is created where all or most teachers can qualify for merit raises, the district may lack sufficient funds to support the program. Those who advocate merit raises with relatively easy-to-achieve requirements are basically pushing for general salary improvement rather than for an incentive scheme for the most able teachers.

Rewards and incentives can be used for purposes other than increasing productivity or retaining teachers. Policymakers may wish to consider using them for shorter-range or more limited objectives. Jacobson reports, for instance, on the successful use of pay incentives to reduce teacher absenteeism in one large New York district.[40] The plan provided a share of incentive funds for each teacher absent fewer than 7 days, the mean number of absences during the year prior to implementation of the plan. Conceivably, incentives could also be used to encourage teachers to tackle new assignments or to undertake challenging projects. A comprehensive review of the research on merit pay by Johnson concluded that it can be an especially effective strategy "for achieving narrow objectives in organizations where pay is already high and working conditions are good."[41]

TEACHER EMPOWERMENT

The case can be made that *teacher empowerment*—or the involvement of teachers in school decision making—acts as an incentive for many teachers. Others might maintain that such involvement is a basic professional right. Since our focus is on local policies that influence teaching and learning, the question arises, Are policies promoting teacher empowerment likely to enhance the quality of instruction and student achievement?

An affirmative answer to this question is based on two arguments. First, school decisions bearing directly on instruction and students are best made by those closest to the classroom. In other words, the quality of these decisions is likely to be higher if teachers are involved. Second, decisions are more likely to be implemented if those affected by them and expected to carry them out participate in their determination. The literature is full of examples of top-level decisions that failed for lack of grass-roots involvement and support.

These two arguments for teacher empowerment are based on several assumptions. The first assumption is that teachers want to be involved in school decision making. The second assumption is that teachers involved in making school-level decisions are capable of transcending their own self-interests. Good decisions are unlikely to be made if teachers resent being involved or if they are unable to focus on students' welfare.

The research suggests that some teachers are interested in school decision making and some are not.[42] Those who are not frequently make the case that it takes precious time away from teaching and planning. They may also point out that collective bargaining assures them of a role in district decision making. In addition some may contend that involvement in decision making does not always ensure influence over those decisions.[43] Teachers resent being asked to attend meetings to discuss issues when they perceive that the ultimate decision will be made by others.

Many school systems have opted for teacher-empowerment experiments in which only a select group of teachers are invited to participate. Consider, for example, recent developments in Pittsburgh. In 1982, Pittsburgh initiated school-level instructional cabinets made up of teachers and administrators. Each cabinet makes decisions concerning instructional methodology, student assignments, use of facilities, allocation of resources, school climate, and staff development. About 15 percent of Pittsburgh's teachers are involved in these school cabinets. These teachers are referred to as "instructional teacher leaders" and relieved of some of their regular teaching loads. In addition, they receive from $500 to $1,500 on top of their base salaries.

Few studies have been conducted to determine the impact of teacher empowerment on teaching and learning. Policymakers who support programs to increase teacher involvement in decision making are advised to make provision for evaluations of these initiatives. As appealing as is the idea of shared decision making, it is by no means apparent that such efforts always yield benefits either for students or for teachers in general.

DETERMINING PERSONNEL POLICIES

Personnel policies are promulgated for a variety of reasons, only some of which deal directly with teaching and learning. In this chapter, we have attempted to identify some of the issues related to teaching and learning that may be encountered when local policymakers address such personnel matters as recruitment, selection, assignment, induction, supervision, evaluation, development, assistance, discipline, rewards, and empowerment. As a result of our efforts, several themes have emerged.

One theme is variation. With any group as diverse as professional educators, it is unlikely that many policies will function equally well for all. Recruitment policies that attract some may actually repel others. Teachers differ as to their preferences for supervision, development, incentives, and involvement in decision making. Given such variety, the policies likely to be most effective are those which are most flexible and adaptable. Rigid personnel policies that permit little latitude on the part of those who must implement them tend to invite disdain and circumvention.

A second theme—actually a manifestation of the first—is the problem of purpose. If the teachers available to school systems were all equally competent, policymakers might not have to concern themselves with accountability. Since evidence indicates, however, that a portion of those hired to teach are incompetent or otherwise unfit, policies are needed to protect students and the general public. As a result, policies have been created that provide for systematic supervision of teachers, annual evaluation, intensive remediation, and discipline. Overemphasis on accountability-oriented policies, however, can undermine another key purpose of personnel policy—professional development. Talented teachers grow to resent policies that treat all teachers as if they were potential problems and that focus resources and administrative energy on the remediation of a relatively small number of troubled teachers. They argue that personnel policies should be aimed at helping competent teachers to grow professionally and feel good about their jobs.

A third theme that emerges from our analysis concerns the assessment of personnel policies. It is difficult to say with any confidence that particular personnel policies actually contribute to improved teaching and learning. This is due, in part, to the variety of factors that influence how teachers will teach and students will learn. No single set of factors—such as personnel policies—is likely to account for much variance in instructional quality or student achievement. As a consequence, it is often difficult to defend or justify many personnel policies. Ironically, the easiest policies to rationalize typically are those that address incompetence. It appears to be easier to specify what we do *not* want instructionally than what we *do* want. Policies that promote competence and growth are more likely to become targets for critics and cost-cutters. It is no coincidence that teachers complain that personnel policies rarely serve to motivate and inspire.

NOTES

1. Randall W. Eberts and Joe A. Stone, *Unions and Public Schools,* Lexington Books, Lexington, Mass. 1984, p. 15.
2. Douglas E. Mitchell and Charles T. Kerchner, "Labor Relations and Teacher Policy," in Lee S. Shulman and Gary Sykes (eds.), *Handbook of Teaching and Policy,* Longman, New York, 1983, p. 220.
3. Charles T. Kerchner, "A 'New Generation' of Teacher Unionism," *Education Week,* January 20, 1988, p. 36.
4. Albert Shanker, "Charter Schools: Option for the Other 80 Percent," *The School Administrator,* November 1988, p. 72.
5. Ronald W. Rebore, *Personnel Administration in Education,* 2d ed., Prentice-Hall, Englewood Cliffs, N.J., 1987, p. 339.
6. Donald A. Myers, *Teacher Power,* Lexington Books, Lexington, Mass, 1973, p. 25.
7. Daniel L. Duke, *School Leadership and Instructional Improvement,* Random House, New York, 1987, p. 109.
8. Arthur E. Wise, Linda Darling-Hammond, and Barnett Berry, *Effective Teacher Selection,* Rand, Santa Monica, Calif., 1987, pp. 80–90.
9. Ibid., pp. 84–85.
10. Ibid., p. 86.
11. Ibid., p. 42.
12. Rebore, op. cit., p. 132.
13. Ibid., p. 83.
14. M. W. McLaughlin et al., "Why Teachers Won't Teach," *Phi Delta Kappan,* vol. 67, no. 6, February 1986, p. 426.
15. Rebore, op. cit., p. 129.
16. Wise et al., op. cit., p. 93.
17. Richard J. Stiggins and Daniel L. Duke, *The Case for Commitment to Teacher Growth: Research on Teacher Evaluation,* State University of New York Press, Albany, 1988, pp. 1–24.
18. Arthur E. Wise, Linda Darling-Hammond, M. W. McLaughlin, and J. T. Bernstein, *Teacher Evaluation: A Study of Effective Practices,* Rand, Santa Monica, Calif., 1984, pp. 144–156.
19. Stiggins et al., op. cit., pp. 137–139.
20. For a detailed discussion of various ways to improve the collection of data on teaching performance, see Duke, op. cit., pp. 103–161.
21. Stiggins et al., op. cit., pp. 131–134.
22. Daniel L. Duke and Richard I. Stiggins, "Beyond Minimum Competence: Evaluation for Professional Development," in Jason Millman and Linda Darling-Hammond (eds.), *Handbook for the Evaluation of Elementary and Secondary Teachers,* Sage, Newbury Park, Calif., 1990, p. 117.
23. Duke, op. cit., p. 295.
24. Duke et al., op. cit., p. 128.
25. Stiggins et al., loc. cit.
26. Milbney Wallin McLaughlin and R. Scott Pfeifer, *Teacher Evaluation,* Teachers College Press, New York, 1988, p. 69.
27. Ibid.
28. Glen D. Fielding and H. Del Schalock, *Promoting the Professional Development of Teachers and Administrators,* Center for Educational Policy and Management, Eugene, Ore., 1985, p. 16.

29. Wise et al., *Teacher Evaluation: A Study of Effective Practices,* pp. 1–37.
30. Ibid., pp. 151–156.
31. James A. Gross, *Teachers on Trial,* ILR Press, Ithaca, N.Y., 1988, p. 12.
32. Ibid.
33. Dan C. Lortie, *Schoolteacher,* University of Chicago Press, 1975, p. 101.
34. Ibid., p. 102.
35. *Former Teachers in America,* Metropolitan Life Insurance Company, New York, 1985, pp. 19–20.
36. Samuel Bacharach and Stephen Mitchell, "The Sources of Dissatisfaction in Education Administration: A Role-Specific Analysis, *Educational Administration Quarterly* 19, no. 1 (Winter 1983): 101–128.
37. Alec M. Gallup and Stanley M. Elam, "The 20th Annual Gallup Poll of the Public's Attitudes toward the Public Schools," *Phi Delta Kappan,* September 1988, p. 44.
38. *Education Week,* February 22, 1989, p. 5.
39. Frank W. Shaw, "A Summary of Legal Implications of Teacher Evaluations for Merit Pay and a Model Plan," *Educational Administration Quarterly* 21, no. 1 (Winter 1985): 66.
40. Stephen L. Jacobson, "Pay Incentives and Teacher Absence: One District's Experience," *Urban Education,* January 1989, pp. 377–391.
41. Susan Moore Johnson, "Incentives for Teachers: What Motivates, What Matters," *Educational Administration Quarterly* 22, no. 3 (Summer 1986): 69.
42. Daniel L. Duke and Bruce Gansneder, "Teacher Empowerment: The View from the Classroom," *Educational Policy* 4, no. 2: 145–160.
43. Daniel L. Duke, Beverly Showers, and Michael Imber, "Teachers and Shared Decision Making: The Costs and Benefits of Involvement," *Educational Administration Quarterly* 16, no. 1 (Winter 1980): 93–106.

10

Issues in School Policy

We have had the opportunity to examine a variety of areas in which local educational policymakers can exert influence. Chapters 2 through 8 demonstrated that much can be done locally to create policies that either facilitate or inhibit teaching and learning. In the present chapter, the focus will shift to the policymaking process itself. What is known about local educational policymaking and efforts to transform these into practice?

To address this question, we first look at the development of local policies. Who contributes to the process? Along with school board members, the key groups that may become involved include teachers, school administrators, parents, and students. The role and impact of each of these groups is reviewed in light of recent research. The second part of the chapter deals with policy implementation. Getting people to comply with policies constitutes a major challenge for many school systems. Studies of educational innovation are reviewed in order to learn more about ways to ensure that locally developed policies are actually implemented. Before addressing the issues of policy development and implementation, however, it may be helpful to look briefly at the contemporary context for local policymaking.

THE CONTEMPORARY CONTEXT FOR POLICYMAKING

The opening chapter noted that American society can be characterized as a culture of localism. The idea that local citizens should determine how the children of their community are to be educated is regarded reverentially as a cornerstone of the republic. Despite the almost sacred quality ascribed to local control, the twentieth century has witnessed a steady erosion of local prerogatives—at least until recently. From the New Deal through the "great society," the standard prescriptions to cure domestic ills—from illiteracy to crime—were massive infusions of government money, bureaucratic expertise, and federal and state policies. By the end of Lyndon Johnson's administration, however, serious questions began to be raised over the efficacy of centrally dictated responses to local concerns. Calls for a reversal of "big government" reached a crescendo during the Reagan and Bush presidencies.

In his unprecedented Education Summit at the University of Virginia in September of 1989, President Bush insisted that the key to educational reform in the United States was a reduction in the amount of red tape and regulations to which local educators were subject. His prescription called for local initiatives unfettered by governmental policies and a set of overarching national goals to which educators could be held accountable. In the wake of the Education Summit, several states announced their intention to waive many of their regulations for any school district that demonstrated an ability to achieve general state education goals. South Carolina, for example, proposed releasing top-scoring districts from state policies governing staffing, class scheduling, and class structure.[1] While state governors seem to have no intention of leaving *all* educational decisions to local discretion, they have recognized, along with federal officials, that pervasive problems such as those facing today's schools cannot be resolved solely from above. Only the commitment of local educators and other citizens can ensure that reform occurs.

A collection of new as well as familiar terms are currently being used by state and federal policymakers to express their growing determination to decentralize a substantial amount of educational decision making. These terms range from *restructuring* and *shared governance to teacher empowerment, shared decision making,* and *school-based management.* While each term is subject to multiple interpretations, a common thread running through all of them is the idea of expanding opportunities for teachers, parents, and other local groups to play a role in guiding their schools.

THE DEVELOPMENT OF LOCAL POLICIES

One aspect of local schooling where the impact of decentralization is being felt is policy development. At one time, local policy development was the job of elected or appointed school boards, working in conjunction with appointed or elected superintendents. One reason why this book is necessary is that school boards and superintendents have come to rely increasingly on the input and involvement of others in the policy-development process. Let us briefly examine several school systems where such reforms have been extensive.

One of the boldest experiments in decentralization can be found in Dade County, Florida. This school system, the nation's fourth largest, is committed to school-based management and shared decision making. Individual schools interested in these concepts are invited to submit proposals providing for the active participation of school staff in both the development and the implementation of school policy. In 1987–1988, the first year of the program, thirty-three schools submitted such proposals. While their proposals varied, each entailed a school-based budget system, in-service training in shared decision making, and provisions for team management. Teachers in most of the pilot schools were assured a role in setting school policies regarding staff selection, scheduling, evaluation, and curriculum. The school district facilitated the introduction of school-based management in these schools by providing them with lump-sum budgets to be allocated according to their individual concerns.[2] In addition, the schools could request waivers from district or state regulations such as those governing the hiring of certified teachers. The district provided funds to enable the schools to undertake staff development related to the implementation of school-based management and shared decision making. The schools participating in the program are free to propose any governing structure they wish so long as teachers are involved in school planning and policymaking.

The Dade County Public Schools have also tried to reduce the dropout rate among at-risk students and raise student achievement by encouraging twelve inner-city schools to work closely with the teachers' union (United Teachers of Dade), the Urban League of Greater Miami, Miami-Dade Community College, and a local foundation. Called Partners in Education, the program provides for five-member committees to be established at each school. Consisting of the principal, an assistant principal, the union steward, and two teachers elected by the faculty, these committees develop proposals to help at-risk students. The entire faculty is then expected to approve and implement the proposals.

Across the continent, in another large school system faced with problems of rapid growth and declining student achievement, Los Angeles is experimenting with a shared decision-making model imported from West Germany.[3] Known as the "team/small-group model," it entails devolving greater authority on small teams of teachers. Each team works with the same group of students for several years, thereby ensuring continuity, teacher familiarity with student concerns, and close relations between teachers and students. The teacher teams enjoy considerable autonomy over the policies by which they operate.

Restructuring is not reserved for huge school systems like Dade County and Los Angeles. While the need for decentralization may be greater in such systems, smaller school districts are also finding reforms of the kind mentioned above valuable. The Prince William County Public Schools in northern Virginia is a suburban-rural district. The reasons why this district is striving to implement school-based management are expressed well in a philosophical statement that opens a district planning document.

> School-based management is an educational concept designed to improve the quality of education. School-based management can best be defined as a process by which decisions directly affecting the school are moved from the central office to the local school building.
>
> School-based management as defined by the Prince William County Public Schools is intended to become "a system of management by which the individual school becomes a self-directed, responsible, and educationally accountable entity within the parameters established by the division superintendent, and where decisions are economical, efficient, and equitably facilitate learning."
>
> The concept of school-based management is predicated on the assumption that the individual building is the most manageable unit for providing quality education. The primary producers of high quality learning environments are school administrators, teachers, and participating parents. Research indicates the principal is a primary factor in determining the quality of education in any specific building. In the Prince William County School-Based Management Plan, principals will serve as the "middle managers" within a team composed of the superintendent and the associate superintendents. As the manager of the total program in the building, the principal will be given the responsibility and the authority necessary to produce desirable educational outcomes. School-based management will place accountability with the principal to produce desirable educational outcomes.[4]

While the Prince William plan acknowledges the value of teacher and parent involvement, it specifies that the principal shall be the key figure in all school decision making. Among the decisions for which Prince William principals have responsibility are the allocation of funds, the selection and allocation of staff, and the determination of staff development needs and programs. The school system reserves to itself the right to establish a uniform curriculum and the bases for evaluating personnel.

As is the case in many school districts that are attempting to decentralize, Prince William's plan calls for piloting school-based management in selected schools and modifying subsequent efforts in light of what is learned during the pilot phase. Provisions have also been made to train all administrators in such critical areas as school-based budgeting, writing building planning documents, and disaggregating and evaluating data on student achievement. Principals who participate in the school-based management program are expected to create a school improvement team consisting of faculty and community representatives.

Prince William, Dade County, and Los Angeles are not isolated examples. Across the United States, school systems are attempting to involve more people in the policymaking and policy-implementation processes. Chicago recently called for the establishment of parent boards for most of its schools. These boards are expected to select principals and help determine school policies. Other school systems have invited local business executives to play a role in school affairs. St. Louis is experimenting with ways to give young people a greater voice in policymaking. Conventional wisdom supports these efforts to decentralize on the pragmatic grounds that failure to involve the groups that will be affected by school policies reduces the likelihood that these policies will accomplish their purpose. Let us see what guidance on decentralization can be gleaned from research.

TEACHERS

In Chapter 9 we discussed teacher empowerment and concluded that little was known about the relationship between teacher involvement in school decision making and the quality of teaching and learning in that school. There is one study that attempted to link teacher involvement and student attitudes.[5] When thirty-five sixth-grade classes in twelve California schools were investigated, it was found that teachers who were more involved in school decision making tended to have students with more favorable attitudes toward school. Another 4-year study of 2,000 British students in fifty primary schools showed that teacher involvement in decisions concerning the assignment of students and teachers to classes was positively associated with student progress.[6] And a study of Houston teachers reported some relationship between teachers' feelings of powerlessness and eventual job "burnout."[7] The bulk of research on teacher involvement, however, has focused on the extent to which teachers are or desire to be involved in school decision making rather than on outcomes of that involvement. As was noted in the preceding chapter, teachers are involved to varying degrees, depending on factors such as personal preference, school organizational structure, and the commitment of the principal.

It should be noted that lack of extensive evidence linking teacher involvement in school decision making and better teaching or greater student achievement is not necessarily a reason to disregard decentralization. Effectiveness is not the only criterion for judging such reforms. A system of representative democracy does not always produce timely or appropriate decisions, but we do not react by eliminating the system. Teacher involvement in school decision making may be an ethically defensible course of action, regardless of whether it produces better teaching and learning.

It is worth noting that teachers are not always anxious to participate in local policymaking. Research provides an understanding of this reluctance. Lortie, in his classic study of Dade County teachers, for instance, found that teachers devalued activities which they perceived as not relating directly to their work with students.[8] Duke, Showers, and Imber reported that teachers in five California secondary schools frequently chose to avoid school decision-making opportunities because they felt that others ultimately controlled the final decision.[9]

If local policymakers wish to encourage shared decision making, therefore, they should be certain that (1) the decisions concern matters of consequence to teachers and (2) the teachers perceive that they actually have influence over the final decision. Duke and Gansneder offer an additional suggestion. Having analyzed data on over 3,000 teachers and found that some teachers desired more involvement than others, the researchers concluded that school officials may wish to concentrate less on across-the-board increases in teacher involvement and more on a careful matching of opportunities for involvement with the interests of individual teachers.[10]

As noted previously, Dade County's efforts to involve teachers in decision making have been among the most extensive in the country. The school district evaluated its efforts following the first year of the School-Based Management/Shared Decision-Making (SBM/SDM) project.[11] School climate in the thirty-three pilot schools was found to be comparable to national norms, based on the Purdue Teacher Opinionnaire. Teachers noted small increases in their level of involvement and seemed to favor collegial approaches to school operation. Principals tended to feel that SBM/SDM provided a better approach to defining school problems and identifying solutions. They also indicated that their relations with teachers had improved as a result of the project.

One yet-to-be-tested possibility is that shared decision making is more important at some times or under some conditions than it is at other times or under other conditions. In other words, the perceived need and/or the actual benefit of shared decision making may not be constant over time and situation. Perhaps shared decision making is least critical when a high degree of trust characterizes relations between teachers and administrators or when there are few pressing concerns of interest to teachers. Teachers may place greater value on assurances that they will be consulted on matters affecting them than they do on provisions requiring their continuous involvement in school governance.

SCHOOL ADMINISTRATORS

Teachers are not the only group with a stake in local policymaking. School administrators, parents, and students may also want to be involved in the process to some degree. While research on the impact of their involvement is not abundant, studies that have been conducted confirm that increased participation by these three groups may affect schools in desirable ways.

Consider the case of school administrators. School-effectiveness studies referred to elsewhere in this book have shown that influence over school decisions need not be regarded as a zero-sum game in which one group's gains necessarily come at another's expense. In fact, schools with good reputations often are characterized by high levels of involvement in school policymaking by building administrators, parents, and teachers.[12]

School officials who recognize the validity of school-effectiveness research have expanded the role of building administrators, among others, in local policymaking. In other schools, where officials have been slower to decentralize, some evidence exists that building administrators have taken the initiative on their own. In a study of principals in the Chicago area, for example, a team of researchers found that a variety of strategies were employed by principals in an effort to avoid central-office red tape.[13] These strategies ranged from "gentlemen's agreements" between principals to intentional delinquency on deadlines to "management by loophole." In some cases, principals faced with potential crises issued spontaneous policy statements. An example of the last strategy was the principal who, upon being confronted by a parent angered that her child had been left alone at 4:30 P.M. when school officially closed, issued a statement that school custodians would henceforth watch students after school closing until their parents could pick them up. The central office was not pleased with the policy but realized it was the only way to avert a confrontation with concerned parents who worked late and occasionally had difficulty picking up their children on time.

One issue raised by this example of principal initiative is the extent to which school systems can tolerate policy variations across schools. Individual schools cannot be permitted to circumvent district policies completely or to deviate so greatly from local policy norms that questions of equity arise. Students must be assured of a reasonably comparable education no matter what school they attend within a local jurisdiction.

PARENTS

Equity concerns may be prompted not only by the unilateral actions of building administrators, but also as a result of parental pressures. Not surprisingly, research on parent involvement finds that parents tend to think in terms of what is best for their own children.[14] Such interest, carried to an extreme, can lead to the creation of policies that benefit only a particular school or group of students. The past 3 decades have witnessed the rise of many parent-based groups representing such special-interests as handicapped students, gifted students, Chapter 1 students, students in certain extracurricular activities, and students belonging to particular ethnic and racial groups. While sometimes these groups simply press for services comparable to those received by other children, in other cases they seek special treatment. Frequently, representatives of parent groups get elected to boards and appointed to school committees. As schools and districts try to expand opportunities for parental involvement in school decision making, they must guard against domination of these processes by any particular group.

Schools and districts must also prevent the opposite kind of problem—perfunctory parent involvement. As is the case with some teachers, parents may feel that efforts to involve them in school policymaking are intended more as a safety valve or public relations ploy than a sincere attempt to share authority. In his comprehensive review of the research on parent involvement, Fullan found that many parent advisory committees were totally inactive or virtually powerless.[15] Where advisory committees functioned effectively, parent roles were specified, training was provided, and parent coordinators were appointed to facilitate involvement.[16]

STUDENTS

Student involvement in school decision making is not as widespread as is parent involvement, particularly at the elementary school level. There are indications, however, that schools can benefit when students are given a role in developing certain kinds of policy. For example, McPartland and McDill reported a measurable increase in students' opposition to violence and vandalism in schools where the students had participated in developing discipline policies.[17] The generally low level of student behavior problems in many alternative schools has been attributed, in part, to a high degree of student involvement in school decision making.[18] A challenge for school officials committed to expanding student involvement in policymaking is identifying the decisions and policies in which students are interested and to which they are able to contribute.

ADVICE ON DEVELOPING SCHOOL POLICIES

It must be acknowledged that conclusive evidence of widespread positive outcomes from shared decision making does not currently exist. Where researchers have looked at the impact of broad-based involvement, there are some indications of favorable results, but hardly enough to justify regarding shared decision making as a potent intervention to improve teaching and learning. The primary justification for shared decision making appears, instead, to be ideological. Teachers, school administrators, parents, and students should participate in determining school policies because they are affected by these policies and therefore deserve a voice in their creation. Such a view of policymaking forms the very essence of democratic theory. In governing schools, policymakers should not forget that upholding shared values can be more important than efficiency or effectiveness.

A variety of steps can be taken by school officials to increase the likelihood that shared decision making will be regarded positively by those expected to participate. One step involves setting aside sufficient time to examine issues, weigh alternatives, and debate decisions. Shared decision making that requires teachers to leave class and parents to leave work is unlikely to be viewed favorably. Such measures as building meeting time for teachers into the regular school schedule and providing child care for parents attending evening meetings indicate to these groups that school officials really care about their participation.

Training is a second important step. People are not born with the ability to be effective participants in decision making. They can benefit from studying and practicing decision making, agenda setting, consensus building, problem solving, and policymaking. Understanding group dynamics and the constraints under which school systems operate can help raise the level of interaction among participants and reduce wasted time and effort. School administrators and board members may need special training in how to share authority and facilitate decision making involving diverse groups.

POLICY IMPLEMENTATION

Hall and Hord have helped educators think of change as a process rather than an event—a process involving a series of relatively distinct steps.[19] In particular, they distinguish between the development of new ideas and their implementation. The folklore of schooling suggests that many ideas painstakingly developed by groups of educators are never successfully implemented. The same certainly can be said for school policies. In this section, we examine some of the factors which bear on the implementation of school and district policies.

Implementing new policies often requires individuals to change well-established patterns of thought and behavior. As Sarason has documented so well, such change is extremely difficult.[20] Teachers and administrators develop routines to help them cope with the stresses and complexities of their work. Over the years, these routines come to be taken so much for granted that people are often unaware of their existence. Any new policies that call for deviation from these routines are likely to be met with resistance. To inhibit change further, there is the obvious message that individuals who have been in a system for a while must not have been very effective if change is needed. These individuals understandably have a vested interest in resisting change.

Hall and Hord, in their work on the Concerns-Based Adoption Model (CBAM), found that resistance to change can be overcome, but not without considerable time, energy, and training.[21] In one case study of a 5-year effort to implement a new mathematics curriculum, they observed that at any given time during the early phases of implementation, different teachers were unlikely to possess the same information about the innovation. A primary challenge for school officials was ensuring that all staff members acquired the same information. Opportunities were provided for teachers to clarify their understanding of the scope and purposes of the new curriculum. Several staff members served as change facilitators, identifying concerns and discussing ways to address them. Staff development workshops were conducted so that teachers could familiarize themselves with the new textbooks and supplementary materials. At the end of the first year of implementation, when problems arose concerning how students were to be grouped for instruction and how they were to be evaluated, several teachers and facilitators were asked to spend the summer working on a record-keeping system to alleviate the problems. The impression left by the case study is that implementing change requires a plan, ample time, oversight, and patience. Having individuals whose chief responsibility is to facilitate change can also be a crucial element of successful innovation.

It is interesting to note that Hall and Hord's research does not stress any of the mechanisms—evaluation, supervision, rewards, and sanctions—by which leaders traditionally attempt to ensure compliance. Their image of effective implementation is collegial in nature. Should efforts to achieve compliance through collegiality fail, leaders presumably might consider using one or more of the traditional mechanisms. Unfortunately, little research is available to indicate which of these mechanisms is most effective.

In one of the few studies of policy compliance at the school level, Peterson, Murphy, and Hallinger questioned superintendents in twelve school districts that had reported mean student achievement scores higher than predictions based on student characteristics.[22] The superintendents were asked to describe the mechanisms on which they relied to ensure compliance with district policies in "technical-core" domains, such as instruction and curriculum. In seven of the districts, policies mandated that all teachers use a specific instructional model. To ensure compliance with this mandate, superintendents indicated that they relied on such strategies as ongoing staff training in the required model, incorporation of the model into school and teacher goals, and evaluation of principals based on teacher compliance.[23] One superintendent said he expected his directors to visit classrooms every day to check on implementation of the district teaching model. Several superintendents reported using their district's teacher-evaluation system to monitor the use of the prescribed model. Three superintendents indicated they reviewed all teacher evaluations personally, while four others reported reading at least some annual evaluations. Teacher dismissal was regarded by most superintendents as the ultimate sanction in cases of non-compliance.

This study suggests that superintendents of high-achieving districts are willing to use a variety of mechanisms to ensure that key district policies are implemented. Presumably, principals have fewer compliance options than do superintendents. As a result, it is crucial for principals interested in successful implementation of district policies to secure the support of their supervisors. Principals who promulgate policies without first checking with the central office may be embarrassed to discover later that the superintendent is unprepared to support them in a noncompliance case.

McLaughlin looked at studies of policy implementation across various levels and jurisdictions and concluded that their success probably depends, in the final analysis, on two broad factors—local capacity and will.[24] *Local capacity* encompasses the resources, both fiscal and material, and the expertise to implement new policies. *Will* involves the "attitudes, motivation, and beliefs that underlie an implementor's response."[25] She observes that will—or commitment to a policy— is apt to be a function of an implementor's assessment of the value or appropriateness of a policy.

Building a school's capacity to implement policy can be a challenge because resources are often scarce and training is time-consuming, but generating the will to implement poses an even greater challenge. Will is unlikely to be affected by threats and directives. For implementors to value a particular policy, they must either find it meaningful or trust those who urge them to implement it. In both cases, leadership can be critical. Duke defines *leadership* as that which brings meaning to the collective actions of people.[26] Fullan suggests that the "meaning" need not always precede the action, however.[27] McLaughlin cites a study where teachers were urged by their principal to interact with low-income parents on matters of homework. Reluctant at first, the teachers made the attempt anyway and, as a result, changed their minds about the contribution these parents could make to their children's schooling.[28]

Drawing on the research available, we can offer local policymakers several suggestions for increasing the likelihood that district and school policies will actually be implemented. The first suggestion concerns the matter of commitment. Notwithstanding the possibility that commitment can sometimes *follow* implementation, the most prudent course for policymakers appears to be generating support for new policies *prior* to their implementation. The means for generating support include involvement of policy implementors in policymaking (discussed earlier) and inspiring leadership—the kind associated with terms like *vision* and *mission*. Blase's research on teachers' views of school politics suggests, though, that perceived favoritism on the part of school leaders can undermine any efforts to implement policies.[29]

A second suggestion concerns local capacity for policy implementation. Capacity is related, in part, to human energy. Since energy is not an inexhaustible resource, policymakers should be careful not to create more policies than the staff is capable of implementing. Chapter 8 raised the possibility, for example, that some school-discipline plans encompass more rules than can be enforced by existing staff. In effect, these plans invite teacher noncompliance and student disobedience by failing to focus energies on a reasonable set of school rules. To avoid ever-expanding sets of school policies, local policymakers are advised to conduct periodic policy audits to eliminate policies that are no longer necessary, have failed to achieve their intended purpose, or were never implemented successfully.

The final suggestion derives from McLaughlin's conclusion that policy implementation depends on a balance of support and pressure.[30] Pressure, in the form of traditional compliance mechanisms such as evaluation and supervision, is most likely to be needed, she notes, in settings where consensus on the merits of a new policy is lacking or where the policy is aimed at relatively weak beneficiaries. Those responsible for overseeing policy implementation under such circumstances should be prepared to monitor implementors to ensure that they understand the intent and the provisions of the policy. Such follow-through efforts may be time-consuming for school personnel, but without them, the likelihood of successful implementation is considerably reduced.

Support for policy implementation differs from pressure in that it focuses on encouragement, recognition of effort, clarification of purposes, troubleshooting, and the like. Efforts to be supportive might lead a school administrator, for example, to ask teachers if a new policy should be modified because of unforeseen problems encountered during implementation. It is recommended that policymakers never lose sight of the fact that those responsible for implementing most school policies are professionals. As such, they deserve to be treated as partners in the process of policy development and implementation.

Notes

1. Ellen Flax, "S.C. Board Adopts Regulatory Relief of Top-Scoring Schools," *Education Week*, November 22, 1989, pp. 1, 16.
2. Many of the items related to Dade County were derived from Anne Lewis, *Restructuring America's Schools*, American Association of School Administrators, Arlington, Va., 1989, pp. 158–161; and Peter I. Cistone, Joseph A. Fernandez, and Pat L. Tornillo, Jr., "School-Based Management/Shared Decision Making in Dade County (Miami)," *Education and Urban Society*, August 1989, pp. 393–402.
3. Debra Viadero, "L.A. School Embraces a West German Import," *Education Week*, November 1, 1989, pp. 1, 10.
4. We are indebted to the Prince William superintendent, Dr. Ed Kelly, for sharing this planning document with us.
5. Alice Z. Seeman and Melvin Seeman, "Staff Processes and Pupil Attitudes: A Study of Teacher Participation in Educational Change," *Human Relations* 29, no. 1 (1976): 25–40.
6. Peter Mortimore, Pamela Sammons, Louise Stoll, David Lewis, and Russell Ecob, *School Matters*, University of California Press, Berkeley, 1988, p. 225.

7. Anthony Gary Dworkin, *Teacher Burnout in the Public Schools,* State University of New York Press, Albany, 1987, pp. 34–41.

8. Dan C. Lortie, *Schoolteacher,* University of Chicago Press, 1975, pp. 200–202.

9. Daniel L. Duke, Beverly Showers, and Michael Imber, "Teachers and Shared Decision Making: The Costs and Benefits of Involvement," *Educational Administration Quarterly* 16, no. 1 (1980): 93–106.

10. Daniel L. Duke and Bruce Gansneder, "Teacher Empowerment: The View from the Classroom," *Educational Policy* (forthcoming).

11. Robert A. Collins, "Interim Evaluation Report—School-Based Management/Shared Decision-Making Project, 1987–88," Dade County Public Schools, Miami, 1988.

12. Daniel L. Duke, *School Leadership and Instructional Improvement,* Random House, New York, 1987, pp. 236–257; Sara Lawrence Lightfoot, *The Good High School,* Basic Books, New York, 1983.

13. Van Cleve Morris, Robert L. Crowson, Cynthia Porter-Gehrie, and Emanuel Hurwitz, *Principals in Action,* Charles E. Merrill Publishing Company, Columbus, Ohio, 1984, pp. 147–162.

14. Michael Fullan, *The Meaning of Educational Change,* Teachers College Press, New York, 1982, pp. 196–203.

15. Ibid., p. 201.

16. Ibid., pp. 201–202.

17. J. M. McPartland and E. L. McDill, "The Unique Role of Schools in the Causes of Youthful Crime," Report No. 216, Center for Social Organization of Schools, The Johns Hopkins University, Baltimore, 1976.

18. Daniel L. Duke and Cheryl Perry, "Can Alternative Schools Succeed Where Benjamin Spock, Spiro Agnew, and B. F. Skinner Have Failed?" *Adolescence* 13 (Fall 1978): 375–392.

19. Gene E. Hall and Shirley M. Hord, *Change in Schools,* State University of New York Press, Albany, 1987, pp. 1–21.

20. Seymour B. Sarason, *The Culture of the School and the Problem of Change,* 2d ed., Allyn and Bacon, Boston, 1982, pp. 95–117.

21. Hall et al., op. cit., pp. 52–106; 285–327.

22. Kent D. Peterson, Joseph Murphy, and Philip Hallinger, "Superintendents' Perceptions of the Control and Coordination of the Technical Core in Effective School Districts," *Educational Administration Quarterly,* February 1987, pp. 79–95.

23. Ibid., p. 85.

24. Milbrey Wallin McLaughlin, "Learning from Experience: Lessons from Policy Implementation," *Educational Evaluation and Policy Analysis* 9, no. 2 (Summer 1987): 172.

25. Ibid.

26. Daniel L. Duke, "The Aesthetics of Leadership," *Educational Administration Quarterly* 21, no. 2 (Winter 1986): 7–27.

27. Michael Fullan, "Performance Appraisal and Curriculum Implementation Research," manuscript for the Conference on Performance Appraisal for Effective Schooling, Ontario Institute for Studies in Education, 1986.

28. McLaughlin, op. cit., p. 173.

29. Joseph J. Blase, "The Politics of Favoritism: A Qualitative Analysis of the Teachers' Perspective," *Educational Administration Quarterly,* May 1988, p. 173.

30. McLaughlin, loc. cit.

11

The Importance of School Policy

The purpose of this book has been to investigate local school policy and determine its relevance as a distinct area of inquiry within the broader field of educational policy studies. No attempt has been made to review every domain of school policy. For example, local policies associated with such important subjects as retention and extracurricular activities have not been addressed. Rather than encyclopedic coverage, our intent has been to select a variety of policy domains which have been studied sufficiently to merit analysis and discussion.

In this concluding chapter, we look back over the preceding chapters in order to assess the importance of local school policy as an area of inquiry separate from state and federal policy. Our effort yields three major findings:

1. Local educators and board members exercise discretionary authority over a wide range of policies related to teaching and learning.
2. Research indicates that local school policies can have a direct bearing on the quality of teaching and learning.
3. Many local policies do not conform to our conception of good policy in that they place certain groups of students at a disadvantage.

These findings suggest that local school policy deserves the serious attention of researchers, practitioners, and prospective school leaders. Let us examine each of our findings more closely.

DISCRETIONARY AUTHORITY

The popular image of increasingly centralized state education systems and an ever-intrusive federal government does not seem completely justified when we analyze the policy domains covered in this book. What we discover is that local educators have a wide range of policy options. It would appear that local policy choices constitute a potentially valuable focus of study for researchers seeking to account for differences in effectiveness across schools and districts.

Consider the domain of curriculum as an example. Local board members often determine curriculum goals and priorities in the process of developing mission statements, annual goals, and long-range plans. During these activities they confront such issues as the desirability of a core curriculum for all students, the merits of electives, and the value of interdisciplinary offerings. Courses and curriculum objectives are typically decided locally, as are the designations for particular courses (advanced placement, honors, remedial) and the type of credit attached to their successful completion. Locally developed policies may even encompass textbook selection and minimum time allotments for specific subjects.

In the domain of scheduling, educators may allocate time for instruction in a variety of ways, including:

- Self-contained, graded instruction (all or part of the day)
- Nongraded instruction (all or part of the day)
- "Pullout schedule" (rotational or fixed period)
- No "pullouts" (all special services delivered in class)
- Parallel block schedule
- Intensive schedule (one course at a time)
- Rotating extra-period day
- Slide concurrent schedule
- Flexible modular schedule
- Trimester schedule
- Block plan

Scheduling choices vary somewhat across grade levels. At the elementary school level, concerns center on how to accommodate the delivery of special services, such as Chapter 1, special education, and music. At the middle school level, decisions frequently focus on how to permit interdisciplinary teams of teachers to work with the same group of students for a "block" of time. At the high school level, the attention of policymakers is often devoted to the number of periods in the day and the possibility of creating longer periods of time for certain courses (for example, labs and seminars).

We found, during the course of our study, that one policy decision often begets others. The initial, or focal, policy decision may be referred to as the *primary policy*. Additional policies that must be developed to ensure the successful implementation of primary policies are called *supporting policies*. A supporting policy related to scheduling may involve the availability of transportation to and from high school for students involved in extended-day schedules. Another supporting policy may relate to reimbursement for teachers employed on extended-day schedules. In order to appreciate fully the discretionary authority of local policymakers, we must consider both primary and supporting policies.

Instructional grouping is a third policy domain in which a variety of options exist. Policies governing grouping practices can focus on within-class grouping and across-class grouping (or *tracking*). Grouping policies may be intended to maximize student differences within groups (as is the case with cooperative-learning programs) or to minimize student differences (as is the case with ability grouping in reading or mathematics).

Local educators and board members find themselves increasingly occupied with developing policies concerned with at-risk students. Here, again, the range of options is great. Programs for at-risk 'students fall into four categories, depending on their primary purpose—remedial-compensatory, preventive, nonacademic, and disciplinary. Some programs, such as campus-based health clinics and day-care centers, generate considerable controversy. Besides developing primary policies for at-risk students, local educators must often develop supporting policies dealing with issues such as eligibility, student expectations, staffing, and funding.

The evaluation of student performance is another area where local policy-makers enjoy considerable discretion. Depending on the school system, they must decide on any or all of the following:

- Type of grading system
- Acceptable criteria for grading student performance
- Weight given to particular grading criteria
- Range of scores associated with letter grades
- Score or grade needed to pass a course or earn credit
- Score or grade needed to move from one grade level to another
- Bases for grading the performance of students of differing ability levels
- Extent to which individual teachers will control the criteria for acceptable student performance
- Provisions for appealing and changing a grade
- Weight to be given for grades in honors or advanced-placement courses
- Bases for determining a student's rank in class
- Grading options such as pass/fail

Policies in the area of homework are not as extensive as those related to the evaluation of student performance, but they nonetheless represent a range of choices for local educators. Schools and districts increasingly are developing policies covering the purposes, amount, scheduling, and grading of homework. In addition, policies are sometimes adopted to cover assistance for students having difficulty with homework and the consequences for those who fail to complete homework.

Student discipline and attendance are two areas in which local policymakers have traditionally enjoyed great discretion. Though policies in these areas are now subject to external review for the purpose of protecting the civil rights of students, they still tend to be developed at the school and district levels. In its judgment on the issue of corporal punishment, the Supreme Court upheld the principle of local control for matters pertaining to the management of student behavior. Local policies encompass issues such as the purposes of school discipline, school and classroom rules, the consequences for disobedience, the conditions under which the consequences can be administered, the procedures used to enforce rules and ensure due process, and the definition of excused and unexcused absences.

Personnel policies—the last policy domain addressed in this book—are also characterized by considerable local discretion, although somewhat less than for the preceding domains. Local educators and board members set policies governing teacher recruitment, selection, assignment, induction, supervision, evaluation, development, assistance, discipline, recognition, and empowerment—but within the constraints of state and federal laws regarding due process and affirmative action. Also, because personnel policies are often arrived at through collective bargaining and formalized by contract, it is unlikely that many variations will be found among schools within the same school district. Such variations are more likely to characterize the other policy domains.

In sum, we find compelling evidence indicating that local educators and board members enjoy considerable latitude when it comes to guiding teaching and learning in their districts and schools. But what is the educational significance of these options?

CHOICES OF CONSEQUENCE

Local policymakers may be free to make a variety of policy choices, but such discretionary authority is no guarantee that their choices will be of any great consequence. It could be argued, after all, that state and federal policymakers determine all the important policies, leaving only the trivial ones to local educators and board members. In this section, we review our preceding analyses in order to assess the importance of policy choices made at the school and district levels.

Policies related to the content and organization of the curriculum are consequential by anyone's estimate. While some of the most important curriculum policies are set at the state level, local policymakers also have opportunities to make critical decisions. For instance, when school boards define their district's mission and designate annual goals, they provide the basis for determining which content areas will be protected during periods of retrenchment. Decisions regarding course and subject matter objectives influence areas of instructional emphasis for teachers and, consequently, student performance on local and external examinations. Policies dealing with course and content approval set the parameters for curriculum growth and affect the public's perception of school responsiveness to shifting societal concerns.

Time is a fundamental resource with which educators work. Research frequently has shown a direct relationship between the time teachers and students spend on a subject and how well the students learn it. Scheduling policies that influence how teaching time will be allocated are therefore likely to have an impact on teaching effectiveness and student achievement. While state authorities sometimes decide how much time must be devoted annually to required parts of the curriculum, local educators and officials usually establish school schedules, which in turn dictate how teachers and students will spend each school day. As Chapter 3 suggested, the choice of a schedule can influence such consequential matters as students' access to special ("pullout") programs, opportunities for extended instruction, the use of specialists and support personnel, the availability of electives, class size, and instructional grouping practices.

How students are grouped is a third area where local policymakers are able to affect the quality of teaching and learning. Grouping strategies have been found, under certain circumstances, to affect students' self-esteem, socialization, and academic learning. While research on the impact of ability grouping has yielded mixed results, there is general agreement that the quality of instruction can vary according to whether students are grouped homogeneously or heterogeneously. Teachers often prefer to teach homogeneous groups of students. Recent studies of cooperative-learning groups, however, suggest that student achievement need not suffer when classes are subdivided into heterogeneous groups of students.

Alternative schools, remedial classes, counseling programs, and a host of other special offerings for at-risk students are yet another consequential outgrowth of local policies. While it is true that these programs are not necessarily successful with every at-risk student, they clearly serve the needs of many young people who otherwise would fall further behind their peers, become resentful and frustrated, and eventually drop out of school. Evidence exists that selected programs not only keep students in school and out of trouble, but also remediate academic deficiencies.

Local policies pertaining to grading and reporting student performance have a direct bearing on the lives of students. Consider, for example, policies as to whether to grade students on their conduct and attendance, as well as on their academic achievement. Or policies requiring that grades reflect a student's accumulated scores, rather than his or her level of performance at the end of the school year. Decisions of great importance to students—such as whether to award academic credit, promote to the next grade, or permit to graduate—are based on grades.

Homework policies indicate how students are expected to spend part of their time outside of school. Evidence exists that homework can contribute to student achievement, but not for all students and not all types of homework. It appears that the positive impact of homework on student outcomes increases with the age of the student. The value of homework is least apparent at the elementary school level.

The quality of teaching and learning is a function, in part, of the orderliness of the school. Policies related to school discipline and attendance can play a major role in creating environments conducive to good instruction and serious study. Learning is less likely to occur in schools where students feel unsafe, disruptions go unchecked, and students are not taught rules and appropriate conduct. On the other hand, there is reason to believe that schools can have too many discipline policies as well as too few. In such cases, discipline can seem to be an end in itself, rather than a means to productive learning. Discipline policies are most likely to play a constructive role when (1) they are developed with input from students and teachers, (2) they are perceived to be fair, and (3) they are applied consistently. Discipline policies are necessitated, in part, by crowded conditions and the absence of close relations between teachers and students. Small schools and alternative programs can function with fewer discipline policies because the teachers and students have more opportunities to get to know each other.

Personnel policies are another example of locally developed policies that matter. The quality of teaching depends upon the quality of the teachers, which is influenced by the policies governing teacher recruitment, selection, and remuneration. Policies related to teacher supervision and development should help teachers become and remain competent and committed.

All in all, the quality of teaching and learning in a school can be affected both directly and indirectly by a variety of local policies. Of course, where the potential exists for benefit, so too exists the possibility for harm. Failure to adopt policies—or the adoption of poorly constructed, punitive, or purely political policies—can place teachers and students at a decided disadvantage. Finally, nowhere is the need for careful consideration of local policies greater than in the education of at-risk students.

IN SEARCH OF "GOOD POLICY"

In the opening chapter, we characterized a "good" school policy as one that increases the likelihood that school goals will be achieved without adversely affecting any particular group of students. On the basis of our subsequent analysis, it appears that many school policies should be reviewed to determine their impact on at-risk students. For example, local policies that limit course offerings in subject matter areas likely to interest non-college-bound students or that deny graduation credit for remedial coursework increase the likelihood that at-risk students will find school inhospitable. Do policies ensure that the cultures of all students are treated fairly and with respect? Have efforts been made to see that all students have access to the curriculum content necessary to advance successfully to the next grade-level or stage of schooling? Are policies in place that mandate close alignment of course content and standardized tests so that students will not be evaluated on material to which they have never been exposed?

Some school policies specify schedules that seem to be premised on the false assumption that all students require roughly the same amount of time to learn. Schedules that overly fragment the school day can interfere with the learning of students who need prolonged periods of time with one teacher. These students may be capable of progress, but only as long as they do not have to cope with too many teachers and too many sets of expectations.

Grouping policies may also work to the disadvantage of certain students. Evidence exists that students in basic or vocational tracks, for instance, often receive less rigorous and well-organized instruction than do their counterparts in academic tracks. If anything, these young people need instruction that is *more* rigorous and well-organized! Grouping policies that tacitly permit the isolation of students on the basis of race, ethnicity, language, or handicap pose additional problems. Local policymakers must ask themselves whether grouping practices in any way limit the access of certain students to essential curriculum content or high-quality instruction. They may need to create special policies to ensure that grouping practices are periodically reviewed and evaluated.

Even policies supporting special programs for at-risk youth can jeopardize their opportunity to gain an education. Some of these programs seem to be directed more at salvaging state aid (when tied to student attendance) than at providing prospective dropouts with meaningful instruction. In weighing the costs versus the benefits of special programs for at-risk students, local policymakers need to ask themselves whether expectations for these students should be the same as, or different from, those for other students. In light of recent concerns raised over grouping policies, local policymakers must also weigh the advantages and disadvantages of separating at-risk students from their peers. The matrix on page 146 provides a framework within which to consider policy options for the at-risk student.

The matrix suggests that local policymakers who strive to uphold our conception of "good policy" need to consider four approaches to the education of at-risk students. Is it in the best interests of some, or all, at-risk students to require that they

1. attend conventional* programs and meet conventional* expectations?
2. attend modified programs and meet conventional expectations?

*Conventional, in this sense, refers to "that which is available to, or expected of, most students in a school."

TYPE OF PROGRAM FOR AT-RISK STUDENTS

	Conventional	Modified
Conventional	1	2
Modified	3	4

EXPECTATIONS FOR AT-RISK STUDENTS

3. attend conventional programs and meet modified expectations?
4. attend modified programs and meet modified expectations?

To be able to compare the costs and benefits of conventional and modified programs for at-risk students, local policymakers must examine existing policies related to such matters as reporting student performance, homework, school discipline, and teacher personnel. As our analyses indicate, policies in each of these areas have the potential to place at-risk students at a disadvantage. For example, a school district with a policy that prevents students from earning graduation credit for work completed in remedial courses may be discouraging needy students from seeking assistance. Local policymakers should examine existing policies carefully to determine their impact on at-risk students. To do so, they may need to raise questions such as the following:

- Is it fair to evaluate at-risk students on the basis of the same criteria used to evaluate other students?
- To what extent do the grading practices of certain teachers discourage at-risk students?
- Do homework policies work to the disadvantage of students who lack home environments conducive to study?

- What opportunities for homework assistance are available to at-risk students in the conventional program?
- Are at-risk students punished more severely for breaking school rules than other students?
- Do punishments tend to compound the problems of at-risk students?
- Is an effort made to teach at-risk students how to behave responsibly?
- Do personnel policies recognize and reward teachers who work effectively with at-risk students in conventional programs?
- Does the teacher-evaluation system ensure that teachers adjust instruction to the needs of individual students?
- Do policies governing staff and professional development ensure that teachers are kept apprised of new research on at-risk students?
- Do policies regarding teacher assignment ensure that only capable teachers are assigned to work with at-risk students?

The fact that local school policies can play a significant role in the education of at-risk students—as well as other students—suggests that school officials should undertake periodic policy audits. Policies that fail to serve the interests of particular groups of students should be modified or eliminated. In cases where policies cannot be altered, it may be necessary to create supporting policies to ensure that existing policies do not disadvantage particular groups. Only in these ways can schools be truly responsive to the needs of all young people.

FINAL THOUGHTS

Our analysis of local school policy indicates that it is indeed a subject worthy of study. Teachers, school administrators, and board members must be aware of the potential impact of their decisions regarding such matters as scheduling, grouping, special programs, curriculum, grading, homework, discipline, and personnel. We hope that this volume helps promote such awareness.

We also hope that this book convinces school reformers and those engaged in school improvement projects to make local policy an important focus of attention. The history of educational change suggests that innovative programs that are implemented without careful consideration of existing policies are unlikely to succeed. Even though the impetus for reform may come from state or national initiatives, local policymakers still hold the key to effective change.

In the process of examining local school policy, we have discovered several issues that merit the attention of policy researchers. We know that local policymakers have a variety of options, but we do not know the extent to which their choices actually vary across schools and districts. What percentage of schools, for instance, prescribe parallel block scheduling, heterogeneous grouping, nightly homework assignments, and so on? Is there a core of common policies related to teaching and learning that characterize all or most effective schools?

The preceding questions suggest that local policies can be treated as independent variables in studies of school effectiveness. By comparing policies in schools where students experience relatively high and low levels of success, we can appreciate more fully the impact of local policymaking. It is unlikely that the ultimate outcome of such inquiry will be "one best" set of policies for all schools and districts. A more likely finding is that local policies associated with effective teaching and learning vary somewhat, depending on factors such as grade level, student diversity, resources, state policies, and local norms.

Another issue requiring the attention of policy researchers is the possible interaction of different policies. Local policies tend to be developed in response to specific concerns. Often these concerns are more political than professional. Rarely is careful thought given to the impact of new policies on existing policies. As a result, it is possible for a new policy to cancel out the effect or undermine the intent of an existing policy. Taken individually, any local policy may appear logical and feasible. Considered cumulatively, local policies may turn out to be contradictory or impractical. Work is needed on methods to determine the feasibility of new policies and predict their impact on existing policies.

Until more is known of local policy, we shall be unable to appreciate fully the impact of local control on American education. Local citizens and educators cling to the belief that they are in the best position to know what is good for the young people of their communities. The policies they develop and endorse are the formal expressions of this belief. Only by studying local school policies in a comprehensive and systematic way will we ever be able to determine if the belief is well-founded.

Appendix A

EXAMPLE OF A COURSE-APPROVAL POLICY FROM FAIRFAX COUNTY, VIRGINIA

Regulation 3202
Instructional Services;
Student Services and
    Special Education;
Vocational, Adult, and
    Community Education Services

CURRICULUM AND INSTRUCTION
Standard Instructional Program
Approval of New Courses
This regulation supersedes Regulation 6110.2.

I. PURPOSE

To establish requirements and procedures for the approval of new courses.

II. DEFINITION OF A NEW COURSE

A *new course* is any credit or noncredit course or other program of instruction that a principal wants to begin and that has not been included in the course selections offered to students in that school in either of the past two school years.

III. REQUIREMENTS FOR APPROVAL OF A NEW COURSE

No new course shall be announced to the school community, offered for student enrollment, or included in the school's program of instruction until approved in accordance with the procedures established in this regulation.

IV. PROCEDURE FOR REQUESTING APPROVAL TO ADD TO THE SCHOOL'S OFFERINGS A COURSE PREVIOUSLY APPROVED BY THE STATE DEPARTMENT OF EDUCATION AND IN THE FAIRFAX COUNTY PUBLIC SCHOOLS' CURRENT LIST OF APPROVED COURSES

The principal shall make a written request to the area superintendent not less than 30 calendar days prior to the date on which the principal wishes to announce that the course will be offered. The request shall not include any course currently being taught as part of an approved pilot project. The request shall include the Fairfax County Public Schools' course number, the course title, and the units of credit. The area superintendent shall approve or disapprove the principal's request.

V. PROCEDURES FOR REQUESTING APPROVAL OF A NEW COURSE NOT ON THE FAIRFAX COUNTY PUBLIC SCHOOLS' CURRENT LIST OF APPROVED COURSES AND FOR WHICH NO ADDITIONAL FUNDING OR STAFFING OR THE TRANSFER OF AUTHORIZED FUNDING OR STAFFING WILL BE REQUIRED. (FINAL APPROVAL BY THE DIVISION SUPERINTENDENT REQUIRED)

A. Before requesting approval of the course, the principal or other staff members shall work with the area office, teachers, guidance counselors, and the school community to determine the need for and desirability of beginning the new course.

B. The principal shall submit the request to the area superintendent not less than

1. 65 calendar days before the date on which the principal wants to announce the course if state approval will be required, or

2. 45 calendar days before the day on which the principal wants to announce the course if state approval will not be required, unless later submission dates are approved by the area superintendent.

C. The request shall include all of the following:

1. The title of the proposed course and a description of the course content, including objectives

2. A statement of whether the course is to be required or elective; whether it is to be offered during the regular school term, summer session, or both; the grade levels at which the course will be offered, the nature of the student group for which the course has been planned, the estimated enrollment in the course, the units of credit to be awarded, and the specific Fairfax County or Virginia graduation requirement that the course will meet, if any; and any special conditions that will apply to the offering of the course

3. The names of the basal texts and supplementary materials to be used and whether or not these materials have been approved

4. The certification and endorsements that will be required for the instructor

5. A statement of the evaluation procedures for determining the effectiveness of the course

D. If the area superintendent approves the request, he or she shall forward the request to the assistant superintendent for instructional services or the assistant superintendent for vocational, adult, and community education services, as appropriate, who shall coordinate the request with the departments of instructional services; student services and special education; vocational, adult, and community education services; financial services; personnel services; management information services; and general services; and the State Department of Education as appropriate. If the area superintendent disapproves the request, he or she shall inform the principal.

E. The assistant superintendent for instructional services or the assistant superintendent for vocational, adult, and community education services shall forward a copy of the request to the assistant superintendent for student services and special education, who shall determine the amount and kind of credit that may be approved for the course.

F. The assistant superintendent for instructional services or the assistant superintendent for vocational, adult, and community education services shall coordinate the final review and action by the division superintendent and shall notify in writing the principal, the area superintendent, and appropriate assistant superintendents of the final decision. The notification shall include, if approval is granted, the approved course number, title, the amount of credit and applicability to graduation requirements, whether or not approval has been granted to add the course to Fairfax County Public Schools' current list of approved courses, and any conditions applicable to the offering of the course.

G. If the course is approved on a pilot basis, the principal/program manager shall submit the results of the evaluation to the area/assistant superintendent when the pilot has been completed together with a recommendation concerning the placement of the course on the Fairfax County Public Schools' list of currently approved courses.

VI. PROCEDURES FOR REQUESTING APPROVAL OF A NEW COURSE NOT ON THE FAIRFAX COUNTY PUBLIC SCHOOLS' CURRENT LIST OF APPROVED COURSES AND FOR WHICH ADDITIONAL FUNDING OR STAFFING OR THE TRANSFER OF AUTHORIZED FUNDING OR STAFFING WILL BE REQUIRED (FINAL APPROVAL BY THE SCHOOL BOARD REQUIRED)

A. Before requesting approval of the course, the principal or other staff members shall work with the area office, teachers, guidance counselors, and the school community to determine the need for and desirability of beginning the new course.

B. The principal shall submit the request to the area superintendent with the principal's budget request for the fiscal year in which the new course is to be taught unless a later submission date is approved by the area superintendent. The request shall include

1. the appropriate budget forms for any additional funding or staffing and for any transfer of existing funding or staffing that is required.

2. a memorandum describing in detail all additional fiscal resources required, all requests for transfer of existing funding or staffing, and the location of each item in the budget documents.

3. the title of the proposed course and a description of the course content, including objectives.

4. a statement of whether the course is to be required or elective; whether it is to be offered during the regular school term, summer session, or both; the grade levels at which the course will be offered, the nature of the student group for which the course has been planned, the estimated enrollment in the course, the units of credit to be awarded, and the specific Fairfax County or Virginia graduation requirement that the course will meet, if any; and any special conditions that will apply to the offering of the course.

5. the names of the basal texts and supplementary materials to be used and whether or not these materials have been approved.

6. the certification and endorsements that will be required for the instructor.

7. a statement of the evaluation procedures for determining the effectiveness of the course.

C. If the area superintendent approves the request, he or she shall forward the request to the assistant superintendent for instructional services or the assistant superintendent for vocational, adult, and community education services, as appropriate, who shall coordinate the request with the departments of instructional services; student services and special education; personnel services; management information services; and general services; and with the State Department of Education, as appropriate. If the area superintendent disapproves the request, he or she shall inform the principal.

D. The assistant superintendent for instructional services or the assistant superintendent for vocational, adult, and community education services shall forward a copy of the request to the assistant superintendent for student services and special education, who shall determine the amount and kind of credit that may be approved for the course.

E. The assistant superintendent for instructional services or the assistant superintendent for vocational, adult, and community education services shall coordinate submission of the request for final review and action by the division superintendent if the course is proposed as a pilot, as well as for action by the school board if the course is proposed for divisionwide use. The assistant superintendent shall notify in writing the principal, the area superintendent, and appropriate assistant superintendents of the final decision. The notification shall include, if approval is granted, the approved course number, course title, the amount of credit and applicability to graduation requirements, whether or not approval has been granted to add the course to the Fairfax County Public Schools' list of currently approved courses, and any conditions applicable to the offering of the course.

F. If the course is approved on a pilot basis, the principal/program manager shall submit the results of the evaluations to the area/assistant superintendent when the pilot has been completed together with a recommendation concerning the placement of the course on the Fairfax County Public Schools' list of currently approved courses.

VII. PROCEDURE FOR APPROVAL OF A NEW COURSE PROPOSED BY AREA OR CENTRAL STAFF

A. A proposal for a new course developed by area staff members shall be submitted to the area superintendent and shall follow the appropriate approval procedures described in Sections V or VI above.

B. A proposal for a new course developed by central staff members shall be submitted to the assistant superintendent for instructional services; the assistant superintendent for student services and special education; or the assistant superintendent for vocational, adult, and community education services, as appropriate, and shall follow the appropriate approval procedures described in Sections V and VI above.

Appendix B

Example of a Dual Progress Plan in a Middle, Junior, or Senior High School

Student:_____   Homeroom Teacher:_____

Grade Level:_____

Reporting Periods: 1   2   3   4   5   6

Subject   (underline):

    Language Arts/English

      Reading

      Spelling

      Penmanship

      Grammar

    Social Studies

    Mathematics

    Health

    Science

    Art

    Music

    Exploratory (if appropriate) _____

    Physical Education

    Stanine-based primarily on mastery tests/quizzes

Grade_____*Example: 5-B_____

    Letter based primarily on teacher's opinion of stanine mark and observed behaviors of the student

EXPLANATION OF DUAL PROGRESS MARKS TO PARENTS

I. Your child's grade in each academic area, except in selected courses, should be viewed as a dual evaluation expressed in stanine and process assignments as explained below.

    A. *Stanine* designates the competitive level of achievement of your child within his or her grade level. A *grade level* usually consists of a large group of students who have attended school for the same number of years.

---

*The student's grade is a combination of stanine and the teacher's subjective opinion of the stanine mark.

9: Designates the top 4 percent of each group.

8, 7: Designates the upper 19 percent of each group.

6, 5, 4: Designates the average, or 54 percent of each group.

3, 2: Designates the lower 19 percent of each group.

1: Designates the lower 4 percent of each group.

B. A letter grade designates the process or performance your child has demonstrated in a subject area in relation to what his or her teachers judge he or she could be doing.

A: Pupil seems to be working to maximum ability and shows a great deal of motivation, interest, and self-direction.

B: Pupil strives diligently to do all that is assigned and appears to be motivated and consistently reliable.

C: Pupil does satisfactory work, but it is felt that better work should be expected. Selected work habits need attention.

D: Pupil is not doing all the required work, and it is believed that he is capable of doing higher-quality work. The teacher is prepared to assist this student if he or she will cooperate.

E: Teacher is unable to make a professional judgment because of some reason such as being a new student in the school or having too many absences.

X: Pupil demonstrates little interest in his work; very few assignments are completed. An Individualized Education Plan (IEP) is being developed for the student.

II. Grades in physical education are based almost entirely on the effort demonstrated by the individual student.

III. Performance in elective courses or exploratory areas has been evaluated according to the following scale:

H: High quality of work

S: Satisfactory quality of work

N: Improvement needed*

Appendix C

To DeKalb Students:

The DeKalb County School System provides a comprehensive program of educational services. Your educational environment must be favorable if you are to take full advantage of these opportunities. Good discipline is essential to a productive and meaningful learning environment.

The best discipline is self-discipline. To perform as a responsible member of the DeKalb student body, you will need to be familiar with the discipline program which has been established to ensure equity and fairness to all students.

The general purpose of this brochure is to acquaint you, your fellow students, your parents, and citizens of the DeKalb School District with regulations governing student conduct. The specific purpose of this brochure is to emphasize the importance of

- maintaining an atmosphere for learning which is protected from interruption and harassment;
- providing you and other students, along with your parents, with regulations of the school system and with information concerning the possible penalties for violations of these regulations;
- providing uniformity of approach and disciplinary procedures;
- encouraging your parents to discuss with you the material contained in this brochure, to help you understand the required behavior in the schools of DeKalb.

You will have an opportunity to discuss the details of DeKalb's approach to discipline when you and your classroom teacher review the contents of this brochure. If you have questions concerning the disciplinary procedures, do not hesitate to ask your teacher or principal.

You and every DeKalb student will have a better educational opportunity when we work together to understand and achieve the goals which will enable us to provide you with a good learning environment.

Robert R. Freeman
Superintendent

DISCIPLINARY OFFENSES AND DISPOSITIONS

This brochure has been prepared in accordance with the Discipline Procedures of the DeKalb County School System. It contains important information for school personnel, students, parents and citizens. Included in the brochure is an outline of disciplinary offenses with the various dispositions relating to these offenses. (Dispositions are in italic type.) Local school rules may supplement but not conflict with this disciplinary brochure.

Disciplinary action will include appropriate hearings and reviews and, in all cases, the rights of individuals will be ensured and protected. Disciplinary actions, including detention, corporal punishment, inhouse instruction, short- and long-term suspensions, transfer to Hamilton Alternative School, and expulsion, will be administered consistently throughout the DeKalb School System.

---

1. USE AND/OR POSSESSION OF TOBACCO
   Possession or use of smoking tobacco, chewing tobacco, snuff, or any other tobacco-related product.
   Penalty may range:
   a. 1st offense: Conference with student and/or parent.
   b. 2nd offense: Three-day (3-day) suspension, warning, place on probation.
   *c. 3rd offense and subsequent offense(s): Charge with violation of probation. Required that the student be sent before the Student Evidentiary Hearing Committee, which may result in expulsion.

   A student is deemed to be in possession of an illegal and/or banned item(s) under this section when such item(s) is found on the person of the student, in his/her possessions, or in his/her locker on school property or on property being used by the school or at any school function or activity, or any school event held away from the school, or while the student is on his/her way to or from the school.

*2. ALCOHOL
   *a. Sale or attempted sale and/or distribution of alcohol, or substances represented to be alcohol by the seller or distributor and/or thought to be alcohol by the buyer or receiver, on school property in a student's vehicle on school property or in any vehicle a student brought on school property, or property being used by the school, at a school function, on property used by the school with permission of the owner, at any school event held away from the school, or while the student is on his/her way to or from school.

   Penalty may range from short-term suspension to permanent expulsion. Required that the student be sent before the Student Evidentiary Hearing Committee.

   Police may be contacted.

   *b. A student is in violation of this section if in possession of alcohol or substances thought to be alcohol or represented to be alcohol by the student on school property, in the student's vehicle on school property or in any vehicle a student brought on school property or property being used by the school, when the item is found on the person of the student, in his/her possessions, or in his/her locker, at a school function on property used by the school

---

*Offenses preceded by an asterisk carry a mandatory requirement that the area superintendent be consulted before charging the student.

with permission of the owner, at any school event held away from the school, or while the student is on his/her way to or from school.

Penalty may range from short-term suspension to permanent expulsion.

Students who are found to be in possession of alcohol for a first offense only and who are not charged with the sale or distribution of alcohol will be suspended for ten (10) days, pending a formal hearing, and referred to the Student Evidentiary Hearing Committee for disposition of their case. In a first offense, if a student is found guilty, the Student Evidentiary Hearing Committee may provide that a portion of the student's sentence may be waived upon successful completion of the MACAD (SUPER) Program.

Police may be contacted.

*c. Being under the influence of (or using) alcohol on school property in the student's vehicle on school property or in any vehicle a student brought on school property, or property being used by the school, at a school function, on property used by the school with the permission of the owner, at any school event held away from the school or while the student is on his/her way to or from school.

Penalty may range:
1st offense: Ten-day (10-day) short-term suspension, with an option of attending and completing an authorized SUPER Program and a six-day (6-day) short-term suspension.
2nd and subsequent offenses: Penalty may range from short-term suspension to permanent expulsion. Required that the student be sent before the Student Evidentiary Hearing Committee.

*3. WEAPONS AND/OR EXPLOSIVE DEVICES

A student shall not supply, possess, handle, use, threaten to use, or transmit any weapon or any other tool or instrument capable of inflicting bodily injury as a weapon. The term "weapons," "tools," or "instruments" shall include by way of illustration, but is not limited to, the following enumerated items: any loaded or unloaded firearm (e.g., pistol, blank pistol, signal pistol, starter pistol, revolver, rifle, shotgun, stun-gun, pellet or BB gun, look-alike firearms, etc.); any knife (e.g., Bowie, Dirk, lock-blade, hunting, pen, pocket, switchblade, utility, knives of any size); any razor (e.g., straight, regular, retractable, etc.); any defensive device (e.g., gas repellant, mace, stun-gun, chemical sprays, etc.); any "martial arts" device (e.g., chinese star, nunchaku, dart, etc.); or any tool or instrument which school staff could reasonably conclude as being a violation of the intent of this offense section, which by way of illustration, shall include, but is not limited to, blackjack, chain, club, metal/brass or any artificial knuckles, night stick, pipe, studded or pointed bracelets, ax handles, etc.).

A student shall not supply, possess, handle, use, threaten to use, or transmit any explosive device or item that ejects or releases a spray, foam, gas, spark, fire, smoke, odor, etc. By way of illustration, such devices or items shall include, but are not limited to, bullets, ammunition of any type, fireworks of any type and size, smoke bombs, paint bombs, stink bomb, any type of homemade bomb, or item which by virtue of its shape or design gives the appearance of any of the aforementioned (e.g., fake bombs, fireworks fuses, etc.).

A student is deemed to be in possession of an illegal and/or banned item(s) under this section when such item(s) is found on the person of the student, in his/her possessions, in his/her locker, in a student's vehicle on school property or in any vehicle a student brought on school property or on property being used by the school, at any school function or activity or any school event held away from the school.

Penalty may range from short-term suspension to permanent expulsion. Required that the student appear before the Student Evidentiary Hearing Committee.

Parents and police will be notified in every instance of weapons where the law is violated.

*4. THREATENING PERSON OR PROPERTY OF FACULTY OR STAFF MEMBER AND/OR CAUSING INAPPROPRIATE BODILY CONTACT
Penalty may range from short-term suspension to permanent expulsion. Immediate suspension, pending a formal hearing to determine guilt or innocence. If student is found guilty, a ten-day (10-day) suspension and mandatory recommendation for a hearing before the Student Evidentiary Hearing Committee.

Police may be notified.

*5. DRUGS/SUBSTANCES
For the purpose of this brochure, the term "drugs" shall mean all substances including, but not limited to, prescription drugs, over-the-counter drugs, lookalike drugs, inhalants, pills, tablets, capsules, and all other legal and/or illegal drugs or substances. Any student required to take medication while at school will follow the procedures provided by a school administrator prior to possessing and using medication on school property.

*a. Sale or attempted sale and/or distribution of drugs, or substances represented to be drugs by the seller or distributor and/or thought to be drugs by the buyer or receiver, on school property, in a student's vehicle on school property or in any vehicle a student brought on school property or property being used by the school, at a school function, on property used by the school with permission of the owner, at any school event held away from the school, or while the student is on his/her way to or from school.

Penalty may range from short-term suspension to permanent expulsion. Required that the student be sent before the Student Evidentiary Hearing Committee.

Police may be contacted.

*b. A student is in violation of this section if in possession of drugs or substances thought to be drugs or represented to be drugs by the student on school property, in the student's vehicle on school property or in any vehicle a student brought on school property or property being used by the school, when the item is found on the person of the student, in his/her possessions, or in his/her locker, at a school function, on property used by the school with permission of the owner, at any school event held away from the school, or while the student is on his/her way to or from school.

Penalty may range from short-term suspension to permanent expulsion.
Students who are found to be in possession of drugs for a first offense only and who are not charged with the sale or distribution of drugs will be suspended for ten (10) days, pending a formal hearing, and referred to the Student Evidentiary Hearing Committee for disposition of their case, In a first offense, if a student is found guilty, the Student Evidentiary Hearing Committee may provide that a portion of the student's sentence may be waived upon successful completion of the MACAD (SUPER) Program.

Police may be contacted.

*c. Being under the influence of (or using) drugs on school property, in a student's vehicle on school property or in any vehicle a student brought on school property or property being used by the school, at a school function, on property used by the school with the permission of the owner, at any school event held away from the school, or while the student is on his/her way to or from school.

Penalty may range:
1st offense: Ten-day (10-day) short-term suspension with an option of attending and completing an authorized SUPER Program and a six-day (6-day) short-term suspension.
2nd and subsequent offenses: Penalty may range from short-term suspension to permanent expulsion. Required that student be sent before the Student Evidentiary Hearing Committee.

*d. Possession and/or distribution of drug-related paraphernalia. Drug-related paraphernalia includes, but is not limited to, pipes, water pipes, clips, rolling papers, etc., and other items used or related to drug use.

Penalty may range:
1st offense: Ten-day (10-day) short-term suspension with an option of attending and completing an authorized SUPER Program and a six-day (6-day) short-term suspension.
2nd and subsequent offenses: Penalty may range from short-term suspension to permanent expulsion. Required that the student be sent before the Student Evidentiary Hearing Committee.

Police may be contacted.

6. PROPERTY
a. Destruction of and/or threats to destroy school or public property which may include such actions as setting fires and/or attempts or threats to destroy, damage or deface school property or property used by the school with the permission of the owner.

Penalty may range from detention to expulsion. Student must make restitution before readmittance to school.

b. Theft and/or attempted theft; extortion or attempted extortion; possession of stolen property; vandalism; destruction or defacement of public or private property located on school premises, at a school function, on property used by the school with the permission of the owner, at any school event held away from school, or while the student is on his/her way to or from school.

Penalty may range from detention to expulsion. Student must make restitution before readmittance to school.

c. Loss, destruction, defacement, and/or other abnormal wear of textbooks, library books, and other media center materials.

Penalty will include restitution assessed according to guidelines for student accountability for textbooks and library/media center materials.

7. VIOLENCE INVOLVING ACTUAL PHYSICAL CONTACT
*a. Offenses involving extreme physical violence. Parents must be contacted and referral may be made to appropriate resource personnel.

Penalty may range from short-term suspension to expulsion. Required that the student be sent before the Evidentiary Hearing Committee.

b. Fighting, threatening, and/or intimidating another student(s) with violence.

Penalty may range from detention to a recommendation that the student appear before the Student Evidentiary Hearing Committee, which may result in expulsion.

Parent(s) must be contacted and referral may be made to appropriate resource personnel.

Police may be contacted.

8. RUDE AND DISRESPECTFUL BEHAVIOR OR REFUSAL TO CARRY OUT INSTRUCTION OF FACULTY OR STAFF
a. Rude and disrespectful behavior.

Penalty may range from a verbal reprimand to a referral to the Student Evidentiary Hearing Committee, which may result in expulsion.

Parent(s) must be contacted and referral may be made to appropriate resource personnel.

b. Refusal to carry out instruction of faculty or staff.

Penalty may range from a verbal reprimand to a referral to the Student Evidentiary Hearing Committee, which may result in expulsion.

Parent(s) must be contacted and referral may be made to appropriate resource personnel.

9. UNLAWFUL ABSENCES AND/OR TRUANCY
Lawful absences are defined by Georgia law:

a. Illness

b. Death in family
c. Religious holiday
d. Instances in which attendance could be hazardous as determined by the DeKalb School System
e. Service as page in legislature

Penalty may range from detention to expulsion. Parent(s) must be notified and a referral to the appropriate resource personnel.

After five (5) unlawful absences or truancy days, chronic offenders must be referred to appropriate resource personnel. After ten (10) unlawful absences or truancy days, the student may be required to appear before the Student Evidentiary Hearing Committee. A referral to the Student Evidentiary Hearing Committee for this offense must include a written report from appropriate resource personnel.

NOTE:

1. *Academic work missed due to* lawful *absences can be made up when the student returns to school.*
2. *Academic work missed due to* unlawful *absences cannot be made up when the student returns to school unless permission is granted by the principal prior to the absence.*
3. *Make-up work in cases of suspension or expulsion is covered in glossary items 9, 10, and 13.*

10. SKIPPING CLASS OR REQUIRED ACTIVITIES
    Penalty may range from detention to expulsion. Parent(s) must be contacted and referral may be made to the appropriate resource personnel. After five (5) violations, the student may be referred to the Student Evidentiary Hearing Committee. A referral to the SEHC for this offense must include a written report from appropriate resource personnel.

11. CLASSROOM DISTURBANCE
    Penalty may range from detention to a recommendation that the student appear before the Student Evidentiary Hearing Committee, which may result in expulsion. The parent(s) must be contacted and referral may be made to appropriate resource personnel.

12. SCHOOL DISTURBANCE
    Acts which cause substantial disruption of the school environment and/or threaten the safety or well-being of other students, which may include sit-downs, walk-outs, rioting, picketing, trespassing, inciting disturbances, threats, pranks, or actual violence during period of disruption.

    Penalty may range from detention to a recommendation that the student appear before the Student Evidentiary Hearing Committee, which may result in expulsion depending on circumstances and the degree of the school disturbance. The parent(s) must be contacted and referral may be made to appropriate resource personnel.

13. USE OF PROFANE, VULGAR, OBSCENE WORDS OR GESTURES; INDECENT EXPOSURE; POSSESSION AND/OR DISTRIBUTION OF PROFANE, VULGAR, OR OBSCENE MATERIAL; OR OTHER SIMILAR MATERIALS, ITEMS, OR GESTURES
    Penalty may range from detention to a recommendation that the student appear before the Student Evidentiary Hearing Committee, which may result in expulsion depending on circumstances and the degree of the school disturbance. The parent(s) must be contacted and referral may be made to appropriate resource personnel.

14. FAILURE TO ACCEPT DISCIPLINARY ACTION
    Penalty may range from detention to a recommendation that the student appear before the Student Evidentiary Hearing Committee, which may result in expulsion depending on the circumstances and the degree of the school disturbance. The parent(s) must be contacted and referral may be made to appropriate resource personnel.

15. CHRONIC TARDINESS
    Penalty may range from detention to a recommendation that the student appear before the Student Evidentiary Hearing Committee, which may result in expulsion. After a student is tardy five (5) times, he/she must be referred to the appropriate resource personnel and parent(s) must be notified. After a student is tardy ten (10) times, a referral to the Student Evidentiary Hearing Committee may be made.

    A referral to the Student Evidentiary Hearing Committee for this offense must include a written report from appropriate resource personnel.

16. MISBEHAVIOR ON BUS
    Penalty may range: Conference with teacher, parent-teacher conference, parent conference, detention, inhouse instruction, short-term suspension, removal from bus from one to ten days (1–10 days), to referral to Student Evidentiary Hearing Committee, which may result in removal from the bus for more than ten (10) days.

17. THREATENING OR INTIMIDATING STUDENT(S), BUT NOT INVOLVING ACTUAL PHYSICAL CONTACT
    Penalty may range: Detention, inhouse instruction, short-term suspension, parent conference. Parent(s) must be contacted and referral made to the appropriate resource personnel.

18. GAMBLING
    Penalty may range: Detention, inhouse instruction, short-term suspension, parent conference. Parent(s) must be contacted and referral made to the appropriate resource personnel.

19. REPEATED VIOLATIONS/MISBEHAVIOR; VIOLATION OF PROBATION
    a. Repeated violations of school rules and/or repeated misbehavior

Penalty may range from short-term suspension to a referral to the Student Evidentiary Hearing Committee, which may result in expulsion. Prior to this charge being made, parent(s) must have been notified of the misbehavior, the student warned of possible consequences, and a referral made to appropriate resource personnel. A referral to the Student Evidentiary Hearing Committee for this offense must include a written report from appropriate resource personnel.

b. Violation of probation (Violation of probation means committing any offense outlined in the brochure while on school and/or systemwide probation.)

Penalty may range from short-term suspension to expulsion. Before a student is readmitted after suspension or expulsion, consequences related to violation of probation must be explained to the student and parent(s).

20. PARKING AND TRAFFIC VIOLATIONS ON CAMPUS
    Each student who chooses to park a vehicle at a DeKalb County school parking lot must purchase a parking permit. Students who purchase a parking permit will be given a decal sticker and assigned a numbered parking space. A copy of the DeKalb County School Parking and Traffic Regulations will be issued to each student at the time of the registration. Parking permits are good for one quarter only and must be renewed quarterly. Students are responsible for their vehicle contents. Parking a car on campus subjects it to search upon reasonable suspicion of a violation of any offense covered in this discipline brochure.

    Penalty for violation of parking and traffic regulations may range: Revocation of parking permit, having a car towed off campus at student's expense, detention, inhouse instruction, or short-term suspension. Reckless driving could result in a referral to the Student Evidentiary Hearing Committee, which may result in expulsion.

21. LOITERING AND/OR GOING ON ANY SCHOOL CAMPUS WITHOUT AUTHORIZATION/TRESPASSING
    A student is not allowed to enter the premises of a school other than his/her school, unless prior permission is received from an administrator of the school to be visited. A student may not enter any school building on weekends or after school hours without authorization.

    Penalty may range from short-term suspension to recommendation that the student appear before the Student Evidentiary Hearing Committee, which may result in expulsion. NOTE: When a student refuses to leave school property and/or returns to school property after being instructed by school staff to leave the property, the matter will be referred to the police. The police will be informed of repeated offenders.

22. PROVIDING FALSE INFORMATION
    This offense covers, but is not limited to, such acts as falsifying school records, forging signatures, and making false statements.

Penalty may range from short-term suspension to recommendation that the student appear before the Student Evidentiary Hearing Committee, which may result in expulsion.

23. INAPPROPRIATE BODILY CONTACT BETWEEN OR AMONG STUDENTS IN-CLUDING, BUT NOT LIMITED TO, SEXUAL CONTACT
Penalty may range from a conference with student, parent(s), administrator, and appropriate resource personnel to a recommendation that the student appear before the Student Evidentiary Hearing Committee, which may result in expulsion, depending upon circumstances.

24. CRIMINAL LAW VIOLATION
A student who has been formally charged with violation(s) of criminal law and whose presence on school property may endanger the welfare and/or safety of other students, faculty, or staff, or whose presence may cause substantial disruption at school, may be subject to disciplinary action.

Penalty may range from immediate short-term suspension to a recommendation that the student appear before the Student Evidentiary Hearing Committee, which may result in expulsion, depending on circumstances.

25. BEHAVIOR NOT OTHERWISE COVERED IN THIS BROCHURE
The DeKalb School System reserves the right to punish behavior which endangers the welfare and/or safety of other students faculty, or staff; or causes substantial disruption to good order and discipline in the schools, even though such behavior is not specified in the written student discipline offenses.

Penalty may range from a conference with student, parent(s), administrator, and appropriate resource personnel to a recommendation that student appear before the Student Evidentiary Hearing Committee, which may result in expulsion, depending upon circumstances.

26. CONDUCT OUTSIDE OF SCHOOL HOURS OR AWAY FROM SCHOOL
Any conduct outside of school hours or away from school which may adversely affect the educational process or endanger the health, safety, morals, or well-being of other students, teachers, or employees within the school system.

Penalty may range from immediate short-term suspension to a recommendation that student appear before the Student Evidentiary Hearing Committee, which may result in expulsion, depending on circumstances.

27. STUDENT IDENTIFICATION CARD VIOLATION
All DeKalb County high school students must carry school I.D. cards while on school property and at any school event. A suspected non-student with no I.D. card will be asked to leave the school grounds, with police assistance if needed. Students who are not in possession of their I.D. cards are in violation of this section.

Penalty may range:
1st offense: Warning and payment for new identification card.

2nd offense: Three-day (3-day) detention, payment for new identification card, and probation.

3rd and subsequent offense(s): Short-term suspension to expulsion. Before a student is readmitted after suspension or expulsion, consequences related to further such offenses must be explained to the student and parent(s).

GUIDELINES FOR STUDENT ACCOUNTABILITY FOR TEXTBOOKS AND LIBRARY/MEDIA MATERIALS

It is the responsibility of the DeKalb County Board of Education to provide for each student a wide assortment of textbooks and library/media center materials. It is the responsibility of the student to be accountable for instructional materials loaned to him/her during the school year. In recent years, however, local school inventories have reflected substantial and growing losses in learning materials loaned or assigned to students. In order to ensure that sufficient learning materials in good condition are available for all DeKalb students, the DeKalb County Board of Education adopted a policy for student accountability for textbooks and library/media center materials. In order to enforce this policy fairly and equitably, the guidelines which follow shall be administered throughout the DeKalb County School System.

I. TEXTBOOKS

A. Lost textbooks

Students who lose textbooks shall be assessed according to the established depreciating scale.

B. Damaged textbooks

Students who return textbooks which exhibit wear in excess of that which could be attributed to normal use shall be assessed according to the damage.

II. LIBRARY/MEDIA CENTER MATERIALS

A. Lost library/media center materials

Students who lose books or other library/media center materials shall be assessed for the item based on its cost at the time of purchase. In addition, an assessment of $1.00 shall be made for catalog card sets and processing.

B. Damaged library/media center materials

Students who return books or other library/media center materials which exhibit wear in excess of that which could be attributed to normal use shall be assessed according to the damage.

III. FAILURE TO PAY FOR LOST AND DAMAGED TEXTBOOKS AND LIBRARY/MEDIA CENTER MATERIALS

Students shall be issued a second textbook with the same title only after payment for the first textbook has been received.

Students shall be given an "I" (Incomplete) in the class where payment for lost or damaged textbook(s) has not been received. The grade earned shall carry no credit until the record has been cleared.

Summary Offense and Disposition Chart

Violation	Disposition Range	Comments
1. Tobacco	(a) 1st Offense—conference (b) 2nd Offense—suspension/probation (c) 3rd Offense—possible expulsion	
*2. Alcohol		
*(a) sale/distribution	Suspension to expulsion	Police may be conta…
*(b)possession	Suspension to expulsion	Police may be conta…
*(c)use/influence	Suspension to expulsion	
*3. Weapons	Suspension to expulsion	Police may be conta…
*4. Threatening staff	Suspension to expulsion	Police may be conta…
*5. Drugs		
*(a) sale/distribution	Suspension to expulsion	Police may be conta…
*(b) possession	Suspension to expulsion	Police may be conta…
*(c) use/influence	Suspension to expulsion	
*(d) paraphernalia	Suspension to expulsion	
6. Property destruction	Detention to expulsion plus restitution	
7. Violence		
*(a) extreme violence	Suspension to expulsion	Police may be conta…
(b) fighting	Detention to expulsion	
8. Rude and disrespectful/refusal to follow instructions	Verbal reprimand to expulsion	
9. Unlawful absences/truancy	Detention to expulsion	Resource personnel
10. Skipping class	Detention to expulsion	
11. Classroom disturbances	Detention to expulsion	
12. School disturbance	Detention to expulsion	
13. Profanity/vulgar gestures/indecent exposure/obscene material	Detention to expulsion	
14. Failure to accept disciplinary action	Detention to expulsion	
15. Chronic tardiness	Detention to expulsion	Resource personnel
16. Misbehavior on bus	Conference to suspension	
17. Threatening (without physical contact)	Detention to suspension	
18. Gambling	Detention to suspension	
19. Repeated violations		
(a) repeated misbehavior	Suspension to expulsion	Resource personnel
(b) violation of probation	Suspension to expulsion	
20. Parking/traffic violation	Loss of permit to expulsion	
21. Loitering/trespassing	Suspension to expulsion	Police may be conta…
22. False information	Suspension to expulsion	
23. Inappropriate bodily contact	Conference to expulsion	
24. Criminal law violation	Suspension to expulsion	
25. Behavior not otherwise in brochure	Conference to expulsion	
26. Conduct outside of school hours/away from school	Suspension to expulsion	
27. Student identification card violation	Warning to expulsion	Student pays for new…

*Offenses preceded by an asterisk carry a mandatory requirement that the area superintendent be co… before charging the student. (Please refer to previous pages for fuller discussion of each offense.)

Students who fail to pay for lost or damaged library/media center materials shall lose the privilege of checking out additional materials. However, students may continue to use the learning resources within the confines of the library/media center.

Students who transfer within the school system shall be subject to the same application of policy at their new school. (Example: New textbooks shall be issued and check-out privilege in the library/media center shall be granted only if records have been cleared in the previous school.)

If a student transfers out of the DeKalb County School System while owing for learning materials, the student's withdrawal/transfer form, report card, and transcript shall be withheld until payment has been cleared.

Students completing elementary school shall be issued a certificate of promotion only after their records have been cleared.

Students who are not financially able to pay for lost or damaged textbooks and/or library/media center materials shall be allowed to provide payment in the form of voluntary services. Arrangements for voluntary services must be made with the local administrator.

GLOSSARY OF TERMS

1. INFORMAL HEARING
   Student is informed verbally of charges and given a chance to explain his/her action. Parent is usually not present for the informal hearing but is informed of charges and action taken by administrator. Informal hearings are used in suspending for one (1) to three (3) days and for assignment to inhouse instruction for one (1) to three (3) days.

2. FORMAL HEARING
   Parents, students and any witnesses for the student or administration will meet with the principal or his/her designee. The formal hearing must be held before a student is suspended for more than three (3) days.

3. WAIVER OF ATTENDING FORMAL HEARING
   Parents may sign a waiver if parents cannot attend or do not elect to attend the formal hearing. *In the event parents or student do not attend the hearing, it will proceed as scheduled.*

4. HEARING OFFICER
   Any local administrator or their designee, without prior knowledge of the event, who conducts the proceedings.

5. DETENTION
   Student is retained outside of regular school hours. Student must be given twenty-four hours' (24-hours) notice so that transportation can be arranged.

6. ALTERNATIVE INSTRUCTION
   a. Inhouse instruction

The student is removed from regular classes but is assigned to an alternative instructional provision in the local school. Student's assignments are sent to the student by the teachers. The student may not attend or participate in any extracurricular activities while assigned to inhouse instruction.

b. Alternative school

The student is removed from the local school but is allowed to attend the alternative school for instruction. Student may not return to local school campus or attend any activities of the local school while at the alternative school.

7. MACAD PROGRAM
See SUPER Program

8. SUPER PROGRAM (Metro-Atlanta Council on Alcohol and Drugs)
This program on drug education is conducted by the Metropolitan Atlanta Council on Alcohol and Drugs for DeKalb students who are first-time offenders of Offenses 2c, 5c, and 5d in this discipline brochure. The program may also be offered in certain other instances, at the discretion of the Student Evidentiary Hearing Committee for offenses under sections 2 and 5. Students may voluntarily participate in this program.

9. SHORT-TERM SUSPENSION
Short-term suspension is one (1) through ten (10) days' suspension out of school that is imposed by the local school administrator and/or a local hearing officer. Short-term suspensions that exceed three (3) days require a formal hearing. Student and/or parents may request the school's assistance in providing the make-up work for the missed class time. In a three-day (3-day) suspension, this work may be made up when the student returns to school. In a ten-day (10-day) suspension the assignments shall be available on the fourth (4th) day of the suspension, if requested by the student and/or parents.

10. LONG-TERM SUSPENSION
Long-term suspension means the suspension of a student out of school or from the bus for more than ten (10) days. Any suspension of more than ten (10) days may be assigned only by the Student Evidentiary Hearing Committee or by the Board of Education. Student may make up work when returning to school.

11. STUDENT EVIDENTIARY HEARING COMMITTEE
A panel of administrators, psychologists, social workers and special educators, hear evidence presented by the school system, the student, and parents when a student is referred to the Student Evidentiary Hearing Committee by the local school principal or his/her designee. This committee has the authority to make decisions ranging from returning the student to the local school through permanent expulsion.

12. DARC
The Disciplinary Action Review Committee (DARC) is authorized to consider and rule on special requests from students, parents and/or legal guardians,

and school administrators. Any action of the DARC is subject to modification by the superintendent and is appealable to the DeKalb County Board of Education.

13. EXPULSION

   Expulsion is the removal of a student from all units of DeKalb County school property and activities beyond the current quarter for a specified period of time. *Permanent expulsion* is an option of the Student Evidentiary Hearing Committee; a student and parent may apply for readmittance six months after being expelled permanently. This action may be taken only by the Student Evidentiary Hearing Committee or by the Board of Education. School work may not be made up or credit received.

14. PROBATION

   A student found guilty of certain offenses may be placed on probation by the local school administrator and/or by the Student Evidentiary Hearing Committee. Probation represents a trial period during which a student violating school and/or school system rules is subject to further disciplinary action, including possible referral to the Student Evidentiary Hearing Committee.

IMPORTANT INFORMATION

1. Students under suspension or expulsion are not allowed on school campus or at school functions.

2. Students are to notify an administrator or staff member when illegal or suspected illegal items, dangerous items, or other items banned from school are found in the school building, on the school campus or on the school bus. Students are advised not to pick up or handle these items, unidentified items, or items not belonging to them.

3. Due to the immaturity of elementary students, administrators may use discretion in determining and resolving "fights, classroom disturbances, and obscene words and gestures."

4. School administrators and/or their designated representatives possess the authority to conduct a reasonable search of students, their possessions, their lockers, and their automobiles when on school property, on property being used by the school, at any school function or activity, or at any school event held away from the school if it is established there is reasonable suspicion of the student being in violation of an offense in this brochure if a search is appropriate to that offense. The administrator is required to have only reasonable suspicion to conduct such searches. Two school employees, at least one of whom is an administrator, and the student or parent should be present during any vehicle search when an administrator is on campus. When an administrator is not on campus, the campus supervisor is authorized to search a vehicle provided: (1) reasonable suspicion is established, (2) an administrator's

approval has been given, (3) student and/or owner is present, and (4) another school employee or a law enforcement officer is present. If the student and/or his/her parent(s) or guardian refuse to allow the search, the police will be called and the matter turned over to them.

5. A student is deemed to be in possession of an illegal and/or banned item(s) when such item(s) is found on the person of the student, in his/her possessions, in his/her locker, in a student/s vehicle on school property, or in any vehicle a student brought on school property, on property being used by the school, at any school function or activity, or any school event held away from the school.

6. A student on his/her way to or from school, at any school function or activity (or any school-related activity), or at any school event held away from the school is under the jurisdiction of school authorities and is subject to the rules and regulations as stated in the Student Discipline Brochure.

7. Seniors and seventh graders under suspension or expulsion through spring quarter will not be allowed to participate in any school-sponsored activities, including the prom, graduation exercises, or baccalaureate ceremonies, except that a student may, *for good cause,* petition the Disciplinary Action Review Committee to participate. The committee's decision shall be final.

8. Victims of certain alleged student misconduct must file a written complaint with the local school administration and with the Board of Education, describing the alleged incident and the injury or damage sustained. The alleged instances of misconduct on which written complaints must be filed are as follows:

   a. An alleged assault or battery by a student upon any teacher, other school official, or employee.

   b. An alleged assault or battery by a student upon another student, if, in the discretion of the school principal, the alleged assault or battery could justify the expulsion or long-term suspension of the student.

   c. Substantial damage alleged to be intentionally caused by student on school premises to personal property belonging to a teacher, other school official, employee, or student, if, in the discretion of the school principal, the alleged damage could justify the expulsion or long-term suspension of the student.

9. DeKalb School Board policy states that the *minimum* penalty that shall be invoked by the Student Evidentiary Hearing Committee is one full-quarter expulsion from all units, except Hamilton Alternative School, of the DeKalb School System for any student found guilty by the Student Evidentiary Hearing Committee of:

   a. The sale or attempted sale and/or distribution of drugs or alcohol, or substances represented to be drugs or alcohol by the seller and/or thought to be drugs or alcohol by the buyer or receiver, on school property, at a school function, on property used by the school with permission of the owner, at any event held away from the school, or while the student is on his/her way to or from school, or

b. Extreme physical violence involving actual physical contact with another person, to be determined by the Student Evidentiary Hearing Committee.

10. Students should recognize their responsibility to know the contents of this discipline brochure and to ask faculty or staff members for any clarification. All students, regardless of age, are subject to the rules and regulations of the DeKalb County School System. Students will be taught the brochure and will be given a written test on the contents.

11. Students must understand that items listed under Offense 3, weapons and/or explosive devices, in this discipline brochure present an immediate and real danger to students, faculty, and staff, and can also damage a school's learning climate and reputation.

12. Students found guilty of being accessories to any violation of school rules are subject to the same penalties as students who are actively involved in committing such offenses.

STATEMENTS ON DUE PROCESS, STUDENT RIGHTS AND RESPONSIBILITIES, AND STUDENT ORGANIZATIONS

"Students in school, as well as out, are persons under the Constitution. They are possessed of fundamental rights which the State must respect, just as they themselves must respect their obligations to the State."

(United States Supreme Court)

DUE PROCESS

Due process will include the appropriate hearings and reviews and, in all cases, the rights of individuals will be ensured and protected.

STUDENT RIGHTS AND RESPONSIBILITIES

A student has full rights and citizenship as defined by the Constitution of the United States and assumes the responsibility to take positive actions relative to this Constitution; the laws of the State of Georgia; and the policies, rules and regulations of the DeKalb County Board of Education.

STUDENT ORGANIZATIONS

All student organizations must follow guidelines and procedures governing the creation and operation of such organizations and groups in accordance with the policies of the DeKalb County Board of Education.

DEKALB COUNTY BOARD OF EDUCATION

Norma W. Bergman, Chairman
David Williamson, Vice Chairman
Elizabeth Andrews
Phil McGregor
Donna L. Wagner
H. Paul Womack, Jr.
Lyman D. Howard
Robert R. Freeman, Superintendent

PREPARED BY THE DIVISION OF PROGRAM DEVELOPMENT AND STAFF ASSESS-
MENT

It is the policy of the DeKalb County Board of Education not to discriminate
on the basis of age, sex, race, color, religion, national origin, or handicap in its
educational programs, activities, or employment policies.

Bibliography

Abadzi, Helen: "Ability Grouping Effects on Academic Achievement and Self-Esteem: Who Performs in the Long Run as Expected," *Journal of Educational Research*, 79, no. 1 (1985): 36–40.

Agnew, E. John: "The Grading Policies and Practices of High School Teachers," paper read at American Educational Research Association Annual Meeting, March 31–April 4, 1985, Chicago. ED259022.

Anderson, John K.: "Intensive Scheduling: An Interesting Possibility," *The Clearing House*, September 1982, pp. 26–28.

Anderson, Linda M. et al.: "A Qualitative Study of Seatwork in First Grade Classrooms," *Elementary School Journal* 86, no. 2 (1985): 123–140.

Bacharach, Samuel, and Stephen Mitchell: "The Sources of Dissatisfaction in Educational Administration: A Role-Specific Analysis," *Educational Administration Quarterly* 19, no. 1 (1983): 101–128.

Barr, Rebecca, and Robert Dreeben: *How Schools Work,* University of Chicago Press, 1983.

Barth, Richard P. "Reducing Nonattendance in Elementary Schools," *Social Work in Education* 30, no. 3 (1984): 151–166.

Beady, Charles, and Robert Slavin: "Making Success Available to All Students in Desegregated Schools," *Integrated Education,* (September–December 1980), p. 28.

Bellanca, James A.: *Grading,* National Education Association, Washington, 1977.

Berke, J. S., and M. W. Kirst: "Intergovernmental Relations: Conclusions and Recommendations," in J. S. Berke and M. W. Kirst (eds.), *Federal Aid to Education: Who Benefits? Who Governs?* Heath, Lexington, Mass., 1972.

Berliner, David C.: "The Half-Full Glass: A Review of Research on Teaching," in Philip L. Hosford (ed.), *Using What We Know About Teaching,* Association for Supervision and Curriculum Development, Alexandria, Va., 1984.

Blake, Howard V.: "Class Size: A Summary of Selected Studies in Elementary and Secondary Schools," Ed.D. dissertation, Teachers College, Columbia University, New York, 1954.

Blase, Joseph J.: "The Politics of Favoritism: A Qualitative Analysis of the Teachers' Perspective," *Educational Administration Quarterly* 24, no. 2 (1988): 152–177.

Bloom, Benjamin S., et al.: *Taxonomy of Educational Objectives,* New York, Longmans Green, 1st ed., 1956.

Boyd, William Lowe: "The Politics of Curriculum Change and Stability," in J. Victor Baldridge and Terrence Deal (eds.), *The Dynamics of Organizational Change in Education,* McCutchan, Berkeley, Calif., 1983.

Bracey, Gerald W.: "The Social Impact of Ability Grouping," *Phi Delta Kappan,* May 1987, pp. 688–689.

Brookover, Wilber, et al.: *School Social Systems and Student Achievement,* Praeger, New York, 1979.

Brophy, Jere E., and Joyce G. Putnam: "Classroom Management in the Elementary Grades," in Daniel L. Duke (ed.), *Classroom Management,* NSSE Yearbook, 1979.

Butts, Freeman R., and Lawrence Cremin: *A History of Education in American Culture,* Holt, New York, 1953.

Cahen, Leonard S., et al.: *Class Size and Instruction,* Longman, London, 1983.

———— et al.: *Class Size Research: A Critique of Recent Meta-Analyses,* Educational Research Service, Arlington, Va., 1980.

Canady, Robert Lynn: "A Cure for Fragmented Schedules in Elementary Schools," *Educational Leadership,* October 1988, pp. 65–67.

————: "Grouping and Time Management Strategies Designed to Improve Reading and Instruction," *ESSAYS: Management Strategies for Improving Reading Instruction,* McGraw-Hill, Monterey, Calif., 1980, n. pag.

————: "Parallel Block Scheduling: A Better Way to Organize a School," *Principal,* January 1990, pp. 34–36.

————: "Programming for Flexibility: Attack the Class Size Issue and Fragmented School Programs with These Scheduling Ideas," *AIGE Forum,* Spring 1981, pp. 1–7.

———— and Phyllis R. Hotchkiss: "School Improvement Without Additional Cost," *Phi Delta Kappan,* November 1984, pp. 183–184.

———— and Alfred R. Butler, IV: "Designing a Middle School Schedule," *American Middle School Education,* Fall 1981, pp. 29–35.

———— and Elaine Fogliani: "Cut Class Size in Half Without Hiring More Teachers," *The Executive Educator,* August 1989, pp. 22–23.

———— and Phyllis R. Hotchkiss: "Scheduling Practices and Policies Associated with Increased Achievement for Low-Achieving Students," *The Journal of Negro Education,* Summer 1985, pp. 344–355.

———— and Jane R. McCullen: "Elementary Scheduling Practices Designed to Support Programs for Gifted Students," *Roeper Review: A Journal on Gifted Education,* February 1985, pp. 142–145.

———— and John T. Seyfarth: *How Parent-Teacher Conferences Build Partnerships,* Phi Delta Kappan Educational Foundation, Bloomington, Ind., 1979.

Carroll, John B.: "A Model of School Learning," *Teacher's College Record* 64 (1963): 723–733.

Carroll, Joseph M.: "The Copernican Plan: Restructuring the American High School," *Phi Delta Kappan,* January 1990, pp. 358–365.

Catterall, James S.: "An Intensive Group Counseling Dropout Prevention Intervention: Some Cautions on Isolating At-Risk Adolescents Within High Schools," *American Educational Research Journal* 24, no. 4 (1987): 521–540.

———— and David Stern: "The Effects of Alternative School Programs on High School Completion and Labor Market Outcomes," *Educational Evaluation and Policy Analysis* 8, no. 1 (1986): 77–88.

Church, Robert L., and Michael W. Sedlack: *Education in the United States,* Free Press, New York, 1976.

Cistone, Peter I., et al.: "School-Based Management/Shared Decision-Making in Dade County (Miami)," *Education and Urban Society,* August 1989, pp. 393–402.

Clark, David L.: "High School Seniors React to Their Teachers and Their Schools," *Phi Delta Kappan,* March 1987, pp. 503–509.

Class Size, Research Summary 1951–68, National Education Association, Research Division, Washington, 1968. ERIC Document Reproduction Service, ED 032 614.

Cohen, Michael: "Restructuring the Education System: Agenda for the 90's," unpublished paper.

Collins, Robert A.: "Interim Evaluation Report—School-Based Management/Shared Decision Making Project, 1987–88," Dade County Public Schools, Miami, 1988.

Cooper, Harris: *Homework,* Longman, New York, 1989.

———: "Synthesis of Research on Homework," *Educational Leadership,* November 1989, pp. 85–91.

Cuban, Larry: "The 'At-Risk' Label and the Problem of Urban School Reform," *Phi Delta Kappan,* June 1989, pp. 780–801.

Darling-Hammond, Linda: "Valuing Teachers: The Making of a Profession," *Teachers College Record* 87, no. 2 (1985): 209.

Dawson, Margaret: "Beyond Ability Grouping: A Review of the Effectiveness of Ability Grouping and Its Alternatives," *School Psychology Review* 16, no. 3 (1987): 348–369.

DiPrete, Thomas A.: *Discipline and Order in American High Schools,* National Center for Education Statistics, Washington, 1983.

Dougherty, Van: *The First Step: Understanding the Data,* Education Commission of the States, Denver, 1987.

Doyle, Walter: "Are Students Behaving Worse Than They Used to Behave?" *Journal of Research and Development in Education* 2, no. 4 (1978): 3–16.

Duke, Daniel L.: "The Aesthetics of Leadership," *Educational Administration Quarterly* 21, no. 2 (1986): 7–27.

———: "Looking at the School as a Rule-Governed Organization," *Journal of Research and Development in Education* no. 4 (1978): 116–126.

———: "Punishment," *International Encyclopedia of Education,* Pergamon, London, 1985.

———: *The Retransformation of the School,* Nelson-Hall, Chicago, 1978.

———: "School Discipline Plans and the Quest for Order in American Schools," in Delwyn P. Tatum (ed.), *Management of Disruptive Pupil Behavior in Schools,* Wiley, London, 1986.

———: *School Leadership and Instructional Improvement,* Random House, New York, 1987.

———: "School Organization, Leadership, and Student Behavior," paper commissioned by the Office of Educational Research and Improvement, U.S. Department of Education, 1986.

——— and Jon Cohen: "Do Public Schools Have a Future? A Case Study of Retrenchment and Its Implications," *The Urban Review* 15, no. 2 (1983): 89–105.

——— and Bruce Gansneder: "Teacher Empowerment: The View from the Classroom" *Educational Policy* 4, no. 2 (1990): 145–160.

——— and Vernon F. Jones: "Two Decades of Discipline—Assessing the Development of an Educational Specialization," *Journal of Research and Development in Education* 17, no. 4 (1984): 25–35.

——— and Adrienne M. Meckel: "Student Attendance Problems and School Organization: A Case Study," *Urban Education* 15, no. 3 (1980): 325–358.

——— and Irene Muzio: "How Effective Are Alternative Schools? A Review of Recent Evaluations and Reports," *Teachers College Record,* February 1978, pp. 461–484.

——— and Cheryl Perry: "Can Alternative Schools Succeed Where Benjamin Spock, Spiro Agnew, and B. F. Skinner Have Failed?" *Adolescence* 13, no. 51 (1978): 375–392.

——— and Richard I. Stiggins: "Beyond Minimum Competence: Evaluation for Professional Development," in Jason Millman and Linda Darling-Hammond (eds.), *Handbook for the Evaluation of Elementary and Secondary Teachers,* Sage Books, Newbury Park, Calif., 1990.

——— et al.: "Teachers and Shared Decision Making: The Costs and Benefits of Involvement," *Educational Administration Quarterly* 16, no. 1 (1980): 93–106.

Dunlop, John: "Negotiating Student Discipline Policy," *Today's Education* 68, no. 2 (1979): 29.

DuPuis, Victor, and Bernie Badialdi: "Classroom Climate and Teacher Expectations in Homogeneously Grouped Secondary Schools," *Journal of Classroom Interaction* 23, no. 1 (1987–88): 28–33.

Dworkin, Anthony Gary: *Teacher Burnout in the Public Schools,* State University of New York Press, Albany, 1987.

Dworkin, Ronald: *A Matter of Principle,* Harvard University Press, Cambridge, Mass., 1985.

Eberts, Randall W., and Joe A. Stone: *Unions and Public Schools,* Lexington Books, Lexington, Mass., 1984.

Emmer, Edmund T.: "Classroom Management and Discipline," in Virginia Richardson-Kochler (ed.), *Educators' Handbook,* Longman, New York, 1987.

English, Fenwick: "Pull-Outs: How Much Do They Erode Whole-Class Teaching?" *Principal,* May 1984, pp. 32–36.

Epstein, Joyce L.: "Homework Practices, Achievements, and Behaviors of Elementary School Students," *Report No. 26,* The Johns Hopkins University Center for Research on Elementary and Middle Schools, July 1988.

Evans, Ellis D.: "A Developmental Study of Student Perceptions of School Grading," paper read at Society for Research in Child Development Biennial Meeting, April 25–28, 1985, Toronto. ED 256 482 PS 015 078.

Faber, Charles, and Gilbert F. Shearron: *Elementary Administration,* Holt, New York, 1970.

Farr, Roger, and Michael A. Tulley: "Do Adoption Committees Perpetuate Mediocre Textbooks?" *Phi Delta Kappan,* March 1985, pp. 467–471.

Fielding, Glen D., and H. Del Schalock: *Promoting the Professional Development of Teachers and Administrators,* Center for Educational Policy Management, Eugene, Ore., 1985.

Finley, Merrilee: "Teachers and Tracking in a Comprehensive High School," *Sociology of Education* 57, no. 4 (1984): 233–243.

Firestone, William A., et al.: *The Progress of Reform: An Appraisal of State Education Initiatives,* The Center for Policy Research in Education, New Brunswick, N.J., 1989.

"First Grade Reading: Who Learns and Who Doesn't?" *The Harvard Education Letter,* January 1987, pp. 4–5.

Flax, Ellen: "S.C. Board Adopts Regulatory Relief of Top-Scoring Schools," *Education Week,* November 22, 1989, pp. 1, 16.

Floden, Robert E., et al.: "Instructional Leadership at the District Level: A Closer Look at Autonomy and Control," *Educational Administration Quarterly* 24, no. 2 (1988): 96–124.

Flummerfelt, Dan R.: "Getting the Best of Both Worlds," *NASSP Bulletin,* December 1986, pp. 118–119.

"The Forgotten Half," *Final Report of the William T. Grant Foundation Commission on Work, Family and Citizenship,* William T. Grant Foundation, Washington, D.C., 1988.

Former Teachers in America, Metropolitan Life Insurance Company, New York, 1985.

Fullan, Michael: *The Meaning of Educational Change,* Teachers College Press, New York, 1982.

Gallup, Alec M.: "The 18th Annual Gallup Poll of the Public's Attitudes Toward the Public Schools," *Phi Delta Kappan,* September 1986, pp. 44–50.

Gameron, Adam: "Organization, Instruction, and the Effects of Ability Grouping," *Review of Educational Research* 57, no. 3 (1987), pp. 341–345.

Garet, Michael S., and Brian DeLany: "Students, Courses, and Stratification," *Sociology of Education* 61, no. 2 (1988): 61–77.

Glass, Gene V., et al.: *School Class Size,* Sage Publications, Beverly Hills, Calif., 1982.

Glasser, William: *Schools Without Failure,* 1st ed., Harper and Row, New York, 1969.

Glatthorn, Allan A.: *Curriculum Leadership,* Scott, Foresman, Glenview, Ill., 1987.

Gold, Martin, and David W. Mann: *Expelled to a Friendlier Place,* University of Michigan Press, Ann Arbor, 1984.

Goldberg, Miriam L., et al.: *The Effects of Ability Grouping,* Teachers College Press, New York, 1968.

Goldman, Jeri J.: "Flexible Modular Scheduling: Results of Evaluations in Its Second Decade," *Urban Education,* July 1983, pp. 191–209.

Good, Thomas L., and Jere E. Brophy: *Looking in Classrooms,* 4th ed., Harper and Row, New York, 1987.

Goodlad, John L.: *A Place Called School,* McGraw-Hill, New York, 1984.

Gottfredson, Gary D., and Denise C. Gottfredson: *Victimization in Schools,* Plenum Press, New York, 1985.

———— and Lois G. Hybl: "An Analytical Description of the Principal's Job," *Report No. 13,* The Johns Hopkins University Center for Research on Elementary and Middle Schools, 1987.

Green, Thomas F.: "The Economy of Virtue and the Primacy of Prudence," *American Journal of Education* 96, no. 2 (1988): 127–142.

Gross, James A.: *Teachers on Trial,* ILR Press, Ithaca, N.Y., 1988.

Guba, Egon G.: "The Effect of Definition of Policy on the Nature and Outcomes of Policy Analysis," *Educational Leadership,* October 1984, pp. 63–70.

Hall, Gene E., and Shirley M. Hord: *Change in Schools,* State University of New York Press, Albany, 1987.

Hargreaves, D. H., et al.: *Deviance in Classrooms,* Routledge & Kegan Paul, London, 1975.

Harrison, Charles: *Public Schools USA,* Williamson Publishing, Charlotte, 1988.

Hawkinson, Howard: "Hatch School—Not at Risk," *Phi Delta Kappan,* November 1984, pp. 181–182.

Hencley, Stephen P., *The Elementary School Principalship,* Dodd, Mead, New York, 1970.

Hirsch, E. D., Jr.: *Cultural Literacy,* Houghton Mifflin, Boston, 1987.

Hollingsworth, Ellen Jane, et al. *School Discipline: Order and Autonomy,* Praeger, New York, 1984.

Hudgins, H. C., Jr., and Richard S. Vacca: *Law and Education.* 2d ed. The Michie Company, Charlottesville, Va., 1985.

Hughes, Larry W., and Gerald W. Ubben: *The Elementary Principal's Handbook,* Allyn and Bacon, Boston, 1984.

Intermediate and Secondary Teacher's Guide: Grading and Reporting to Parents, Fairfax County Public School, Fairfax, Va., 1987.

"Is the A to F Grading Scale Obsolete?" *Torchbearer* 26, no. 3. (1987).

Jacobson, Stephen L.: "Pay Incentives and Teacher Absence: One District's Experience," *Urban Education,* January 1989, pp. 377–391.

Jennings, Lisa: "Disparities in Pupils' Treatment Persist, Rights Study Finds," *Education Week,* December 14, 1988, p. 5.

Johanningmeier, Erwin V.: *Americans and Their Schools,* Rand McNally, Chicago, 1980.

Johnson, David, et al.: *Circles of Learning: Cooperation in the Classroom,* Interaction Book Company, Edina, Minn., 1986.

Johnson, Susan Moore: "Incentives for Teachers: What Motivates, What Matters," *Educational Administration Quarterly* 22, no. 3 (1986): 54–79.

Kauffman, James M., et al.: "Arguable Assumptions Underlying the Regular Education Initiative," *Journal of Learning Disabilities* 21, no. 1 (1988): 6–11.

Keith, T. Z.: "Time Spent on Homework and High School Grades: A Large-Sample Path Analysis," *Journal of Educational Psychology* 74, 2 (1982): 248–258.

Kelly, A. V.: *Mixed Ability Grouping: Theory and Practice,* Harper and Row, London, 1978.

Kemmerer, Frances: "The Allocation of Student Time," *Administrator's Notebook* 27 (1978–79), n. pag.

Kerchner, Charles T.: "A 'New Generation' of Teacher Unionism," *Education Week,* January 20, 1988, p. 36.

Kirschenbaum, Howard, et al.: *Wad-ja-get? The Grading Game in American Education,* Hart, New York, 1971.

Kirst, Michael W.: "Policy Implications of Individual Differences and the Common Curriculum," in Gary D. F. Fenstermacher and John I. Goodlad (eds.), *Individual Differences and the Common Curriculum,* NSSE Yearbook, pt. 1, 1983.

Klein, Karen: "The Research on Class Size," *Phi Delta Kappan,* April 1985, pp. 578–579.

Komoski, Kenneth: "Needed: A Whole-Curriculum Approach," *Educational Leadership,* February 1990, p. 78.

Kulik, C. C., and J. Kulik: "Effects of Ability Grouping on Secondary Students: A Meta-Analysis of Evaluation Findings," *American Educational Research Journal* 19, no. 3 (1982): 415–428.

Kulik, James A., and Chen-Lin C. Kulik: "Effects of Ability Grouping on Student Achievement," *Equity and Excellence* 23, nos. 1–2 (1987): 22–30.

LaConte, Ronald T., and Mary Anne Doyle: *Homework as a Learning Experience,* National Education Association, Washington, 1986.

Lele, Jackson F., Jr., and K. Wayne Pruitt: *Providing for Individual Difference in Student Learning: A Mastery Learning Approach,* Charles C. Thomas, Springfield, Ill., 1984.

Levine, Daniel U. (ed.), *Improving Student Achievement Through Mastery Learning Programs,* Jossey-Bass, San Francisco, 1985.

Levine, Daniel U., and Joyce Stark: *Instructional and Organizational Arrangements for Improving Achievement at Inner City Schools,* ERIC Document Reproduction Service, 1981, ED 221, 636.

Lewis, Anne: *Restructuring America's Schools,* American Association of School Administrators, Arlington, Va., 1989.

Liggett, Lee B.: "Discipline by Grade Reduction and Grade Denial Based on Attendance," in M. A. McGhehey (ed.), *School Law in Contemporary Society,* National Organization on Legal Problems of Education, 1980.

Lightfoot, Sara Lawrence: *The Good High School,* Basic Books, New York, 1983.

Lipsky, Michael: *Street-Level Bureaucracy: Dilemmas of the Individual in Public Service,* Russell Sage Foundation, New York, 1980.

Lortie, Dan C.: *Schoolteacher,* University of Chicago Press, 1975.

Madgic, Robert F.: "The Point System of Grading: A Critical Appraisal," *NASSP Bulletin,* 72, no. 507 (1988), 29–34.

Mager, Robert Frank: *Preparing Instructional Objectives,* rev. 2d ed., Lake Management and Training, Belmont, Calif., 1984.

Majestic, Ann: "Disciplining Students for Out-of-School Misconduct," *School Law Bulletin* 19, no. 2 (1988): 6–11.

Mann, Carleton Hunter: *How Schools Use Their Time,* Teachers College, New York, 1928.

Marsh, David D., and Allan Odden: "Key Factors Associated with the Effective Implementation and Impact of California's Educational Reform," unpublished paper.

Marshall, John D.: "Teaching's Most Taxing Traditions: Reflections on Evaluation and Grading," occasional paper, The University of Texas at Austin, Spring 1983. SP 025 945.

McLaughlin, Milbrey Wallin: "Learning from Experience: Lessons from Policy Implementation," *Educational Evaluation and Policy Analysis* 9, no. 2 (1987): 171–178.

——— et al.: "Why Teachers Won't Teach," *Phi Delta Kappan,* February 1986, p. 426.

——— and R. Scott Pfeifer: *Teacher Evaluation,* Teachers College Press, New York, 1988.

McPartland, James M., and Edward L. McDill: "The Unique Role of Schools in the Causes of Youthful Crime," *Report No. 216,* The Johns Hopkins University Center for Social Organization of Schools, 1976.

Menacker, Julius C., et al.: "Legislating School Discipline: The Application of a Systemwide Discipline Code to Schools in a Large Urban District," *Urban Education* 23, no. 1 (1988): 12–23.

Mercer, Cecil D.: *Children and Adolescents with Learning Disabilities,* Charles E. Merrill, Columbus, 1979.

Meyer, John, et al.: "Research on School and District Organization," in J. Victor Baldridge and Terrence Deal (eds.), *The Dynamics of Organizational Change in Education,* McCutchan, Berkeley, Calif., 1983.

Mirga, Tom: "Explosion in School Lawsuits has Ended, 2 Unpublished Studies Find," *Education Week,* November 30, 1988, p. 1.

Mitchell, Douglas E., and Charles T. Kerchner: "Labor Relations and Teacher Policy," in Lee S. Shulman and Gary Sykes (eds.), *Handbook of Teaching and Policy,* Longman, New York, 1983.

Moles, Oliver (ed.): *Strategies to Reduce Student Misbehavior,* U.S. Department of Education, 1989.

Morris, Van Cleve, et al.: *Principals in Action,* Charles E. Merrill, Columbus, Ohio, 1984.

Mortimore, Peter, et al.: *School Matters,* University of California Press, Berkeley, 1988.

Myers, Donald A.: *Teacher Power,* Lexington Books, Lexington, Mass., 1973.

Neale, Daniel C., et al.: *Strategies for School Improvement,* Allyn and Bacon, Boston, 1981.

Nelson, Joe, et al.: "New Futures for America's Children," in Frank I. Macchiarola and Alan Gartner (eds.), *Caring for America's Children,* Academy of Political Science, New York, 1989, p. 217.

Newfield, John, and Virginia B. McLyea: "Achievement and Attitudinal Differences among Students in Regular, Remedial, and Advanced Classes," *Journal of Experimental Education* 52, no. 1 (1982): 47.

Noland, Theresa Koontz, and Bob L. Taylor: "The Effects of Ability Grouping—A Meta-Analysis of Research Findings," paper read at American Educational Research Association Annual Meeting, April 16–20, 1986, San Francisco. Reproduction supplied by ERIC ED 269 451.

Nottingham, Marv: "Grading Practices—Watching Out for Land Mines," *NASSP Bulletin,* April 1988, p. 27.

Oakes, Jeannie: *Keeping Track: How Schools Structure Inequality,* Yale University Press, New Haven, 1985.

———: "Keeping Track, Part 2: Curriculum Inequality and School Reform," *Phi Delta Kappan,* October 1986, pp. 148–153.

Odden, Allan, and David Marsh: "How Comprehensive Reform Legislation Can Improve Secondary Schools," *Phi Delta Kappan,* April 1988, pp. 593–598.

O'Donnell, Holly: "ERIC/RCS: Homework in the Elementary School," *Reading Teacher,* November 1989, pp. 220–222.

Pallas, Aaron M., et al.: "The Changing Nature of the Disadvantaged Population: Current Dimensions and Future Trends," *Educational Researcher,* June/July 1989, pp. 16–22.

Peterson, Kent D., et al.: "Superintendents' Perceptions of the Control and Coordination of the Technical Core in Effective School Districts," *Educational Administrative Quarterly* 23, no. 1 (1987): 79–95.

Pizzo, Peggy: "Slouching Toward Bethlehem: American Federal Policy Perspectives on Children and Their Families," in Edward F. Zigler et al. (eds.), *Children, Families, and Government,* Cambridge University Press, Cambridge, England, 1983, p. 12.

Pomeroy, Richard, and Trevor Johnson: "Friendship Choices and Self-Image: An Investigation of Group Cohesiveness and Perceptions of Remedial Children in Comprehensive School," *Educational Review* 35, no. 1 (1983): 51–58.

Purkey, Stewart C., and Robert A. Rutter: "High School Teaching: Teacher Practices and Beliefs in Urban and Suburban Public Schools," *Educational Policy* 1, no. 3 (1987): 375–394.

Rachlin, Jill: "The Label That Sticks," *U.S. News & World Report,* July 3, 1989.

Ralph, John: "Improving Education for the Disadvantaged: Do We Know Whom to Help?" *Phi Delta Kappan,* January 1989, pp. 395–401.

Rebore, Ronald W.: *Personnel Administration in Education,* 2d ed., Prentice-Hall, Englewood Cliffs, N.J., 1987.

Resnick, Daniel P., and Lauren B. Resnick: "Understanding Achievement and Acting to Produce It: Some Recommendations for the NAEP," *Phi Delta Kappan,* April 1988, pp. 578–579.

Rinne, Carl H.: "Grading and Growth: Answer to an Editorial," *Educational Leadership,* January 1975, p. 248.

Roberts, Arthur D., and Gordon Cawelti: *Redefining General Education in the American High School* Association for Supervision and Curriculum Development, Alexandria, Va., 1984.

Robinson, Glen E., and James H. Wittebols: *Class Size Research: A Related Cluster Analysis for Decisionmaking,* Educational Research Service, Arlington, Va., 1986.

Rollins, Sidney P.: *Developing Nongraded Schools,* F. E. Peacock, Itasca, Ill., 1968.

Rosenthal, Robert, and Lenore Jacobson: *Pygmalion in the Classroom; Teacher Expectation and Pupils' Intellectual Development,* Holt, New York, 1968.

Rupley, William H., and Timothy R. Blair: "Primary Teachers' Assignment and Supervision of Students' Reading Seatwork," *Reading Psychology* 7, no. 4 (1986): 279–288.

Sarason, Seymour B.: *The Culture of the School and the Problem of Change,* 2d ed., Allyn and Bacon, Boston, 1982.

Saville, Anthony: *Instructional Programming,* Merrill, Columbus, Ohio, 1973.

Schorr, Lisbeth B.: *Within Our Reach: Breaking the Cycle of Disadvantage,* Anchor Books, New York, 1988.

Schwille, John, et al.: "State Policy and the Control of Curriculum Decisions," *Educational Policy,* March 1988, pp. 29–50.

Sedlak, Michael W., et al.: *Selling Students Short,* Teachers College Press, New York, 1986.

Seeman, Alice Z., and Melvin Seeman: "Staff Processes and Pupil Attitudes: A Study of Teacher Participation in Educational Change," *Human Relations* 29, no. 1 (1976): 25–40.

Sendor, Benjamin: "You May Discipline Kids for 'Acting Up' Outside of School, But Don't Lower Their Grades," *The American School Board Journal,* March 1985, p. 23.

Shanker, Albert: "Charter Schools: Option for the Other 80 Percent," *The School Administrator,* November 1988, p. 72.

Shapson, Stan M., et al.: "An Experimental Study of the Effects of Class Size," *American Educational Research Journal* 17, no. 2 (1980): 141–151.

Sheppard, Lorrie A., and Mary Lee Smith: "Synthesis of Research on Grade Retention," *Educational Leadership,* May 1990, pp. 84–88.

Sigurdson, Sol E.: "Two Years on the Block Plan: Meeting the Needs of Junior High School Students," *Final Report, Department of Education, Edmonton,* Planning and Research Branch, Edmonton Public School Board, Alberta, Canada, 1982. Reproduction supplied by ERIC, ED 225 946, SP 021 649.

Sizemore, Barbara A.: *An Abashing Anomaly: The High Achieving Predominantly Black Elementary School. Executive Summary,* 1983. ERIC Document Reproduction Service, ED 236 275.

Slavin, Robert E.: "Effects of Individual Learning Expectations on Student Achievement," *Journal of Educational Psychology* 72, no. 4 (1980): 520–524.

———: "Making Chapter I Make a Difference," *Phi Delta Kappan,* October 1987, pp. 110–119.

——— and Nancy A. Madden: "What Works for Students at Risk: A Research Synthesis," *Educational Leadership,* February 1989, pp. 4–13.

Smith, Lee L.: *A Practical Approach to the Nongraded Elementary School,* Parker Publisher, West Nyack, N.Y., 1969.

Snider, William: "Houston School Chief's 'Get Tough' Policy Will Send 40,000 to After-School Tutorials," *Education Week,* February 17, 1988, pp. 1, 25.

"A Special Analysis of 1986 Elementary and Secondary School Civil Rights Survey Data," National Coalition of Advocates for Students, Boston, 1988.

Stiggins, Richard J. "Revitalizing Classroom Assessment: The Highest Instructional Priority," *Phi Delta Kappan,* January 1988, pp. 363–368.

—— and Daniel L. Duke: *The Case for Commitment to Teacher Growth: Research on Teacher Evaluation,* State University of New York Press, Albany, 1988.

—— et al.: "Inside High School Grading Practices: Building a Research Agenda," *Educational Measurement: Issues and Practice* 8, no. 2 (1989): 5–14.

Strang, Ruth: *Guided Study and Homework,* National Education Association, Washington, 1968.

Strother, Deborah Burnett: "Homework: Too Much, Just Right, or Not Enough?" *Phi Delta Kappan,* February 1984, pp. 423–26.

Sweet, Anne P., and Robert Lynn Canady: "Scheduling for a Differentiated Reading Program," *Reading Horizons,* 20, no. 1 (1979) 36–41.

Tanner, Daniel, and Laurel Tanner: *Curriculum Development,* Macmillan, New York, 1975.

Taylor, Barbara: "Let's Pull Out of the Pullout Programs," *Principal* 65 no. 1 (1985): 52.

Thomas, William C.: "Grading—Why Are School Policies Necessary? What are the Isues?" *NAASP Bulletin*, February 1986, pp. 23–26.

U.S. Department of Education, *Becoming a Nation of Readers,* 1985.

U.S. Department of Education, *Schools That Work: Educating Disadvantaged Children,* 1987.

U.S. General Accounting Office: *Education Reform: Initial Effects in Four School Districts,* 1989.

Viadero, Debra: "L.A. School Embraces a West German Import," *Education Week,* November 1, 1989, pp. 1, 10.

Walberg, Herbert J., et al.: "Homework's Powerful Effects on Learning," *Educational Leadership,* April 1985, pp. 76–79.

Wilkinson, Louise Cherry: "Grouping Low Achieving Students for Instruction in Designs for Compensatory Education," Conference Proceedings and Papers, June 17–18, 1986, Washington. Reproduction supplied by ERIC ED 293, 295.

Williams, Michael F.: "The Trimester Scheduling Plan: Flexibility in the High School Curriculum," paper read at American Association of School Administrators Annual Meeting, February 22–25, 1985, Atlanta, Georgia. Reproduction supplied by ERIC ED 266 553, EA 018 250.

Winn, Wyona, and Alfred P. Wilson: "The Affect and Effect of Ability Grouping," *Contemporary Education* 54, no. 2 (1983): pp. 119–125.

Wise, Arthur E.: "Legislated Learning Revisited," *Phi Delta Kappan,* January 1988, pp. 328–333.

—— et al.: *Effective Teacher Selection,* Rand, Santa Monica, Calif., 1987.

—— et al.: *Teacher Evaluation: A Study of Effective Practices,* Rand, Santa Monica, Calif., 1984.

Wise, Robert I., and Betty Newman: "The Responsibilities of Grading," *Educational Leadership,* January 1975, pp. 253–256.

Yeaworth, Rosalee C., et al.: "The Development of the Adolescent Life Change Event Scale," *Adolescence,* 15, no. 57 (1980): 91–98.

Zirkel, Perry A., and Ivan B. Gluckman: "The Constitution and the Curriculum," *Principal,* September 1988, p. 60.

Name Index

Subject Index